Eastern Kayah Li

Eastern Kayah Li

Grammar, Texts, Glossary

David B. Solnit

University of Hawai'i Press

97 98 99 00 01 02   5 4 3 2 1

Library of Congress Cataloging-in-Publication Data

Solnit, David B.
Eastern Kayah Li : grammar, texts, glossary / David B. Solnit.
        p.   cm.
Includes bibliographical references and index.
ISBN 0–8248–1743–5 (alk. paper)
1. Kayah language—Grammar. I. Title.
PL4058.K39S65   1996
495—dc20   96–9271
                                    CIP

Camera-ready copy prepared by David B. Solnit

Contents

Contents

Contents

Contents

Contents

Contents

Contents

Introduction

0.1 Kayah, Karen, Karenni

0.1.1 General Remarks

The language described in this study is an Eastern dialect of Kayah Li. Kayah in turn is a Central Karen language, and Karen is a major subdivision of the Tibeto-Burman branch of Sino-Tibetan. Kayah Li is thus very closely related to languages like Bwe and Brè; less closely to other Karen languages like Sgaw, Pho and Pa-O (Taungthu); more distantly to hundreds of languages including Burmese, Tibetan, Lahu, Yi, Lushai, etc.; and most remotely to Chinese.

Karen is a well-defined subgroup of Tibeto-Burman, with no questionable members. It covers a relatively continuous block of territory extending to either side of the Thailand-Burma border, plus outlying scattered groups of Sgaw in the Irrawady delta. Sgaw is the largest Karen language in number of speakers, with Pho probably second largest. Population figures can only be approximate; one guess for total speakers of Karen languages is between 3 to 4.5 million, with perhaps 300,000 in Thailand. Speakers of Karen languages certainly make up the largest (non-urban) minority ethnicity in both Burma and Thailand. Kayah Li has perhaps 100,000 speakers, all in Burma except for some 1500 in Mae Hong Son province of Thailand.

Karen is distinctive among Tibeto-Burman groups in its SVO syntactic typology, which gives it affinities with the neighboring Mon-Khmer and Tai languages. These affinities are surely areal in nature, and only to be expected of the southernmost Tibeto-Burman group (also nearly the easternmost: only Loloish extends further in that direction). This SVO typology is perhaps one reason that Benedict (1972) separates Karen from Tibeto-Burman, establishing the two as coordinate branches of a larger Tibeto-Karen group. Benedict also cites a few cognates that Karen shares with Chinese but not with Tibeto-Burman, but in my view neither these cognates nor the typological divergence is sufficient evidence for such a separation.

'Central Karen' is essentially a geographic term, which may nevertheless turn out to be a valid unit of linguistic subgrouping as well. It refers to the Karen languages (with the exception of Paku, which is either a dialect of Sgaw or closely related to it) spoken in and immediately adjacent to the area now known as Kayah State, formerly Karenni (more fully, 'The Karenni States'; cf. 'Shan States', now Shan State). These include, besides Kayah, languages that have been referred to as Padaung, Brè, Yintale, Palaychi, Mopwa, and many more. Actually the foregoing is more accurately interpreted as a list of designations than of valid, commensurate ethnic or linguistic groupings. The situation in the Central Karen area is complex in the extreme: the ethnolinguistic groupings are in themselves complex, with extensive 'dialect chain' phenomena, and this is complicated by the nomenclature, which mixes self-designations and exonyms (Matisoff 1986) with abandon. Many of the latter are deictic in nature, with meanings like 'people upstream' or 'westerner', and so naturally change their referents as their users progress upstream, westwards, etc. Residents of the area also are given to statements like 'Manaw is really a kind of Kayah' or 'Yintale is 65% Bre'. The reader is directed to Lehman 1979 for some additional discussion of these matters.

The Kayah are numerically the dominant group in the Central Karen area. This area, as its former name 'Karenni states' suggests, has a history of state-level political culture of a sort, and varying autonomy. It has consisted of between three and five states, with the states of Kyebogyi, Bawlakhe, and Kantarawady having the most continuity. Much of the outer form of Kayah political culture is an adaptation of Shan practices, but without the Buddhist ideology underpinning the Shan sources (Lehman 1967b).

Kayah Li, like most Karen groups, are not typified by any one form of rice culture. This contrasts with such groups as the Tai, who invariably are wet-rice cultivators, or the Hmong, who traditionally practice only swidden, dry-rice culture. Depending on their location, Kayah may practice wet-rice, dry-rice or a combination. They may also grow supplementary crops such as sorghum, for brewing, or sesame, as a cash crop.

The Kayah Li resident in Thailand engage mostly in dry-rice agriculture, as well as some wet-rice culture, and wage labor. Some of my acquaintance also own elephants and derive income from them, at present from transporting tourists, but formerly from working for logging operations. There is memory of employment with these foreign (British?)-run operations having been a source of prosperity for the Kayah.

The variety of Eastern Kayah described here is spoken in villages lying both south and north of Mae Hong Son town in northwestern Thailand; it thus lies on the eastern edge of the Kayah-speaking area. I am not aware of any Kayah Li villages existing east of the main north-south road that runs through Mae Hong Son. There is a slight difference between the Kayah spoken to the north of Mae Hong Son town and that spoken to the south, the two varieties being known to the Kayah Li as kè khu 'upper' and kè kē 'lower'. The language described in the present study is of the 'lower' variety; for a summary of what is known about Kayah Li dialectology see chapter 10. Most of the data presented here was recorded in three villages just to the south of Mae Hong Son town. They are

1. Thā Médɤ̄ Lē Khā (Thai khǔn hûaj dỳa), at an elevation of about 500 meters on a mountain (dɔɔj khǔn hûaj dỳa) on the right bank of the Paai river. thā is 'water', médɤ̄ is a shrub of the genus Ficus (Shan màak lɤ̀, Thai madỳa), lē 'creek, ravine', khā 'apex'; hence 'upper wild-fig creek'.

2. Rùsɔ̄ Lē 'rotten snake creek' (Shan hɔj sɤ̌ thaw, Thai hûaj sỹa thâw 'old tiger creek'), about two-thirds of the way down the mountain.

3. Thā Médɤ̄ Lē Chá 'lower wild-fig creek' (Shan waan hɔj lǝ̀ǝ, Thai hûaj dỳa or bâan hûaj dỳa), on the opposite bank of the river.

Thᴀ̄ Mɛ́dɤ̃ Lɛ̄ Khᴀ̄ is the oldest; people from it later founded Rùsɔ̄ Lɛ̄, and still later some moved farther down to Thᴀ̄ Mɛ́dɤ̃ Lɛ̄ Khᴀ̄ Chá, which I believe was originally a Shan village. In any case its present population is partly Kayah Li and partly Shan.

For all Kayah Li in Thailand there is a high degree of contact with Shan, and a lesser degree with Tai Yuan (Northern Thai) and Standard Thai. The population of all river-valley villages and towns of the area is Shan, with some more recent Tai Yuan and Central Thai immigrants. Local and provincial officials are also largely Tai Yuan and Central Thai. There is much knowledge and use of Shan by the Kayah Li, especially among younger people, and some Shan Buddhist practices are followed. Standard Thai is much less known, since it can only be acquired by attending school. Any literacy is in Standard Thai; there is minimal knowledge of the new Kayah script (9.4.3) or of the Shan script. The Kayah residents of Huai Dya, living mixed with Shan and going most often to Mae Hong Son town, are naturally more integrated into Shan society than those of the other two villages. Their children also attend the local school and so are required to learn Central Thai. However the Huai Dya Kayah maintain connections with the other two villages, returning to them for important Kayah festivals such as the ʔilū New Year's celebration. It should be noted that the presence of Kayah Li in this part of Thailand goes back quite some time; according to their own legendary history, they were here before the Shan and Thai. At any rate the residents of the three villages that I worked in are all Thai citizens.

0.1.2 Names

The Eastern dialects of Kayah might more accurately have been called 'Kayeh', since one of the isoglosses separating the Eastern and Western dialect groups is the correspondence East /E/ = West /ia/. The word for 'person, human', also part of the self-designation of the ethnic group, is thus /kəjā?/ in the Western group and /kəjɛ̄?/ in the Eastern. I have decided to retain 'Kayah', since it has already some currency in Burma, most saliently, perhaps, in the name of Kayah State; and in the Western anthropological and linguistic literature, especially via the writing of F. K. Lehman. From the linguistic and ethnographic point of view, 'Kayah' is as valid and unitary as most other ethnic groupings; also the people themselves recognize their overall identity. For these reasons it is preferable to use a single term for all subgroups and dialects.

I do, however, in most places use the fuller form Kayah Li. Native speakers refer to their language as kəjɛ̄ li ŋò, with kəjɛ̄ 'person, Kayah', li 'red' and ŋò 'speech'; and to themselves as kəjɛ̄ li phú, where phú is a suffix indicating 'member of a class, instance of a category' (cf. klⒶ 'army', klⒶ phú 'soldier'; details in section 3.3.3.1). Eastern speakers do often abbreviate the language name to kəjɛ̄ in the expression ?íbe kəjɛ̄ 'speak Kayah', but kəjɛ̄ li is the full form to which ŋò or phú is added. Using the name Kayah Li in English is also preferred by some speakers of my acquaintance for political reasons. See Lehman 1967a for some of the political background to the use of the names Karen, Karenni and Kayah.

0.1.3 Previous Work

On Kayah. There has been very little published in Western languages concerning either Kayah Li language or culture. The single exception is the writings of F.K. Lehman (1967a, 1967b, 1979), which deal with the Kayah largely from the point of view of theory of ethnicity, but also contain much ethnographic detail, including words and phrases in the Western Kayah dialect of Kyebogyi. Apart from that there are wordlists and phrase books compiled by British colonial officers, also in Western dialects.

On Karen. American Baptist missionaries in Burma during the 19th century created Burmese-based scripts for Sgaw and Pho. Using these scripts they compiled large amounts of lexical data for Sgaw (Wade 1896), and somewhat less for Pho (Purser & Aung 1922, Duffin 1913). Suriya 1986 is a lexicon of Sgaw as spoken in Thailand.

Haudricourt (1946, 1953, 1975) described the basics of the proto-Karen sound system, namely initials and tones. The initial work was based on a comparison of only Pho and Sgaw, using the missionary-compiled lexical material, but subsequently-available data on other Karen languages has largely confirmed Haudricourt's reconstruction.

Jones 1961 is a landmark in Karen linguistics, including a detailed phonology and a structuralist grammatical description of Moulmein Sgaw; shorter phonological descriptions of Bassein Sgaw, Palaychi, Pa-O (Taungthu), and two varieties of Pho; texts; a comparative wordlist of some 800 sets; and a reconstruction of proto-Karen. The phonological descriptions and lexical data are very accurate; unfortunately the reconstruction is fairly eccentric and takes no account of Haudricourt's pioneering work.

Western Bwe or Blimaw was the subject of two articles by the late Eugénie J. A. Henderson; it is hoped that her extensive Bwe-English dictionary will be published very shortly.

0.2 This Book

The language described in this work is that spoken in the three villages described above. Data was also collected from the village Mē Lē (Thai hûaj pòoŋ), north of Mae Hong Son town and not far from the town of Mok Cham Pae (mòok cam pɛɛ). The dialect in this area, called by the Kayah kè khu 'upper' differs slightly from the kè kē 'lower' of the territory south of Mae Hong Son (see Chapter 10 for details). Most of the Upper Kayah data is to be found in the texts, but a few examples are also cited in the grammatical description.

The data was recorded during two field trips. The first, between February 1983 and March 1984, resulted in an earlier version of this grammar which was submitted in November 1986 as my dissertation for the Ph.D. in Linguistics, University of California, Berkeley. The present version incorporates data from a second period of field research covering October 1987 to July 1988.

The book is divided into three sections: grammar, texts, and Kayah Li-English glossary. There is also an English-Kayah index of short glosses.

0.3 Abbreviations and Conventions

0.3.1 Conventions in Glosses

Example sentences are cited as in the following:

(0-1) ʔa chɯ́ ʔɯ́ lɔ̄   pīchəə vē̄te né mi nʌ̄ pɯ

    3s burn smolder exhaust complete 1s-thing Né fire two C:cloth

She burned up two of mine [blankets] (with fire). (272.3)

The form is as follows. First line: Kayah Li sentence; second line, interlinear gloss; third line, free translation followed by a formula indicating the example's source.

Notes on interlinear glosses and free translations:

1. The interlinear glosses are intended only to identify morphemes, not to give a fully accurate translation. More information on the semantics can be found in the free translation, in the Glossary, and for some grammatical morphemes, in the Grammar section.

2. Many-word English glosses of single Kayah morphemes are connected by periods, as hʌ 'lower.garment', dé 'dip.up' (e.g. water). A few morphemically complex words are given glosses for each component, connected by hyphens, e.g. təko 'one-CLF', chāmò 'chicken-female' ('hen' in free translation).

3. Some morphemes whose meanings are not amenable to a one-word English gloss, mostly particles and other 'grammatical' morphemes, are glossed in several ways. Some are given a two- or three-letter mnemonic, such as ʌ́, a Verb Particle (4.3) glossed 'NS' for 'new situation'; and kè~ké, a noun appearing as subject with weather predications, glossed 'AMB' for 'ambient'. A few are simply given a placeholder gloss in the form of a cap-

italized version of their phonemic transcription; e.g. nʌ, a morpheme with nominalizing, demonstrative and other functions, is
glossed as NØ. Classifiers are glossed 'C:x', where x is a short
tag for the class of items counted; e.g. phre, the classifier for
humans, is 'C:hum', and ko, the general classifer, is 'C:gen'.

4. Lexicalized compound words are generally not analyzed; e.g. bé se plɔ is glossed simply as 'eye' without identifying the components bé se 'face' and plɔ 'small round object';
similarly hʌ ca 'lower.garment + upper.garment: clothes' is
glossed simply 'clothes', dɛ sí plɔ 'put + heart: decide' is simply
'decide', and so on. Some of the more transparent compounds
have the component morphemes glossed on the second line, and
the gloss of the whole word appears in the free translation. Examples:

pò	vɛ̀	bése khí
Ysib	Osib	face dark
sibling		blind

5. Pronouns are glossed with numerals, plus 's' for singular and 'p' for plural if number is distinguished. Number is not
distinguished in the third person, but there are three third person
pronouns: a general, more-definite form /a glossed simply as '3';
an indefinite, backgrounded form ʔū glossed '3i'; and a form lū
glossed '3OBV' for 'obviative', which occurs only when preceded by a non-coreferential 3rd-person NP in the same clause
(see 6.3.2, 7.1). Gender is not distinguished by any of the pronouns.

6. Source formulas:

numerals with decimal point, e.g. 345.6	transcribed texts
numerals with slash, e.g. 8/23	elicitation notes
Arabic-point-Roman, e.g. 15.iv	elicitation notes

The contrast between texts and elicitation corresponds for the most part to the difference between spontaneous utterance and speech that is self-conscious, linguistically reflective and in that sense artificial. The only exceptions are scattered instances of short spontaneous utterances that appear in my notes with minimal recorded context. Examples with no indication of source are mostly simple, well-supported patterns for which the available examples are unsatisfactory (e.g. contain material that is irrelevant to the point under discussion, but that would require explanation). I have attempted to keep this last type to a minimum.

Bracketing: Occasionally when constituent structure seems relevant, the following symbols will be used:

‖ . . . ‖   clause boundaries

|. . . | boundaries of the Verb Complex (VC)

⧧   divides NP's, PP, ClfP from each other and from Sentence Particles (clause-final)

[. . .]   embedded clause (usually Attributive Clause)

example:

(0-2) ʔa | khé pò | thuú ⧧ dɤ́ mi klē ⧧ sō   be ⧧ bō ʌ‖
      3   shoot additionally bird   at:U forest among three C:flat and.then
He shot three more birds in the forest, and then . . .

Double slashes are used to indicate change of speaker in examples extracted from conversations, e.g.

(0-3) cwá tōútē // cwá ʔolē phέ
       go   where   go for.fun simply

Where you going? Just going out.

0.3.2 Abbreviations

AMB	ambient noun with weather predications kè ~ kè
at:I	'invisible', entity not in sight, Preposition mú (6.6)
at:U	entity unmarked for visibility, Preposition dɤ́ (6.6)
at:V	visible entity, Preposition bɤ́ (6.6)
AtrC	Attributive Clause (8.1)
BEN	benefactive, Verb Particles pè and pjà (4.3.5)
C:x	Classifier for x
Clf	Classifier
Clf'	Classifier-plus-Quantifier construction (6.1, 6.4)
ClfP	Noun Phrase headed by a Classifier (6.1)
COM	comitative Verb Particle kɅ̄ (4.3.5)
CP.x	Bound couplet-partner of x
DIS	diminitive-instantiating suffix phú (3.3.3.1)
Drv	Directive V-V
Dsc	Descriptive V-V
DUR	Verb Particle pa (4.3.5)
EMPH	various emphatic Verb and Sentence Particles, including jɅ, ní
EXH	'exhorting', Sentence Particle pō (7.2)
go:FH	go away from home, Verb hē

go:TH	go towards home, Verb ka
huh?	prompt-question Sentence Particle ɔ (7.2)
IMP	imperative Verb Particle mʌ (4.3.5)
INS	Intensifier (4.5.2)
INT	Interjection, e.g. ʔa:
IRR	irrealis Sentence Particle pā (7.2)
ITS	prefix ʔa (3.3.2.2.8)
Lz	Localizer Noun
LzP	Noun Phrase headed by a Localizer (6.1, 6.5)
Mod	Modal V-V
NEG	negative Sentence Particle to (7.2)
NEW.LOC	new location, Verb Particle kē̠ (7.2)
NØ	Sentence Particle nʌ (7.2)
NS	new situation, Verb Particle ʎ́ (4.3.5)
OBL	oblique, Preposition nέ (5.5.2.2, 6.6)
OrdNP	Noun Phrase headed by an Ordinary Noun (6.1)
OSib	older sibling
own.accord	do stg on one's own or of one's own accord, Verb Particle dɯ (4.3.5)
PL.AC	plural action, Verb Particle khē̠ ~ lē̠khē̠ (4.3.5)
PsAtrC	Postposed Attributive Clause (8.2)
PTC	unspecified Verb Particle or Sentence Particle
QS	yes/no question, Sentence Particle ē̠ (7.2)
Res	Resultative V-V
RØ	oblique participant involved, Verb Particle rʎ́ (4.3.5)
RØ:	pause, Sentence Particle rʌ (7.2)
s/p	(after numerals 1/2/3) singular/plural

sbdy	somebody
Seq	Sequential V-V
SH	special high, expressive high tone (2.6.4)
SPtc	Sentence Particle (7.2)
stg	something
SUGGEST	Sentence Particle kɔ (7.2)
TRN	transfer of possession, Bound Result Expression pè (4.5)
V-V	Verb plus Verb construction (4.1-2, 4.4)
VC	Verb Complex (4.1, 5.1)
when:FUT	time-when in future, Preposition chá (6.6)
X.big	as big as X, Preposition tí (6.6)
X.long	as long as X, Preposition thɤ ~ tɤ́ (6.6)
YSib	younger sibling
1/2/3	first/second/third person
3i	indefinite backgrounded third person (6.2.1)
3OBV	third person obviative, non-coreferential with a preceding third-person NP (5.3.1)

Transcriptions of non-Kayah languages

Written Burmese	Okell's (1971) recommended transliteration, but with acute accent for creaky tone
Spoken Burmese	as in Okell 1969
Chinese (Mandarin)	Hanyu Pinyin
Kayaw (Brè Karen)	my notes
Pa-O (Taungthu)	Jones 1961 and my notes*

Pho Karen	Jones 1961*
Shan	Egerod 1957, with /p t k/ for Egerod's final /b d g/
Sgaw Karen	Jones 1961*
Thai (Standard)	Haas, with /p t k/ for Hass' final /b d g/

*The Karen languages are transcribed as in Jones 1961, except for the following tonal notations: I use macron for mid level tones (Jones leaves unmarked), and circumflex for the high falling final-creaky tones of Pho and Sgaw (which Jones writes as high tone plus glottal stop).

0.4 Acknowledgments

I am indebted to the members of my dissertation committee: Chuck Fillmore, Kun Chang, and especially Jim Matisoff.

Many friends in Thailand deserve credit of various sorts, among them Professor Suriya Ratanakul, William Young, Bamrung Ruangsawat, Jacques Landy, Philippa Curwen, U Aye Saung, Jennifer Ringstad, Khoo Ooreh, Tim and Helen Van Sumeren, and John and Cathy Hall.

I have benefited greatly from discussions with friends and colleagues at Berkeley and Cornell, including Paul Kay, Farrell Ackerman, Amy Dahlstrom, Knud Lambrecht, Cathy O'Connor, and Julian Wheatley.

I am grateful to J. Fraser Bennett for making the Western Kayah Li script font available. Thanks also to him and to F. K. Lehman, two-thirds of the world community of Western linguistic students of Kayah Li, for all sorts of discussion and practical assistance.

I am indebted to the U.S. Department of Education Fulbright-Hays program for two grants (Doctoral Dissertation Abroad, Southeast Asian research) that made my field research trips possible. I am also grateful to the National Research Council of Thailand, and to the governments of Mae Hong Son and Chiangmai Provinces for assistance during my stays in Thailand. Much of the rewriting of the present volume was supported by the National Endowment for the Humanities and by the Rackham Graduate School of the University of Michigan. Thanks also to an anonymous reader for the University of Hawai'i Press. For assistance with printing, heartfelt thanks to the University of Michigan Language Resource Center and its personnel, especially Marc Siskin.

I am deeply indebted to my major informant Kāmè for long hours of patient work, and to the people of Thʌ Médɤ Lɛ Khʌ, Rùsɔ Lɛ̄ and Thʌ Médɤ Lɛ̄ Chá, who put me up in their homes, told me stories, answered my questions, and allowed me to tape record hours of conversation, story and song.

Last but not least I would like to thank my parents, who discerned my interest in linguistics long before I did, and my wife Linda Tiffany, for support of every kind, both long-distance and close-up.

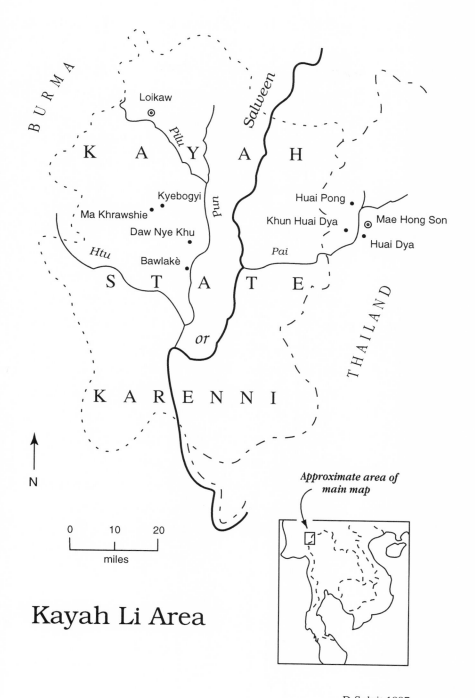

BURMA

Loikaw ◉

K　A　Y　A　H

Pilu

Salween

Kyebogyi •
Ma Khrawshie •

Pun

Huai Pong •
Khun Huai Dya •　　◉ Mae Hong Son

Daw Nye Khu •

Htu

Pai

Huai Dya •

Bawlakè •

S　T　A　T　E

or

THAILAND

K　A　R　E　N　N　I

N

Approximate area of
main map

0　　10　　20
miles

Kayah Li Area

D. Solnit 1997

Part I

Grammar

Chapter 1

Typological Outline

The purpose of this chapter is to provide an overview of the Kayah Li language before launching into detailed description. In doing so I will make use of both standard typological parameters, such as word-order, and of more traditional categories such as 'tonal', hoping to situate the language in the Southeast Asian areal context as well as among human languages in general. A more practical consideration is to familiarize the reader with basic Kayah Li sentence structure and with a short list of high-frequency morphemes, which should ease comprehension of the upcoming example sentences and expressions. For example, since virtually every clause contains at least one pronoun, I give a list of pronouns here so that the reader does not need to hunt out the chapter (6) on Nouns and the NP, where the pronoun system is discussed.

Note that the use of familiar terms like Noun, Verb, Indirect Object, Prepositional Phrase, and so on, should not be taken to mean that the Kayah Li phenomena are identical in every respect to their counterparts of these names in familiar languages like English. They are similar enough that the familiar terms can provide an entry into understanding the item in question, but in every case the full description should be consulted for the points on which the Kayah Li phenomenon is unlike any other phenomenon with the same name.

1.1 Phonology

Kayah Li is a tone language, with some 'tones' including phonation; as well as pitch features. The initial consonant system is moderately complex, including a three-way contrast of voiced/voiceless unaspirate/voiceless aspirate for stops, and stop+liquid clusters. There are no voiceless sonorant or glottalized initials. There are no final consonants, and the rhyme system is fairly simple, consisting mostly of monophthongs and a few diphthongs.

The transcription is generally IPA for segments. Tones are marked with macron ($\bar{x}$) for mid level, acute accent ($\acute{x}$) for high level, grave accent ($\grave{x}$) for low falling, and no mark (x) for low level.

1.2 Morphemes

Most morphemes are monosyllables, but there are a few polysyllables and a rather larger number of prefixed syllables, where the 'prefix', a CV syllable with a drastically reduced inventory of segmental and tonal contrasts, is sometimes an identifiable morpheme and sometimes not. No prefix has a high degree of productivity. There is one productive use of reduplication. There is also a hint of tone-change as a derivational process. Morphophonemic alternations include vowel copying and tone dissimilation in prefixes. Word formation is predominantly by compounding.

1.3 Lexicon

Form classes include Noun, Verb, Preposition, Demonstrative, Quantifier, Verb Particle and Sentence Particle. There is no class of adjectives, the translation equivalents of English adjectives being a subclass of Verb. Classifiers are a special type of bound Noun. Prepositions are few, and many locative meanings are expressed by Localizer Nouns that function as head of the NP object of a preposition. E.g. 'inside the box' is dɤ̀ kɔ̄ kū, literally 'at (dɤ̀) the box's (kɔ̄) inside (kū)'. Sentence Particles, at the end of the clause, mark things like aspect, polarity and illocutionary force; Verb Particles, clustering around the verb, mark aspect, modality, and adverbial notions ranging from the abstract, like 'instead' and 'excessively', to quite concrete, as 'help to V', 'sneak, V stealthily'.

There is notable lexical elaboration in such areas as rice culture, carrying, cutting, and containers. There is no status marking, either in lexical paradigms or in special status-marking morphemes. In this latter characteristic Kayah Li resembles the languages of other non-literate, egalitarian cultures of the area, and differs from those found in literate, stratified cultures such as Thai, Burmese, Khmer and so on.

1.4 Syntax

Word order is SVO, with nominal modifiers preceding heads and verbal modifiers following. For example:

(1-1)   vē ʔikē   du
     1s blanket big
     my big blanket

(1-2)   ne tétabō thʌ̄ ʔo
     2s pencil   water exist
     your ball-point pen

The postposed verbal modifiers in both examples are clauses, the single word du '[be] big' in (1) and thʌ̄ ʔo 'water exists' in (2), tétabō thʌ̄ ʔo being literally 'a pencil that has liquid'.

     Prepositions exist, but they are not of great importance in locative or syntactic function-marking. There is extensive verb serialization, mostly restricted to immediate concatenation of strings of lexical verbs, optionally preceded and/or followed by Verb Particles, the whole being known as the Verb Complex (VC). All larger verb-centered constructions in series are clause sequences, with the exception of one limited V' series.

     Clause structure is:

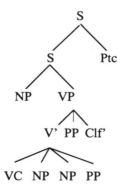

The two NP daughters of V' are Indirect Object followed by Direct Object. Note the preferred position of Clf' (Quantifier +

Clf), regardless of which NP referent it 'counts'. The following would be the normal way to express 'four children have eaten':

(1-3) púcè ʔe thō ʎ dī sí lwī
     child   eat finish NS c.rice C:hum four
Four children have eaten.

Clauses that modify a nominal are called Attributive Clauses (AtrC), not relative clauses since there is no class of relative pronouns. They are of two kinds, postposed as in (1,2) above, and preposed, as:

(1-4) [ʔa ʔe tēú] təhe
    3   eat fish one-C:group
    the group that was eating fish

This illustrates the requirement that the nominal modified by the preposed AtrC must be a Clf', here consisting of the numeral tə- 'one' and the classifier for groups of people he. The preposed AtrC is considered to be nominalized, preserving the generalization that nominal modifiers precede their heads.

1.5 Areal Characteristics

The foregoing mentions many characteristics typical of the linguistic area composed of mainland Southeast Asia and southern China. Among them are lexically contrastive tone, the high correlation between the syllable and the morpheme, the presence of classifiers as a grammatical category, and the prominence of verb serialization. The picture is very much that of the traditional 'isolating' language. Semantically the elaboration of terms for cutting and carrying is typical.

We may also list some negative characteristics. There is

no marking of nouns for case, number or gender. There is no inflection of verbs for tense, person-number agreement, voice, or anything else. In fact there is no inflectional morphology of any kind; the few affixes and other processes (tone change, reduplication) have derivational functions, of low productivity.

1.6 Useful and Common Words

Pronouns:

	Sg	Pl	number unmarked
1	vē	pe	
2	ne	sī	
3	—	—	ʔa, lū, ʔū

The third-person pronouns are all unmarked for number. lū is noncoreferential with a NP that precedes it in the clause; ʔū is backgrounded and indefinite. There is also a rare third-person plural form jesī.

Words for rice:

bó growing and unhusked rice; e.g. bó mɔ̀ 'rice plant'; bó tù 'rice-sheaf'; bóʔe rice after threshing, grains separated from stalks but still in husk

hō rice after pounding to remove husks; 'h.rice' in interlinear glosses

dī cooked rice; 'c.rice' in glosses

Other nouns:

mɔ̀ mother	thwi dog	rū̄ silver, money
phē father	chā chicken	ʔithoə knife
pɔ̀ younger sibling	pù ox	hi house

Some common verbs:

cwá go	thɛ ascend	dʌ́ give; allow
me do	tā fall	nɔ́ use; command
hé say	thō finish	ka go towards home, return
ʔe eat	phjá take	hɛ̄ go away from home
rɛ́ good	du big	ʔo exist, have

Demonstratives:

ʔʌ̄ this

nʌ that

Quantifiers:

tə- one	lwī four	
nʌ̄ two	ŋɛ̄ five	
sō three	pwā every	

Classifiers:

phre ~ sí humans

dō animals

be faceted/winged things (birds, fish, leaves, edged tools, etc.)

mɛ̄ larger semiregular shapes (houses, internal organs, drums
     etc.)

nʌ̄ day

na year

Other common grammatical words:

dɣ̂ unmarked preposition: 'at', 'when'

nɛ́ Preposition marking backgrounded participant, often trans-
     lated as 'and' or 'with'

to negative, clause-final

9

ʌ́ Verb Particle marking change of state, new situation; glossed 'NS'

rʌ́ Verb Particle marking presence of obliquely involved participant

kʌ̄ Verb Particle marking presence of comitative participant; glossed 'COM'

The meaning 'to have' is expressed using the verb ʔo 'exist, be located', the pattern being [[possessor] [possessed] ʔo]. For example,

(1-5) vē rū̃ ʔo sō ba

1s   silver exist three baht

I have three baht. (literally, my money exists three baht)

Chapter 2

Phonology

Kayah Li phonology is best treated in terms of two types of unit, full syllables and prefixes. Full syllables may occur alone, while prefixes must precede a full syllable. The possible constituents of prefixes, both segmental and tonal, are a subset of the inventory of possible constituents of full syllables. Lexical items may consist of various combinations of full syllables and prefixes: se 'fruit' (full syllable), pənè 'buffalo' (prefix + full syllable), sárá 'teacher' (full syllable + full syllable), tərecū 'regularly, all the time' (prefix + full syllable + full syllable), mēləké 'pineapple' (full syllable + prefix + full syllable), hōsɔphɔ̄ 'airplane' (three full syllables), Təkɛluphē [name] (prefix + three full syllables).

A 'prefix' here is defined phonologically, and is not necessarily a morpheme, as in the example pənè 'buffalo', which is a single morpheme. Some prefixes are indeed autonomous morphemes, e.g. tə- 'one' in numeral-classifier constructions such as tədō 'one (animal)'. There are also two elements that are analyzed as suffixes but they are of relatively minor importance (see 2.4, 3.3.3).

11

2.1 Syllable Structure

Setting aside combinations of full syllables, the maximal phonological shape of lexical items can be represented as follows:

$$(2\text{-}1) \qquad \begin{array}{c} t \\ | \\ c \ \ v \end{array} \ \ C_1 \ \ (C_2) \ \ (G) \ \ \begin{array}{cc} T & t \\ | & | \\ V & v \end{array}$$

where both parenthesized upper-case elements and lower-case elements are optional. The minimal full syllable is considered to require an initial consonant, the only exceptions being a very small number of morphemes that I write with no initial, (see note 9 in section 2.2.1 below for a possible special explanation of them). Lower-case c, v and t stand for subsets of the possible realizations of their upper-case counterparts. Note that the linking of tone to V slots here is just a graphic convenience, and does not mean that I hold V to be the tone-bearing unit. cv/t is a prefix, $C_1(C_2)(G)V/T$ is a full syllable, and the rightmost v/t is suffix. For the maximal unit cvC(C)(G)V a convenient term is 'sesquisyllable', i.e. a syllable-and-a-half (the term was coined by James A. Matisoff). In what follows we will first describe full syllables.

T equals a tone; C_1 is any consonant; C_2 is a medial liquid; G is a glide (w or j); and V is a vowel. The combination of $C_1 + C_2$ is further referred to as the initial, which may be simple or cluster according to whether C_2 is present. Similarly G + V is known as the rhyme, simple or complex according to whether G = Ø or not. The presence of C_2 entails the presence of C_1. That is, the following combinations are possible (T present in all): CV,

CGV, C_1C_2V, C_1C_2GV. This list omits the small group of zero-initial syllables, which would be simply V, there being no GV syllables.

2.2 Initials

2.2.1 Simple Initials

	lab	den	alvpal	ret	vel	glot
voiceless unaspirated	p	t	c		k	(ʔ)
voiceless aspirated	ph	th	ch		kh	
voiced	b	d	(j)			
nasal	m	n			ŋ	
voiceless fricative		s				h
voiced continuant	w	l	(j)	r		

Notes on initials:

1. Aspirated stops and affricate are unit phonemes.

2. /c ch/ are alveopalatal affricates [tɕ tɕʰ]. /ch/ is occasionally realized with no stop component, as a slightly aspirated fricative [ɕʰ].

3. /j/ varies between standard palatal glide and voiced palatal fricative, also occasionally appearing as a slightly pre-nasalized alveopalatal affricate [ⁿdʑ], especially in the Low Falling tone.

4. /s/ is an alveolar or dental flat spirant. For some speakers it is strongly dental or even interdental, but this is more characteristic of Western Kayah.

5. /ŋ/ has allophones [ŋʲ~ɲ] (fronted velar or palatal nasal) before front vowels and glide /j/. Otherwise it is velar [ŋ].

6. /b d/ are voiced stops, with little or no implosion. They may be prenasalized in connected speech (i.e. intervocalically, since all Eastern Kayah words end with a vowel).

7. /w/ is usually labiodental [v].

8. /r/ is usually a retroflex approximant similar to Mandarin Chinese /r/. In emphatic speech it may be an alveolar trill. As medial in clusters it is largely or completely devoiced by simultaneous aspiration, approaching [ʂ].

9. A glottal stop that begins the second of two full syllables can be elided, producing a smooth transition between the two vowels. E.g. bó ʔe 'husked rice' can be realized as either [bo⁵⁵ ʔe¹¹] or [boe⁵¹]. It cannot be elided after a prefix, as in words like pəʔá 'mud', kəʔɔ́ 'noisy', pəʔu 'to rot (of wood)', ʔíʔu 'to crow'. When glottal stop is elided between two syllables that have the same vowel, the effect is of a long vowel, with a contour tone if the two tones are different: ʔaplō ʔo 'it has holes' (literally, 'holes exist') may be realized as [ʔəplo:³¹]. Elision is the rule in connected or rapid speech; it usually does not take place after pause or in emphatic speech.

There is idiosyncratic free variation involving glottal stop in two morphemes: [k~ʔ] in /kuklɔ́/ 'head' and /kúklé/ 'swidden'. The glottal stop variant is subject to elision as just described.

There are exceptions to the foregoing, such as the beginning of at least some VP's, where glottal stop cannot be elided. E.g. in the Subject-Verb-Object sentence kəjē ʔé ne 'a person calls you' the VP-initial glottal stop of ʔé 'call' cannot be elided to produce *[kəjɛɛ³⁵ ne¹¹]. On the other hand the sentence ʔaplō ʔo 'it has holes', cited in the previous paragraph as an example of elision, is a Subject-Verb sentence in which the VP-initial glottal stop of ʔo 'exist' does elide. It seems likely that these elision facts are to be accounted for in terms of larger phonological units (e.g. a phonological phrase that does not necessarily copy syntactic structure), but such matters remain to be investigated in Kayah Li.

Distinct from the preceding is a small collection of words that usually have no initial consonant at all, and do not have variants with initial glottal stop. First are five items that never have any initial consonant: the Verb Particles (4.3.5) ʌ́ 'NS [new situation]' and the second syllable of lāí '[not] yet'; the Sentence Particles (7.2) ɛ̄ 'polarity question' and ɔ 'prompt-question'; and the element ʌ that is a common second component of male personal names (6.2.2). Secondly, variation [pʰ~h~Ø] is found in Verb Particle phɛ́~hɛ́~ɛ́ 'simply' and suffix phú~hú~ú 'diminutive/instantiating' (3.3.3) (related to the Noun phú 'child').

The facts described above amount to a two-way contrast. I am treating the two members as (1) glottal stop, which elides under certain conditions; and (2) zero, which in two morphemes varies with [pʰ] and [h]. A few minimal pairs may be cited:

(2-2) ʔɔ 'pond' (Bound Noun): ɔ 'prompt-question' (Sentence Particle). E.g. ma thƛʔɔ 'it's a pond', ma thƛ ɔ 'it's water, huh?'

(2-3) ʔú 'book' (Bound Noun) : ú 'diminutive/instantiating' (suffix). E.g. kəjē liʔú 'Kayah writing', kəjē liú 'the (red) Kayah' (possible variant of the full self-designation kəjē li phú)

In the second example, the first syllable of liʔú 'book' is a different morpheme from the homophonous li 'red'.

The status of this zero initial is of course suspect, since it occurs in such a small number of grammatical morphemes and not in any content morpheme. It is possible that this zero is actually an underlying /h/, deleted under conditions that have still to be elucidated but that, again, are likely a matter of supra-syllabic phonological structure. (in that case the [pʰ~h~Ø] pattern would be simply [pʰ~h], with the [h] variant subject to whatever deletion pattern applies to ƛ ē ɔ and the others).

2.2.2 Cluster Initials

pl   phr
kl   khr

In clusters, there is complementary distribution between aspiration and the l-r contrast; that is, the aspirated stop is only followed by r and the unaspirated stop is only followed by l. Either the aspiration feature or the choice of the following liquid may be treated as redundant. If such mutual determination is considered undesirable, there is one bit of evidence for choosing the l-r difference as fundamental: simple initials with aspiration

16

never occur in the low falling tone, but [phr khr] do quite frequently. In other words, aspiration in clusters has different phonological behavior from aspiration in simple initials. Historically it is in fact the l-r contrast that is significant, with aspiration in Eastern Kayah Li clusters being a side effect of the medial /r/(cf. the Tai languages, where /h/ is common as a reflex of *r).

2.3 Rhymes

2.3.1 Simple Rhymes (the Vowel System)

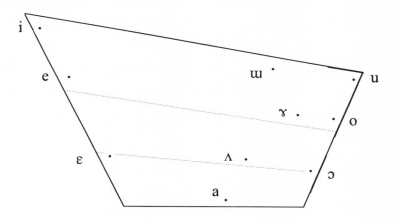

Notes:

1. /i u/ are cardinal [i u].

2. /a/ is a low central [a].

3. /e o/ are slightly higher than cardinal. When unstressed, /e/ may lower. This is especially noticeable in the word /bé se/ 'face', which often sounds more like /bése/.

4. /ɛ ɔ/ are cardinal [ɛ ɔ]; /ɛ/ is not as low as the [æ] of Tai languages which is often transcribed as 'ɛ'.

5. /ɯ/ is a centralized high back unrounded vowel, more central than the similar vowel of standard Thai, but not a fully central [ɨ].

6. /ɤ/ is a slightly centralized upper-mid back unrounded vowel, very similar to the /ɤ/ of Thai and Shan (which is often transcribed 'ə'), and occurring almost exclusively in Thai or Shan loanwords.

7. /ʌ/ is a centralized version of cardinal [ʌ], similar to the English vowel often transcribed with the same symbol (the vowel of but, gum, hug etc.)

8. All vowels except /i u a/ are raised under the low-level and low-falling tones. /ɯ/ is slightly lowered under the high tone.

9. The phonemic status of the three-way contrast /ɯ ɤ ʌ/ is solid only in the high tone, cf.

dɯ́	cut, slice	dɤ́	at	dʌ́	give
tɯ́	just now	tɤ́	chest, box	_	
sɯ́	wrong	sɤ́	insert	_	
chɯ́	kindle	_		chʌ́	clear; ten
jɯ́	shrink	_		jʌ́	(a Verb Particle)

There is also a triplet in the low level tone (not minimal because of different first syllables or prefixes): ʔíplɯ 'fight (of fowl)', təplɤ 'a while', súplʌ 'rope'.

The total number of occurrences of these three vowels in high-tone words is (from about 1800 words) 17 ɯ : 10 ɤ : 6 ʌ. Three of the words with /ʌ/ are particles. In other tones, words with /ɤ/ are rare, and include many Shan/Thai loans, e.g. mɤ̄ 'city' (Shan mə́ŋ = Thai myaŋ), mɛ́ dɤ̄ 'wild fig' (Shan màak lə̀ = Thai madỳa).

Thus these back unrounded vowels are close to having only a two-way contrast conditioned by tone: [ɯ : ɤ] in the high tone, and [ɯ : ʌ] elsewhere.

2.3.2 Compound Rhymes

          wi   wa   we   ja   jo   (jɯ)

The onglides /j- w-/ are usually closer to [e̥] and [o̥] respectively. There is at least one form /pja/ which may result from a fusion of /pe/ + /a/ (see 4.3.5).

/jɯ jo we/ are rare. The first occurs only in one word so far recorded: thā̄ khjɯ 'the Salween river'. /jo/ similarly occurs only in the common word mjō 'type, kind' (from Shan/Burmese). /we/ is more common, but seems confined to Shan and Burmese loanwords, e.g.

cwe habituated; W[ritten] B[urmese] cwài stick fast in, adhere, use habitually, chronic.

pwe celebrate, festival; WB pwài id.

jwe small change; Shan jɔ̄j id. (cf. Thai jɔ̂ɔj 'break up into small particles')

Note that the rhyme spelled '-wai' in WB is pronounced [-wɛ] in modern Rangoon Burmese.

/wa/ occurs with all initials except /v/. /wi/ occurs with all simple initials except /v t n h Ø/. /ja/ occurs only after labial obstruents and simple (non-cluster) velars.

2.4 Tones

The first four tones listed below are major components of the tonal system, while the fifth is decidedly marginal.

mid	⊢	33
low level	L ʔ	11
low falling	⬎ʔ	21
high	⌐ ʔ	55
high falling	⬊ ʔ	52

Examples:

rē across	kō blow away
re all over, at random	ko general classifier
rè trellis	kò wear on head
təré wax	kó do temporarily
cɔ́kəre⁵² otter	chiko⁵² shrimp

The forms given above are those found in isolation or before pause. In this position all but the mid tone end in glottal stop. The low-falling tone starts slightly higher than the low-level, then falls rapidly, passing the bottom of the vocal pitch register and into a brief stretch of creaky voice that shades immediately into glottal stop. Mid tone syllables are slightly longer than those with other tones, but this difference disappears in connected speech. In connected speech the final glottalization disappears from the low level, high and high falling tones but the low-falling tone retains its final creaky voice.

The sentence particles have special characteristics relating to the glottalization feature of tones, in that the distribution of glottalization is often reversed: the mid tone often has final glottal stop, especially in pā 'irrealis'.

Examples:

(2-4) ʔū dʌ́ hē pā to kəjē phú nʌ
     3i give go:FH IRR NEG Kayah DIS NØ
     they won't let them go, the Kayah (331.7)

(2-5) ʔʌ̄ tənʌ̄ pā rʌ phú ʔo nʌ hé nʌ
     this one-C:day IRR RØ child exist NØ say NØ
     One day later she had a child (80.3)

There is also a Sentence Particle, meaning 'only', with the anomalous phonetic shape [toːꜛ¹¹]; i.e. low level tone with long vowel and no final glottal stop. It contrasts with the negative morpheme /to/, also a Sentence Particle, but with the short vowel and pre-pause glottal stop standard to the low level tone. There is evidence that the two particles are in complementary distribution syntactically, as in

(2-6a) rū̄ ʔo ŋēcwè too
     money exist 500   only
     I have only 500 [Baht]. (2/27)

(2-6b) rū̄ ŋēcwè ʔo to
     money 500   exist NEG
     I don't have 500 [Baht]. (2/27)

See 7.2 for details. I use the spelling /too/ for the particle 'only'. This may be taken to reflect a speculation that the form is actually a fusion of two syllables /to/+/o/, which would in fact have the phonetic shape described, given what was said above about the zero initial.

The final glottal stops are considered features of the tone. They are not etymological: neither the low-level nor the low-falling tones descend from *stop-final syllables, while the mid tone does include reflexes of such syllables (see below).

There is a high pitch, sometimes extra-high with falsetto voicing, that occurs as part of an expressive marking for emphasis; see (2.6.4) below.

In a sequence of two mid tone words, the first may have a slightly lowered tone. The beginning of the low-level tone may be raised by a closely preceding high-tone syllable; thus the pitch contours of kúmʌ 'fingernail' and kúmì 'tail' are very similar, and the two words are distinguished (apart from the vowel difference) by the presence of creaky voice in the latter as much as anything else.

There is no tone sandhi properly speaking; i.e. no shift between tones conditioned by the tones of adjacent syllables, often with morphological relevance.

The relative lexical frequency of the tones is as follows: low-level > mid > high > low-falling > high-falling. The high-falling tone is quite rare, occurring most often in animal names and some other polysyllabic morphemes. But minimal pairs can be found:

ple^{52} bat	təple over (turn __, once __)
	təplè one layer; one arrow
di he^{52} kind of frog	di hé frog says
dī bɛ^{52} paper wasp	dī bɛ̄ yellow rice
sɛ^{52} same as	sɛ́ back at, in response

The high-falling tone is the realization of a suffix whose vowel copies the preceding full syllable and whose tone, [52], preempts that of the full syllable. The suffix is written /ə/; this vowel will also be used to write a vowel found in prefixes which likewise copies an adjacent vowel (see next section). For example, 'bat' is written /təpleə/, 'cockroach' is /lɔ kiə/, and so on; see 3.3.3 below for further discussion.

Analyzing the high-falling tone as a suffix helps account for its rarity in the lexicon. A slightly fuller form of the suffix can be seen in the 'upper' (kè khu) dialect of Eastern Kayah (cf. chapter 10). The following also lists Western Kayah cognates for comparison (V̱ signifies breathy voice):

	East (lower)	East (upper)	West
crab	chwa khri^{52}	chwa khreu^{52}	(çuo)
bat	təple^{52}	təpleu^{52}	plé
otter	cɔ^{55} kəre^{52}	cɔ kɛreu^{52}	tsɔ́ kərī
shrimp	chi ko^{52}	—	si kọ́
cockroach	lɔ ki^{52}	—	lɔ kī

The upper Eastern Kayah suffix has its own vowel quality. The Western Kayah cognates show that the preceding full syllables originally had a variety of tones; the regularly corresponding (and synchronically underlying?) forms in East Kayah would be təplé 'bat', cɔ kərē 'otter', chi kò 'shrimp', and lɔ kī 'cockroach'

23

(the Western Kayah 'crab' is cognate only to the first syllable of the East Kayah forms). It is possible that tonal dissimilation has been at work here, with the suffix originally specified for low level tone, and the high tone imposed on the preceding full syllable by dissimilation.

I will not go further in proposing features or any other internal structuring of the tones. However two types of evidence that would be relevant to such proposals may be worth noting from tonal dissimilation phenomena (2.5, 3.3.2, 3.4.2).

(1) Tonal dissimilation treats the low-level and low-falling tones identically, as simply low. One could then abstract away from the four-tone system to a three-way categorization by pitch level, high/mid/low, with the low member further divided by phonation features.

(2) In dissimilation, high tone triggers low, the two low tones trigger high, but mid tone is followed by sometimes high, sometimes low, suggesting that mid tone is unmarked or neutral.

2.5 Phonology of Prefixes

Prefixes are proclitic syllables with a reduced range of phonological values, always preceding a full syllable, with which they form an iambic rhythm (unstressed-stressed). They strongly resemble those units that in Mon-Khmer languages are commonly called minor syllables or preliminary syllables. While some of these proclitic units are clearly identifiable as autonomous morphemes, others are not; but since they all exhibit identical phonological behavior, I use the term 'prefix' for all. See 3.3.1 for further discussion of this point.

24

There are two main types of prefix, ʔi- and Cə-:

1. ʔi- has its tone restricted to low and high, the low tone being slightly higher than the low level tone found in full syllables. Before non-mid tone full syllables this two way contrast is overridden by dissimilatory conditioning: the prefix is high tone if the full syllable is low-level or low-falling, and low if the full syllable is high (or high falling). When the full syllable has mid tone, dissimilation does not apply and the prefix's lexical tone is realized (see 3.3.2.1 for examples and more discussion).

2. For Cə-, C = /p t k/, pitch is low (as with ʔi-, slightly higher than full low level tone), and V is a copy of the vowel of the following syllable, tending towards schwa in connected speech. This type is written Cə, directly preceding its full syllable: pəthɛ 'upwards'; təmjō 'one sort'; kəjē̄ 'person, Kayah' (more in 3.3.2.2 below). Notice that not only tone and vowel, but also the voicelessness and stophood of the initial are predictable: the only features that need underlying specification are those for place of articulation.

For minimal pairs contrasting a disyllabic word (two full syllables) with a sesquisyllabic word (prefix-plus-main-syllable unit), cf. kʌ dā 'spaces between figuration' vs. kədā 'door'; tɔ mɔ̀ 'silk-cotton tree' vs. təmɔ̀ 'sun'.

2.6 Vowel Harmony and Other Processes

This section summarizes various phonological processes exhibited in certain restricted contexts. Some have already been mentioned, some will be more fully described in the following chapter.

2.6.1 Vowel Harmony

The vowel I am writing /ə/ is found only in affixes: prefixes pə-, tə-, kə-, tə- 'one', suffix -ə, and a suffix -ə̄ possibly found in tə¹³ 'some' (see 3.3 below for further discussion of affixes). In all instances it copies the vowel of the full syllable to which it is affixed. In prefixes this vowel is reduced towards schwa as speech tempo increases; in suffixes it merges completely with the vowel of the full syllable.

Vowel harmony in prefixes is found in other Karen languages, such as Western or Blimaw Bwe (Henderson 1961); Kayaw (Brè) has both vowel and phonation harmony in one prefix (Solnit 1989).

2.6.2 Tonal Dissimilation

Occurs in prefix ʔi- and in several other morphemes and morpheme-like elements; see 3.3.2.1. Generally high tone in the full syllable triggers low tone for the prefix, low and low-falling tone full syllables trigger high tone in the prefix. Mid tone full syllables occur with either high or low tone prefixes, with some discernible patterning but never complete predictability.

The suffix -ə also may involve dissimilation, at least etymologically, with the suffix's low tone triggering high tone in the full syllable it attaches to. If this is valid, it shows that dissimilation is controlled more by linear ordering than by full vs. reduced syllable type. That is, it suggests that full syllables determine the tone of their prefixes, not because they are full syllables, but because they are the rightmost element in the phonological unit.

26

2.6.3 Tone Change

This is suggested by some pairs of morphemes, semantically related and homophonous except for tone; e.g. lō 'corpse', ló 'inter, bury'. Like this pair, many include one member with high tone. See 3.4.2 for a full list.

2.6.4 Note on Expressive Phonology

This is not an area that has been investigated in depth, but there is one type of expressive marking that is so common that it is worth a brief description. It is a complex of phonological features that includes:

1) non-lexical high pitch, i.e. high tone regardless of the morpheme's ordinary, lexically specified tone; glossed as SH for 'special high'

2) prolongation of the vowel, indicated by the length mark, e.g. /dɤ́:/

3) extra-high pitch, sometimes indicated by a second tone mark, e.g. /dɤ̋:/

4) falsetto voicing

The list is in implicational order; that is, if a syllable with this expressive marking has prolongation of the vowel, it always has the (non-lexical) high tone as well, but need not have extra-high pitch or falsetto voicing.

This marking indicates, roughly, emphasis. It is largely confined to assertions (not questions), and there seem to be some restrictions on its position in the sentence. At any rate, it does not occur in Subject NP's, and it is not common in the Verb Complex. One very common position is at the beginning of a Prepositional Phrase, as in the following expression that begins many a narrative:

(2-7) dɤ́ː ŋjá   nʌ ma
       at:U long.time-SH NØ be.so
       long, long ago . . .

Here dɤ́ 'at' (unmarked for visibility) has the prolonged vowel and the extra-high tone, and ŋjā 'be a long time' has the expressive high pitch imposed on its lexical mid tone. As this example shows, the expressive marking need not be confined to one item within a unit.

Another common position for this expressive marking is on the first Clf of a Classifier construction, especially in negative assertions as in the following typical exchange (the double slash divides utterances by different speakers):

(2-8) cwá khé ʔitē // khé təcɤ́   to
       go shoot what shoot one-C:kind-SH NEG
       What are you hunting? // Nothing at all!

cɤ, a Classifier meaning 'kind, type, sort', is lexically in the low level tone, but tokens of its occurrence in this expressive high pitch are probably just as numerous as those in its lexical tone.

Chapter 3

Morphemes, Word Formation, Grammatical Categories

3.1 Monosyllabicity

The typical Kayah Li morpheme is monosyllabic. As already stated (2.1), Kayah Li words may consist of various combinations of full syllables and prefixes. In fact each type of unit occurs as a single morpheme: the Kayah Li morpheme may be subsyllabic (i.e. an affix), monosyllabic, polysyllabic, or sesquisyllabic. Of these, true affixes, i.e. those with full morphemic autonomy, are very rare; polysyllabic morphemes are a decided minority; and monosyllables are most probably the majority.

Of the truly polysyllabic morphemes, some fall into semantically definable classes. Loan words, unanalyzable in Kayah Li even if analyzable in the source language, include kho-nokhá 'king' < Shan khŭn hɔ̌ khám ('prince'+'palace'+'gold')= prince of the golden palace); hōsɔphɔ̄ 'airplane' < Shan hɔ́ 'boat' + Burmese (Written) saŋ-bhau 'ship', perhaps influenced by Kayah Li phɔ̄ 'winged insect' and/or by sɔphɔ̄ ba 'galvanized

29

metal for roofing' (airplanes might appear to be made of the same material). Another group consists of names of plants, animals, and insects: mēleké 'pineapple', lehʌ 'teak', kúpè 'butterfly', jɔbébʌ 'mantis'. Others fall into no obvious class: nínè 'real', jèjo 'shadow, image', lāí 'yet'.

Kayah Li morphemes are usefully divided into Free and Bound types. Free morphemes are those capable of functioning as a major clause constituent such as Subject, Object, or main verb (= head of VP; all these terms will be discussed below); Bound morphemes cannot so function alone, but must combine with some other morpheme. A 'word' can then be defined as a minimal Free form.

Kayah Li word-forming processes include compounding and affixation. Affixation is relatively marginal to the system, while compounding is highly productive, playing a central role in all types of nominal constructions. There are various and heterogeneous constructions that could be considered verb compounds; those that are made up entirely of verbs and verb-like elements are discussed in 4.5. This chapter will describe principally nominal compounding, plus a brief mention of verb-noun compounds.

3.2 Compounding

Certain grammatical classes are Bound by definition (e.g. Prepositions, Verb Particles); others include both Free and Bound members (Verbs and Nouns). Compound expressions may contain all possible combinations of Free and Bound morphemes, as exemplified in the following compound nouns:

F + F   síne gun + thi penis —> trigger

mi fire + dā to forge, strike a light —> lighter, flint-and-steel

F + B   thʌ̄ water + mē̄ bamboo-section —> water container

pù ox + po enclosure —> cattle-pen

sɔ tree, wood + klʌ̄ boat —> boat

B + F   tē fish + bū white —> (a kind of large white fish)

B + B   sí heart/mind + plɔ small round thing —> heart (the organ)

tē fish + ú (a suffix) —> fish (general term)

Further discussion of the syntax of modification in the Noun Phrase will be found in Chapter 6.

There are two types of compounds that include one verbal member and function as predicates. Verb-Object compounds are made up of verb plus noun relating to each other as main verb and Object, but with specialized meaning. With nō 'enter':

nō hóhé   attend school

nō jechuə   be a Christian (jechuə Jesus)

For a non-idiomatic version of the former cf. kənō dɤ́ hóhé kū 'go into the school building'. Subject-Predicate compounds include the following:

mi name + du big —>   famous

bése face + khí dark —>   blind

se fruit + ʔo exist —>   useful, meaningful

Cross cutting the Free/Bound contrast is that of versatile versus restricted. Of the preceding examples, pù po consists of two versatile morphemes: pù 'ox' could also combine with ja 'flesh', nɔ̀ 'horn', etc., while po could be preceded by thé 'pig' chā 'chicken', and so on. On the other hand klā̄ 'boat' is a highly restricted morpheme, which never occurs without sɔ 'wood'. Another example of this type is lè sɯ 'shed, granary': lè is a highly versatile element meaning basically 'place for __ ' (see 6.7). sɯ, on the other hand, occurs nowhere but in this compound noun, and if asked to gloss it we can only reply that it stands for that part of the meaning of 'shed' that remains after the meaning of lè is subtracted. The same can be said of klā̄ in 'boat'. For another example consider the form təkhrɯ̄ se, which represents two homophonous morphemes: (1) 'a kind of fruit', (2) 'hail'. But təkhrɯ̄ se cà can only mean 'it's hailing', cà being a highly restricted verb that occurs only with təkhrɯ̄ se as its subject. So pù and sɔ are Free versatile morphemes, po and lè are Bound versatile, klā̄ and sɯ are Bound restricted, and cà is Free restricted.

When restricted morpheme combines with restricted morpheme it becomes increasingly difficult to identify the meanings of the component parts, and the expression verges on being a single polysyllabic morpheme. Often it is not possible to be completely certain that recurrent elements in compounds represent instances of a single morpheme. One example is the syllable do in donē̄ 'tell legends', dodē̄ 'hold out, offer in the hand ', and domɛ́ 'show'. Of the second elements, mɛ́ is 'to look', and dē̄ may be related to the second part of sedē̄ 'come forth (as new fruit)' (se 'to fruit'); do might then be said to have a meaning like 'set forth, offer'. Again, consider:

súplʌ rope	plʌ rope, string (Bound)
súba harvested hemp	ba classifier for sheets, flakes, mats
súsē bamboo splint	sē split with a wedge

A common meaning assignable to sú in these three words might be 'fiber'. This would be distinct from the second syllable of ʔasú 'oil'; but which of the two occurs in kúbísúse 'peanut'? kúbí is the general term for 'bean', so the word is probably to be analyzed as 'bean + oil + fruit' (kúbí-sú-se).

Comparative study may reveal that components of currently unanalyzable polysyllables derive from older full morphemes; e.g. jòlɛmɔ̄ 'squirrel' consists of jò 'rodent, rat' plus unanalyzable lɛmɔ̄; lɛ however may be cognate to Pa-O lí (B₁) 'squirrel' (although the vowel is irregular), while mɔ̄ is cognate to the second syllable of Kayaw jɤ̀ (B₂) mɔ̄ (D₂) 'squirrel'.

3.3 Affixes[1]

3.3.1 General

So far I have defined Kayah Li affixes (prefixes and suffixes) purely in phonological terms. In general linguistic usage an affix is a morpheme, or at least an element having a describable role in morphological processes. In this section we will consider to what extent these items in Kayah Li possess the non-phonological characteristics.

Let us say that an affix is something that is phonologically dependent but morphemically autonomous (i.e. having discoverable semantic and syntactic features); however Kayah Li tends

---

[1] For additional discussion of Kayah Li affixes, see Solnit 1994.

not to combine those two characteristics in a single item. The items that are clearly phonologically dependent are mostly of dubious morphemic autonomy, while those whose morphemic autonomy is most secure tend to be full syllables—not phonologically dependent. It is also worth noting that even when a phonologically dependent item does have identifiable semantic/syntactic features, seldom do the features include those usual among affixes cross-linguistically (marking person, number, tense/aspect; changing category or valence, etc.). Put another way, Kayah Li words that include affixes are either too much like single morphemes or too much like compounds, and the most productive formations are the ones that are most like compounds. For example, the prefix tə- 'one' is a numeral whose co-occurrence with classifiers is exactly like that of any other numeral, except for the phonological dependency represented by the vowel harmony affecting the prefix's vowel.

The remarks in the preceding secion on the difficulty of identifying Bound morphemes in compounds apply with equal force to Kayah Li affixes. The following lists all instances of each prefix of a given phonological shape, subdivided into groups with a plausible common meaning, plus, for each phonological shape, a miscellaneous ungroupable residue.

3.3.2 Prefixes Listed: Type ʔi-

Prefixes of this type are specified for one member of a two-way tonal contrast, high vs. low (see also 2.5). This lexically specified tone surfaces only before mid-tone main syllables, and is shifted by dissimilation before high, low-level and low-falling main syllables.

By sorting words containing these prefixes into groups with discernible common meanings, several distinct morphemes of this ʔi- type can be distinguished.

3.3.2.1 Instrumental ʔi-

One group of words has ʔi connecting a verb with a preceding noun, N+ʔi+V with a general meaning 'N for the purpose of V':

ché sew	sé ʔiché sewing machine (sé large machine)
klē̄ chop keeping contact	jò ʔiklē̄~jò klē̄ chopping block (jò at the base of)
phō chop, pound	kūchɯ ʔiphō foot-operated tilt hammer for pounding rice (kūchɯ mortar)
sē̄ split with a wedge	təthá ʔisē̄ a wedge
dɛ́ dip up (water)	thʌ̄ ʔidɛ́ kū water hole (thʌ̄ water, kū hole)

A second group has only ʔi- + verb, forming names of tools; as if words originally belonging to the preceding group had omitted the initial noun.

mū̄ to hammer, strike	ʔimū̄ a stick (for beating)
thá to plow	ʔithá a plow
ci cut with scissors	ʔíci scissors
pɔ thresh	ʔípɔ a hammer
dū sweep	ʔidū broom

And possibly ʔíkwa 'stick, switch', if related to kɛ́kwa 'be in half', təkwa 'one half' (via 'half piece > piece of branch, stick').

35

The following residue items are separated into nouns and verbs for convenience.

3.3.2.2 ʔi- in Other Nouns

ʔíthɯ 'post', ʔíbɛ 'bamboo shoot', ʔíja 'flesh', ʔíje 'howdah', ʔilū 'the Kayah New Year festival', ʔitē 'what?', ʔíse 'salt', ʔikē 'shawl, blanket', thʌʔíphrè 'whiskey', ʔithoə 'knife', ʔithé 'Crataeva' (Thai phàk kùm, a plant with edible sour leaves; perhaps related to təthé 'centipede'?), ʔíkhu 'earth, the world' (khu 'on the upper surface of' [Localizer Noun, cf. 6.5]).

3.3.2.3 ʔi- in Verbs

ʔílò 'to plant (seeds)', ʔikhré 'to winnow', ʔichɛ́ 'to tell', ʔíʔɛ 'dirty', ʔipiə 'narrow', síʔichē 'afraid' (sí 'heart', chē 'hurt'), ʔíphri 'buy', ʔihí 'to spin (thread)', ʔichá 'pound in a mortar' (chá 'hit with the fist'), ʔíkò 'jab with stg curved' (kò 'chop hole in log with axe'), ʔíkhu 'to wind, as thread on a spool' (khu is Classifier for spools of thread). Note that only síʔichē 'afraid' provides evidence of the underlying low tone, by showing ʔi- before a mid-tone full syllable.

For ʔithɔ́ 'cover as with a blanket', cf. thɔ́ 'id.', a Bound form occurring in complex verbal expressions, e.g. thɔ́ bí 'all covered up' (bí 'shut'), ʔomʌ̄ thɔ́ ʔikē 'sleep covered by a blanket' (ʔomʌ̄ 'lie down, sleep'). Here ʔi- seems to derive a free form from a bound form (for a similar function see ʔa-, 3.3.4).

3.3.2.4 Body Function ʔí-

These verbs denote body movements or functions: ʔítā 'get down, as from a vehicle' (tā 'descend, fall'), ʔícha 'jump', ʔílò 'bathe', ʔícho 'wash (clothes, hair), ʔíla 'call animal by clucking sounds', ʔíchʌ 'urinate', ʔínē 'to fart', ʔíbe 'speak', ʔívī 'to whistle; to scratch [as chicken]', ʔírō 'to sing', ʔíʔu 'to crow'.

3.3.2.5 Kinship ʔí-

With kinship terms, the meaning is 'my own kin': ʔíphē 'my father', ʔímò 'my mother', ʔíphō 'my grandfather'. The unprefixed forms phē mò phō could be used of one's own relatives, of somebody else's, or of an older person being addressed as elder kin out of respect.

3.3.2.6 Other ʔí-

ʔíchē 'sell', ʔíphō~phō 'chop, pound', ʔílū 'combine, unite (cf. Verb Particle lū 'each other, together', 4.3.5). These are the only words so far known to have high-tone ʔí- in verbs not plausibly assignable to the body-function category. For minimal pairs cf. ʔílū 'combine', ʔilū 'New Year festival'; ʔíchē 'sell' and síʔichē 'afraid'.

3.3.3 Cə-

A second type of prefix has the form Cə-, where C = /p t k/, pitch is low (as with ʔi, slightly higher than full low level tone), and /ə/ is the echo-vowel, copying the vowel of the following syllable. Unlike the preceding prefix type, pitch is always low, with no dissimilatory effects. This type, like all prefixes, is written directly preceding its main syllable: pəthɛ 'upwards'; təmjō 'one sort'; kəjē 'person, Kayah'.

3.3.3.1 tə- 'one'

See 6.4.4 below on quantifiers and counting.

3.3.3.2 Directional tə-

təva 'encircling', təka 'curved, hooked, in a curving path', təlwá 'past', təphā 'out of the way', təja 'past going in opposite directions'. Of these the first two are verbs, while the rest are members of a class of bound directional expressions (4.5) which also includes unprefixed items (vɔ 'circumventing', rwá) and one with optional prefix kə- (bé~kəbé 'across'). təka 'curved' occurs optionally unprefixed in sí təka~sí ka 'dishonest' ('heart'+ 'bent'), and may be related to ka 'go towards home' if the latter originally meant 'return, turn around'.

3.3.3.3 tə- in Verbs Denoting Undesirable Personal Qualities

təmwī 'crazy', təklùù 'stunted', təro 'timid', təké 'dwarfed', təklē 'lazy', təkhrɔ̄ 'stupid', təkhwa 'speechless'.

3.3.3.4 Animal tə-

təchē 'elephant', təci 'binturong', təchɔə 'slow loris', təkhwá 'lizard', təklí 'tortoise', təthé 'centipede', tənī 'bee', tədō 'land leech', təmɛ́ 'tusk (of pig)', təmʌ 'mollusc' (mʌ 'shell, kúmʌ 'fingernail').

3.3.3.5 Other tə-

Many other occurrences of tə- do not fit into the preceding groups. The following is just a sample. Verbs: təpē 'kick stg', təkli 'gnaw', təlū 'roll stg up', tənέ 'steep', təcʌ́ 'cool', təcā 'tight', təkhā 'yawn', təplo təpjā 'hurry'; Nouns: təphέ 'cotton', təkɔ̄ 'box', təpwī 'longan'(a fruit), təmɔ̀ 'sun'. There are close to two dozen more.

Alternation of prefixed and unprefixed forms is found in təne 'think about' (with Noun argument), ne 'think that' (with clausal argument).

3.3.3.6 Directional kə- and pə-

These occur with direction verbs only.

kə- means 'Subject changes location', thus ʔa phjá thε 'he picks it up' (phjá 'take', thε 'ascend') versus ʔa phjá kəthε 'he takes it and goes up'. In the first sentence only the (unspecified) Object/Patient moves upwards, while in the second the Subject/Agent moves upwards (and incidentally carries the Object along). (There is also a difference in the grammatical structure: phjá thε is a Resultative V-V, while phjá kəthε is a Sequential V-V; see Chapter 4).

pə- means 'orientation', as in jò pəthε khε 'raise the leg', mέ pəthε 'look upwards', pəhē 'up ahead, in front' (hē 'go from home'). In general the meaning of verbs with pə- does not include a change in location of any entity (in 'raise the leg' the emphasis is on the fact that the leg ends up pointing upwards, not on the motion that results in that state). pə- occurs with most directionals except lɛ 'descend'; the equivalent of the non-occurring *pəlɛ is tālɛ̄, with tā 'fall' and tone-change on lɛ.

kə- appears with orientational rather than moving-Subject meaning in kəkhjā 'backwards', related not to any verb, but to khjā~békhjā 'in back of, behind' (a Localizer, 6.5). A complete list of words with directional kə- and pə- follows:

gloss	base verb	kə-	pə-
go up	thɛ	kəthɛ	pəthɛ
go down	lɛ	kəlɛ	(tālɛ̄)
go out	the	kəthe	pəthe
go in	nō	kənō	pənō
go nearby	thō	kəthō	-
go across	rē	kərē	pərē
move from home	hē	-	pəhē ahead
behind (non-verb)	-	kəkhjā backwards	-

3.3.3.7 Other kə- and pə-

There are a few other occurrences of kə-: kəjē 'person', kəlō 'hill', kədɔ́ 'lid' (dɔ́ 'a wall, to enclose'), kədā 'door' (dā 'crotch, space between'), kəne 'almost', kəʔɔ̄ 'noisy, deafening', kəlwa 'slanted', kəsé 'itch', kəjō 'move, shake', kədó 'dirty (water)', kərē pē 'umbrella', kətha 'magic' (ultimately from Indic gatha).

Other occurrences of pə-: pəhó 'onion', pəcʌ 'to gossip', cō pəriə 'sharp-pointed', pətí and pətɛə both 'small', pəlwī 'cool (air)', pənè 'buffalo', pəkū̄ 'Sgaw Karen'. pəkhrō occurs as couplet-partner (9.2) of the last and possibly designates a particular Karen group, but it may also have little semantic content and function simply to complete a parallelism (see Chapter 9).

40

3.3.4 ʔa-

ʔa is the unmarked third person pronoun (singular and plural are not distinguished; see 6.2.1). An item with the same phonological shape occurs as a prefix. Phonologically it fits the Cə- type of prefix (2.5) in being unstressed, at or near low-level pitch, and with vowel quality approaching [ə]. It is exceptional, though, in not undergoing vowel harmony. I write it directly run-on with the following syllable, e.g. ʔaplɔ 'a seed, its seed'. Although this item is a prefix, some of its functions closely resemble those of the homophonous pronoun; therefore in the following discussion I give some arguments for its independent, non-pronominal status.

With Bound Nouns, ʔa- as it were allows the Noun to occur as a Free form without adding any other semantic coloration.

1. One type of Classifier (see 6.4.3) may function as head of compound nouns; for instance plɔ 'clf for small round things' appears in kɛ́ plɔ 'eggplant seed', bése plɔ 'eye' (bése 'face'), mi plɔ 'light bulb' (mi 'fire'). ʔa- may precede this type of Clf; with plɔ we have ʔaplɔ 'a seed, its seed'. At the level of morphosyntax, ʔa- is in effect a stand-in for any Common Noun (6.1), functioning only to make the whole construction a Free element: like any Bound morpheme, these Nouns require a coconstituent, and ʔa- is merely the most colorless such coconstituent (see 3.3.3.1 for a similar function of the suffix -ú). ʔa-prefixed nouns may also have special properties with respect to referentiality, as will be seen.

2. ʔa- functions similarly with some other Bound Nouns. An example is phē 'male' (to be distinguished from the homophonous Free noun 'father'), occurring in compounds such as hē phē 'Chinese man', phē twà 'handsome man', pù phē 'bull', and chā phē 'cock'. ʔaphē, with prefix ʔa-, can be glossed 'the male one(s)', i.e. the males of some previously mentioned group of animal. Exactly parallel is mò 'female' (Bound, distinct from homophonous Free 'mother') in chā mò 'hen', ʔamò 'the female one(s)'.

Although ʔa- is a prefix, it often seems to have an anaphoric function, calling into question its distinctness from the homophonous pronoun. For example:

(3-1) chāmò   bē   ʔo nʌ be, chāmò   lɔ ʔo sō be,
        chicken-FEM yellow exist two CLF chicken-FEM black exist three CLF
        ʔamò bē   jo cwá ʌ   təbe
          yellow fly go   NS one-CLF
        There are two yellow hens, and three black hens; one of the yellow ones has flown away (27.v)

Here it might seem that ʔa in ʔamò refers back to chā 'chicken'. Another such example is found in a conversation concerning the cultivation of ginger. After several mentions of təʔā 'ginger', several clauses intervene and then the speaker uses the word ʔatʌ 'the rhizome' (i.e. the useful part of the ginger plant).[2] Since tʌ is a general term for tubers, ʔatʌ in another context might refer to potato, yam, or taro.

But closer examination shows the difference between the prefix ʔa- and the pronoun ʔa. Consider example (1): in a Pro-

---

[2] See Solnit 1994 for the full citation of this example.

noun+Noun expression, ʔa would modify mò and the expression would the possessive interpretation standard to Noun-Noun expressions (see 6.3): ʔa mò would mean 'his/her/its mother'. But ʔa in (1) is not a possessive modifier of mò; ʔamò bē in does not mean 'its yellow female'. It is true that ʔamò bē partially depends on the preceding chāmò for its interpretation, but that dependence is not the usual relation of coreference. The following example will make this point clearer:

(3-2) vē sínɛ ʔo, manɛ́ ʔaplɔ ʔo to
     1s gun exist but   exist NEG
     I have a gun, but no bullets. (29.iv)

Again, it would be inaccurate to analyze ʔaplɔ in this example as a possessive construction 'its small-round-thing'. Such an analysis would have to construe ʔa- as coreferential with the preceding sínɛ 'gun', which refers to one gun in particular, that belonging to the speaker. But ʔaplɔ in this sentence does not mean bullets belonging to that particular gun: it does not refer to any bullets in particular, but simply names the general category 'bullet'. It is in reality a sort of abbreviation of the compound Noun sínɛ plɔ 'bullet', but that word does not occur as such in the preceding context. One might argue that this ʔa- designates the same category as the preceding sínɛ, but that is not the same thing as referring to the same entity.

     Prefix ʔa- is also common with Bound names of body and plant parts. For instance, mā 'joint' occurs in khɛmā 'knee', kɔnɔ̄ mā 'knuckle', ve mā 'bamboo joint', and ʔamā, 'joint, bamboo joint'. In ʔaso 'liver', besides allowing for generic meaning, it may be seen as having a disambiguating function: so on its own means 'head louse', and homophonous forms occur in so mɔ̀ 'hemp', he so 'loose soil' (he 'earth') and lɔ̀ so 'tripod for cooking' (lɔ̀ 'stone') as well as others. In plant parts ʔa- often alternates with sɔ 'tree, plant': ʔatʌ 'its tuber, a tuber'; ʔamɔ̀ 'trunk'; sɔché~ʔaché 'thorn'; sɔle~ʔale 'leaf'; ʔarwì 'root'; ʔase~sɔse 'its/a fruit'; ʔalò 'heart (of banana plant)'.

The true prefix ʔa- does not occur with Verbs. The closest thing to an ʔa-prefixed Verb is the optional occurrence of ʔa before stative ('adjectival') verbs in citation form. In this use ʔa is unlike a pronoun in being not fully referential.

There are occasional expressions like ʔa bū ʔíchē lɔ́ʌ 'the white ones have all been sold' [27.xi], which might seem susceptible to interpretation as having the Verb bū 'white' nominalized by ʔa and serving as Subject of a simple clause. But the more common version is of the type ʔa bū [nʌ təhe]ClfP ʔíchē lɔ́ʌ, with the same gloss. This shows that in the actual structure ʔa bū is a clause 'it is.white', functioning as a preposed Attributive Clause (8.1) modifiying the ClfP nʌ təhe 'that group'. Hence ʔa in these examples is a pronoun, not a prefix.

3.3.5 Suffixes

Suffixation is far less evident in Kayah than prefixation. There is indeed no shortage of Bound morphemes that must be postposed to some other morpheme, but they do not parallel prefixes either phonologically (they show no restrictions on possible occurrence of phonemes) or morphologically (they have precisely describable functions). Only two items have been found that qualify as suffixes.

3.3.5.1 Diminutive/Instantiating (ph)ú

phú is a noun meaning 'child'. It is Bound, requiring a preceding personal pronoun if it has the sense 'offspring' (as Thai lûuk): vē̄ phú 'my child', ʔa phu 'his/her/somebody's child'. With the sense 'immature person' (as Thai dèk) it must be followed by cè 'soft, tender, young'.

Related to this noun is a morpheme meaning 'small': dɔ̄ phú 'small village', ŋē̄ phú 'small banana plant'. Although this phú is verb-like in following a modified noun, it never occurs in a predication; the equivalent verb is pətí~pətɛə.

Also related to 'child' is a morpheme with the varying shape phú~hú~ú. Examples are klʌ̄ú ~ klʌ̄phú 'soldier' (klʌ̄ 'army'), kəjē̄ li phú ~ kəjē̄ liú 'the (red) Kayah' (kəjē̄ 'person, Kayah', li 'red'). Here there is no diminuitive meaning; the sense seems rather to be 'member of a class, instance of a category'.[3] That this suffix is distinct from the preceding phú 'small' is shown by the ambiguity of dɔ̄ phú (dɔ̄ 'village'), meaning either 'small village' or 'villager'.

Note especially thu 'bird' and tē̄ 'fish', both Bound nouns that are first syllables in dozens of names for species of bird and fish (and other compounds, e.g. thu pwi 'bird nest'); the generic terms for 'bird' and 'fish' as Free nouns are thuú and tē̄ú respec-

---

[3] A parallel can be seen in Chinese zǐ and èr, whose root meanings are both 'child', but also occur in reduced form as essentially simple markers of noun-hood. èr even loses its syllabicity, being realized as retroflexion, plus other modifications, of the vowel of the main syllable to which it is attached. Closer geographically, cf. modern Burmese hkalèi 'child' going to -hkalèi 'small', and thà 'son', also occurring as 'member of a class' in expressions such as myóuthà 'male city-dweller' (myóu 'city').

tively. In these words -ú functions like the prefix ʔa- (3.3.4), allowing a Bound morpheme to attain Free status without adding any semantic coloration.

3.3.5.2 -ə

The suffix -ə posited as underlying the high-falling tone (1.4) is quite parallel to the prefixes in that it is phonologically dependent and semantically elusive, although there is one sub-group of occurrences that could be called 'animal suffix'. How-ever, while there are abundant examples of main-syllable mor-phemes occurring both with and without a prefix (which provides the best clues to the prefix's meaning), only the following can be offered as such examples with -ə:

chi kó sɔ̄ shrimp paste (sɔ̄ rotten)   chi koə shrimp

ho stealthily   hoə hidden, out of sight

bɛ̄ yellow   dī bɛə paper wasp (cf. phɔ̄
                                        dī housefly)

sɛ́ again, in reaction (Verb Particle) sɛə be the same as (Verb)

3.3.6 Final Remarks on Affixation

It was stated above that Kayah Li syllables tend to be either phonologically dependent or morphemically autonomous, but not both. The preceding sections contain a fairly exhaustive listing of exceptions to this tendency, in the form of phonologi-cally dependent items, some of which have clearly definable morphosyntactic characteristics of their own, and some of which do not. But the vagueness of boundary between those that are clearly morphemically autonomous and those that are clearly not justifies, to my mind, the use of the terms prefix and suffix for all of them. It is likely that additional lexical data will reveal further common-meaning groupings; and prefixes that are now obscure in morphemic identity may once have been autonomous morphemes.

A good example of the latter can be seen in ʔíbe 'speak', whose prefix is a reduction of hé 'call, say' (the main syllable is be 'impinge, affect', a very common result expression). The unreduced form is preserved in Western Kayah hé be 'speak'. This prefix probably has the same source in ʔíchɔ̄ 'berate', if originally hé 'say' plus chɔ̄ 'hard, strong'; and possibly in other verbs of utterance such as ʔíché 'tell' and ʔírō 'sing'.

Undoubtedly many other Kayah Li affixes are relic forms as well. This is a common situation in Tibeto-Burman, as is cyclical prefixation: as old prefixes are lost or fuse with initials, new ones arise (see Matisoff 1978, 1.122 on the 'compounding/prefixation cycle'). E.g. the th- of Kayah thé 'pig', thē 'bear' and thwi 'dog' is in origin an old prefix, the Tibeto-Burman roots being something like *wak, *wam, and *kwiy (in the last case the initial *k- was reanalyzed as a prefix, then dropped before addition of the new prefix t(h)-). Even by proto-Karen times this *th- was assimilated into the initial consonant system; however, it is possible that the Kayah tə- in animal names (3.3.3.4) is a regeneration of the older dental-stop animal prefix.

Proto-Tibeto-Burman prefixes may be grouped into five types: fricative *s-, liquid *r-, stop *b-d-g-, nasal *m-, and *(ʔ)a- (cf. Benedict 1972). Of these the two prefix types of Kayah Li are faithful reflections of the third and fifth, whether direct reflexes or latter-day re-creations. What we seem to have is the persistence of affixation as a system, combined with rapid obsolescence of individual items in the system.

3.4 Other Alternations

3.4.1 Tone Change

There exist pairs of morphemes that have the look of being derivationally related by tone change, although the seeming relation is no doubt a coincidence in some cases. Many, though by no means all, of this type include the high tone as one of the pair, suggesting a former derivational function for that tone. Examples:

thɔ̄ enclosure, container	thɔ́ cover as with a blanket
bɔ̄klé blink	bɔ́khri close the eyes
bō classifier for lengths	khɛ bó leggings[4] (khɛ leg)
cū willing, obey (V)	cú according to (V)
le dē mat	dé to spread
thʌ̄ klō ditch	thɛ́ kló pig trough
təcɛ̄ a bird trap	ché to trap
du big	dúlōʌ́ be older of siblings
lō corpse	ló inter (bury a corpse)
pho clf for places	phó clf for times
sī 2nd person plural pronoun	sí clf for humans (6.4.3)
ma steady, fixed	rā má write down
lɛ descend	tālɛ̄ downwards

---

[4] Part of the Kayah female costume, consisting of large numbers of rings made of lacquered twine, gathered around the knees.

ro be early (in the day)	rō classifier for mornings
chī nʌ̄ chī sē	chī nʌ chī sē (both:) all day and all night (nʌ̄ day, sē night; both are classifiers)
ʔa ro other, another	rò particle denoting plural action by animates (4.3.7)

Note the additional alternation of initial in təcē 'a trap'/ché 'to trap'; this type of alternation is not common in Karen.

The numeral 'ten' also exhibits this pattern: in the numerals 10–19 it is chʎ́, while in 20–99 it is chʌ̄ (see 6.3.4 for details; note the parallel with English ten, which has -teen for the former and -ty for the latter). The etymologically regular form is chʌ̄ (cf. Pa-O təchì, tone A1), indicating that here also the high tone is secondary.

The following possible grouping includes both low-level and mid as well as high tone:

> dε put, place
> dodē hold out, offer
> sedē form, as fruit (sε to fruit)
> dέ to sprout (dέ plu a sprout)

The expressive use of the high and high-falling tones (2.6.4) also qualifies as tone change.

3.4.2 Tonal Dissimilation

This has already been described for the prefix ʔi-; something similar is seen in the following.

kè 'country' (Bound) is related to kè~ké, ambient subject of weather verbs such as cɯ 'rain', rò 'cold', ku 'hot'. kè is the etymologically regular form, with tone B₂ as seen in cognates such as Pa-O khâm. High-tone ké would seem to have undergone dissimilation before the low tones of cɯ/rò/ku; the impression is confirmed by the alternation ké cɯ 'it's raining', versus kè sí cɯ 'it's going to rain' (sí 'want'). However dissimilation fails to apply in kè lɛsé 'it's windy, wind blows'.

'Leg' has the form khɛ, with low-level tone, before mid tone in the compounds khɛ mā 'knee' (mā 'joint'), khɛ kē lē 'hollow of the knee', and khɛ rē 'paw'. It is khē (mid tone) before low-level: khē do 'lower leg', khēkʌ 'thigh', khē le 'foot', khē khi 'shin'. (low-level khɛ is the etymologically regular form).

The element ku~kū~kú appears in many body-part words. The following list indicates the tone of the ku element with a lower-case letter and that of the following syllable with an upper-case letter.

mL	kūʔu	mouth
mL	kūcɛ	earring, long silver Kayah-style
hL	kúkhu	hand
hL	kúmʌ	fingernail (mʌ 'shell')
hL	kúmì	tail
hL	kúklɔ	hold in hand (cf. klɔ́ clf for bunches, bundles)
hL	chākúdi	cock's comb (cf. kūdi stem, handle)
lH	kuklɔ́	head
lH	kuchɔ́	hairpiece
lM	kukhʌ̄	tooth
lM	kusā	sweat
lM	kuphō	nose (phō flower?)
lM	kusē	earring, gold Shan-style

50

hM   kújā   <small>palm</small>

hM   kúdūū   <small>crown of the head</small>

hM   kúlā   <small>necklace</small>

Other possible members of this group, if we assume that the vowel of ku has assimilated to that of the following syllable, are kɔnɔ̄ 'finger/toe', kólo 'hair of the head' (lo 'thread'), kēleko 'ear', and kesé 'itch'. In all of these the dissimilation is more general: the two syllables must have different tones. Notice that the low-falling tone never appears in the first syllable, more evidence of the marked or unusual nature of the low-falling tone. Notice also in kúklɔ 'hold in hand' that the second syllable may exhibit tonal dissimilation as well, if it can be identified with klɔ́ 'clf for bunches, bundles'. The connection would be the notion of a bunch as gathered into the hand; in support is the fact that klɔ́ is used to count bó klɛ 'rice seedlings', which are gathered into small bundles that are held in one hand while transplanting, an important procedure in wet-field rice cultivation.

As was pointed out in the discussion of compounds (3.2.1), the history of these sets of forms may show either descent from a formerly productive and clear-cut process, or coincidental convergence of formerly distinct forms. An example of the latter may be təmɔ̀ 'sun', mɔ́ 'sky', complicated by the existence of mɔ̀, the ambient subject of time-of-day predicates mɔ̀ lī 'early morning' (lī 'light'), mɔ̀ khí 'nighttime' (khí 'dark'), mɔ̀ hé 'evening'. mɔ̀ might seem to be either 'sun' without the prefix or a tonal alternant of 'sky'—or perhaps 'sun' and 'sky' are tonal alternants of each other. These are really two separate etyma, as seen in Pa-O mî (B$_2$) 'sun', mɔ́ʔ (D$_1$) 'sky'. Pa-O has cognates for the second and third time-of-day expressions cited: mî khéʔ 'nighttime', mî hà 'evening'.

3.4.3 Reduplication

Reduplication in Kayah copies the last syllable in a clause, with the meaning 'also, too, either'. Examples:

(3-3) vē ma ʔe kʌ̄ phé thé ja   ja
      1s be.so eat COM simply pig flesh RDP
      I ate only pork, too (as did he).

(3-4) ʔa cwá kʌ̄   kʌ̄
      3 go COM RDP
      He went along too.

(3-5) vē cwá to   to
      1s go NEG RDP
      I won't go either.

(3-6) m̩, síʔichē ké rò he he
      afraid   AMB cold LST RDP
      Mm, I'm afraid it'll be cold, too (e.g. in addition to raining).

The process is largely a simple matter of copying whatever syllable happens to be clause-final, regardless of either form-class or syntactic function. The reduplicated syllables in the above examples include:

    ja 'flesh', a Free Noun, the head of an NP functioning as object
    kʌ̄ 'with, also', a Verb Particle

to 'negative', a Sentence Particle

he 'lest, possible bad situation', another type of Sentence Particle

The only exceptions to this simple rule are: (1) certain clause-final particles may not reduplicate (see 7.2 below); (2) examples like the following:

(3-7) thế phra   kʌ̄   ke   ke ~ thế phra phra ke
     pig to.sound COM perhaps RDP
(both:) It might also be a pig making noise.

Here it seems possible to reduplicate the lexical morpheme phra 'to sound', passing over a grammatical morpheme, the Sentence Particle ke 'possible non-future situation'. More research is needed on this point.

3.5 Form Classes

Below is a list of the form classes of Kayah Li:

Noun. Occurs in the slot __te 'X things, X's things'; can function as Subject, Direct Object, Indirect Object; precedes a modified Noun (with exceptions); can be counted by a ClfP containing a classifier that is lexically/semantically related.

Classifier. Occurs in the slot tə- __ 'one X'; the other essential component of the ClfP; may be considered a special type of Noun.

Verb. Occurs in the slot __lāí to 'hasn't yet X-d'; may function as Predicator, the head of the VC; follows a modified Noun. Includes all the morphemes translating English adjectives. Minor form classes with verblike features include Bound Result Expressions and Intensifiers.

Preposition. Occurs in the slot __ ʔʌ̄ (e.g. bɤ́ ʔʌ̄ 'at this = here', hú ʔʌ̄ 'like this'); introduces the PP.

Quantifier. Occurs in construction with ko 'general classifier' or any other Classifier (preposed or postposed according to the particular Quantifier); is one of the two essential components of the ClfP; includes the numerals.

Demonstrative. Occurs in the slot __ Quantifier-Classifier.

Verb Particle. Occurs in the slot me jɛ̀ ___ NP 'hard to do . . . ' (e.g. me jɛ̀ lāí hi to 'not yet hard to build a house', me jɛ̀ lɤ̀ 'harder to do'); terminates the VC.

Sentence Particle. Occurs in the slot Verb-ClfP__ ; a principal member is to, the negative.

Adverb. Occurs both sentence initially and immediately preceding the Sentence Particles; a small class consisting largely of time expressions.

Class overlaps. In general the two major classes, Noun and Verb, are distinct, yet there are instances of morphemes with dual membership. Note the following:

(3-8) bó se ʔo to
      rice fruit exist NEG
      The rice doesn't have any grains.

(3-9) bó se to
      rice fruit NEG
      The rice doesn't fruit; the rice doesn't put out grains.

(3-10) ʔa se lāí to
      It hasn't fruited yet. (5/4)

Similar overlap is seen in phō 'flower; to flower', ché 'thorn; be thorny'. Note also ʔíbe 'language; to speak'. Ethnic designations may also be interpreted as having membership in both Noun and Verb, in line with two characteristics (see also 6.3.2):

1. Like Nouns, they may modify a following Noun with a meaning of possession (phrè hʌca 'a Shan's clothes, the Shan's clothes'); they may also, like Verbs, modify a preceding Noun, with a meaning like 'X-type, X-style' (hʌca phrè 'Shan-style clothing')

2. They may appear inside the VC, a possibility normally open to Verbs and Verb Particles only (ʔa ʔíbe phrè cè nɔ́ to 'he can't speak Shan at all'). This particular construction is probably to be classified as a Descriptive V-V (4.2.4).

Within the major classes, there are several salient instances of overlap. Among Nouns, there is fairly extensive overlapping between one type of Classifier and Bound Ordinary Nouns (6.4.3.3). An example is mɔ̀, the classifier for smaller plants, which also appears in compounds such as bó mɔ̀ 'rice plant', təkhέ mɔ̀ 'mango tree', ʔamɔ̀ 'trunk, stem'. Among Verbs, there are two special verb classes that include members overlapping with ordinary verbs. Examples are dʌ́ 'let' as Directive Verb, 'give' as ordinary Verb (4.2.3); be 'must' as Modal Verb, 'strike, affect' as ordinary Verb (4.2.5).

Chapter 4

The Verb Complex

4.1 Introduction

The Verb Complex (VC) is the site of the extensive verb serialization of Kayah Li. This serialization is in the form of immediate concatenation, i.e. strings of verbs. The VC can also contain verb particles (VPtc), but these are confined to the initial and final portions of the VC. That is, the general structure is (Ptc) (Ptc) . . . V (V) . . . (Ptc) (Ptc). The only required component and head constituent is a verb. In a verb string the first verb is the head.

Any other sequence of verb-containing constructions is a clause series. What is not found is noun (or NP) arguments intervening between the members of a series of verbs, the single exception being the fairly restricted source construction (5.2). This goes against the cross-linguistic generalization that associates immediate concatention of verbs with verb-final syntax, and verb-noun serialization with verb-medial syntax (Foley & Van Valin 1984, 193; Foley & Olson 1985). Kayah's preference for immediate concatenation is high even in comparison to what is known of the syntax of other Karen languages such as Sgaw and Pa-O.

I will adopt a 'bottom-up' strategy in describing the VC, starting with binary constructions of verb plus verb, abbreviated V-V (4.2), and of verb plus particle (4.3), then describing how these binary constructions combine into larger units (4.4).

The present analysis of the VC depends on a number of concepts, some being features of lexical items occurring in the VC, some being characteristics of the constructions formed by them. These concepts are sketched out below, starting with those applying to lexical items.

1. Verbhood. Possible VC constituents are usefully divided into those which satisfy the definition of full verbs and those which do not, with the latter known as Verb Particles (VPtc). Full verbs are capable of functioning as unitary predicate, or main Verb, of a clause. Most full verbs are also capable of modifying a preceding Noun, and they generally have more concrete meanings than the VPtc. These latter two characteristics can be taken as general guides only; there are some VPtc with surprisingly concrete meanings, such as cwà 'help' (see 4.3.6), and there also exist items that can modify preceding Nouns but cannot be unitary predicates, hence are non-verbs. As a rule VPtc's occur towards the beginning and end of the VC, and do not intervene among Verbs.

2. Syntactic valence. This means specification for co-occurrence with the 'core' grammatical relations Subject, Object and Indirect Object (for specifics of these grammatical relations

see Chapter 5). This specification is said to LICENSE the occurrence of these relations; it is a feature of every verb, and of a few VPtc's as well. Besides the three core grammatical relations, there are also a few cases in which it makes sense to recognize specification for certain oblique grammatical relations, but these will concern us more in Chapter 5 than in this one. Most generally useful is a classification of verbs into V_i, V_t and V_d, taking one, two and three grammatical relations respectively. The valence of the head verb may interact with that of other morphemes in the VC, including both non-head verbs and certain VPtc's, this interaction producing a valence for the VC as a unit.

3. Semantic participant roles (theta-roles, thematic roles, deep Case), also known as arguments. Argument specifications of verbs are said to be realized by grammatical relations in the clause.

I will use familiar terms such as Agent, Patient (not distinct from Theme), Goal, Recipient; but these are more conveniences for description than terms of a formal analysis. What does turn out to be salient and useful in description is a notion of a scale along which participant roles may be ranked. One endpoint is characterized by volitional involvement, sentience, causing, and movement; the other end involves undergoing a change of state, being causally affected and being stationary (relative to another moving participant). The foregoing is an abridgement of Dowty's (1991) list of properties of two role prototypes which he calls Proto-Agent and Proto-Patient; a similar concept is Foley and Van Valin's (1984) Actor-Undergoer scale. The roles specified by multi-argument verbs can be ranked on this scale relative to each other. I will use Foley and Van Valin's terms, Actor for the role with the most Proto-Agent properties and Undergoer for the role with the most Proto-Patient properties; Foley & Van Valin call these 'macroroles'. With Dowty, I assume that the assignment of a given role type to the macroroles is not fixed across verbs; that is, a type such as Patient may be Undergoer with a verb like *fry* as in *Next you fry the onions,* but Actor with a verb like strike in *The arrow struck the target.* In the latter case, the arrow argument has no Actor property but movement, but that is enough for it to outrank the stationary target argument. With all three authors, I assume that the Actor/Undergoer distinction is not neutralized with one-argument verbs: we will have occasion to divide one-argument verbs into those taking Actor and those taking Undergoer.

The following are features of constructions rather than individual items.

4. Ordering. This applies expecially to particles, which are strictly divided into preverbal and postverbal. Even the few postverbal particles that can intervene among verbs (4.3.6) remain to the right of the head verb. Within the pre- and post-verbal types, the VPtc's can also be given a rough classification according to the order in which they occur relative to each other.

5. Argument mapping. This refers to the way that verbs' participant roles are (or are not) realized as syntactic constituents (usually NP) of the clause. The head verb's roles are always realized. If the non-head verb is to realize its roles, they must be mapped onto roles of the first verb. This can be illustrated by the example:

(4-1) ʔa ce li bēʔū

    3   dye red cloth

S/he dyed the cloth red.

Here the first (head) verb ce 'to dye' takes the two arguments realized as the Subject ʔa 'he/she/it' and the Object bēʔū 'cloth'. In addition, bēʔū is understood as functioning as the Patient argument of the second verb li 'red'—the cloth becomes red. I express this fact by saying that the single argument of li is mapped onto the Patient argument of ce; or that the two arguments are mapped to each other. This mapping is most conveniently formulated in terms of the macro-roles Actor and Undergoer (point 3 above). Mapping can be represented as follows, using ce li 'dye red' as an example:

(4-2)   Sbj Obj

         | |

    ce [Ac Un]   li [Un]

           |_ _ _ _|

The dotted line indicates that the Undergoer arguments of the two verbs are mapped to each other. The 'Sbj Obj' notations are linked by vertical lines to the notations of the arguments that they realize: the Subject realizes the first verb's Actor argument, and the Object realizes the mapped pair of Undergoer arguments. One might wonder whether the two Undergoers are realized equally, or whether one is realized directly and the other is somehow parasitic on it; or whether indeed there is any substantive matter at issue. I will not attempt to decide among these alternatives here, but will conventionally link grammatical relations to the argument of the first verb, which may be taken to reflect the priority of the first verb as head constituent.

In some V-V types, the second verb realizes none of its arguments, i.e. there is no mapping (4.2.5, 4.2.6).

If there is mapping, it is predictable which argument of the second verb is mapped: the Actor of a multi-argument verb, or the single argument of a one-argument verb, whether Actor or Undergoer (for an apparent exception to this rule see 4.5.1). On the other hand, the choice of mapped argument of the first verb is not predictable, but depends on the type of V-V. Thus V-V types may have mapping or not, and if they do have mapping there is a further differentiation according to which argument of the first verb is involved. This yields a classification of V-V's into (1) no mapping, (2) Undergoer mapping, (3) Actor mapping, where types (2) and (3) refer to the mapped argument of the first verb.

6. Interpredicate relation. This refers to the relation that is understood to hold between the two events/actions/states named by the two verbs. In the above example the relation between the action of ce 'to dye' and li 'red' is that of causation: the event of dyeing causes the state of redness. Kayah Li V-V's can be classified according to three types of interpredicate relation: causation, sequence/purpose, and modification.

7. Relative openness of the two slots of the V-V. Generally the second position in a V-V can be filled by any verb, subject only to semantic considerations. The first slot in some V-V types is likewise open to any verb, while in other types the first slot is restricted to a special class of verbs. There are also a few

types in which it is the second slot that is restricted. Here again
we use a three-way classification, into Open, Restricted V_1 and
Restricted V_2. Note that the classes of verbs that fill these
restricted positions may have special characteristics in terms of
the other features listed here.

I close this section with some general remarks about the
VC.

This chapter will present many examples from spontaneous speech, but there are also points at which more artificial or
abbreviated examples are necessary. It should therefore be understood that although the minimal realization of the VC is a single
verb, there is a strong preference in actual speech for the VC to
include multiple instances of both verbs and particles. Cf. the following, from a recorded conversation, with three verbs followed
by three VPtc's; the VC is bracketed:

(4-3) [chúi kē ré   kʌ̄   lēkhē pè] vē mi to
       kindle burn good COM PL   BEN 1s fire NEG
       They didn't burn it well for me. (ls.2)

This preference for multimorphemic VC's sometimes makes for
difficulties in determining the verbhood of lexical items. It may
be that the difficulty of finding an example of certain morphemes
as unitary predicators, the criterion for verbhood, reflects the
unlikeliness of an appropriate context rather than a lexical feature
of the morphemes in question.

The VC has the properties of a single word. It does have
its own internal structure, describable in terms of ordering, argument mapping and interpredicate relation (points 4 through 6
above); but it relates as a unit to the rest of the clause, most obvi-

ously in its possession of a single overall syntactic valence. As an example (VC bracketed),

(4-4) ʔa [vī   jo cwá] chā   mò   bē   nʌ rʌ
       3   throw fly go   chicken female yellow Nø Rø
       She threw the yellow hen so that it flew away. (376.3)

This complex VC can be analyzed as [vī [jo cwá]], with inter-predicate semantics of the Causative type holding between both jo 'fly' and cwá 'go' and between vī 'throw' and the unit [jo cwá]. The argument mapping of this VC is as follows (for simplicity, the binary constituent structure just described is omitted from this diagram):

(4-5)   Sbj Obj

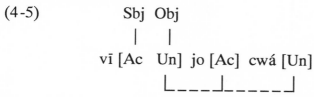

indicating that the Object chāmò bē 'yellow hen' (1) is thrown (2) flies and (3) goes (away). However, this complex internal semantic structure all boils down to the simple two-place syntactic valence specifying Subject and Object, no different from a monomorphemic V_t. Contrast the English translation, in which the syntax reflects much of the semantic structure just described, parceling out into separate clauses the action of throwing, with its two participants, versus that of flying away, with its single participant. The Kayah Li original confines this complexity to the semantics and keeps the syntax simple. Also the Kayah contains no overt indication of the causal relation between the actions of throwing, flying and going; while the English conjunction *so that* makes explicit the causal connection between *threw* and *flew.*

All this has the effect of giving the VC some of the characteristics of a black box, occupying the center of the clause over which it exerts many powerful effects, but difficult to see into or take apart.

4.2 Verb-Verb Constructions

4.2.1 Survey of Construction Types

V-V's are usefully divided into five types, based largely on the semantic relation between the two components. I will first list all five V-V types, with brief characterizations in terms of interpredicate semantics, and a few examples of each. The two V's in each example are underlined.

1. Causative, further divided into Resultative and Directive.

1a. Resultative. The first verb denotes an action, the second verb denotes a result of that action. Examples:

(4-6) ʔū | m<u>ū</u> s<u>ʌ̄</u> | pe
    3i   beat die 1p
They beat us to death. (110.3)

(4-7) belɔ | t<u>ā</u> <u>phé</u>
    glass fall crack
The glass fell and cracked. (10/31)

1b. Directive. The first verb denotes an act of ordering or permitting, the second verb denotes the content of that act, the action ordered or permitted.

(4-8) ʔa n<u>ɔ̄</u>   pā ph<u>úcè</u> mē klúí
    3 command cut child rhythm-pipe
She told the children to cut rhythm-pipes. (42.5)

(4-9) vē <u>dʌ́</u> <u>cwá</u> ne to
     1s let go   2s NEG
     I won't let you go. (3/31)

2. Sequential. The first verb denotes an action, the second verb denotes an action performed after and/or as the purpose of the first.

(4-10) ʔa | <u>ka</u>   <u>dɛ́hʌ̄</u> rʌ́ | ʔaphʌ̄
     3   return ask RØ grandmother
     He went back and asked his grandmother. (93.6)

(4-11) ʔa <u>lɛ</u>   <u>dʌ́</u> lū   ʔíkwa təphre   təko   rʌ
     3 descend give 3OBV stick   one-C:Hum one-C:gen RØ
     He went down and gave each of them a stick (gave them sticks one per person). (459.3)

3. Descriptive. The first verb denotes an action, the second verb gives an adverb-like modification of the action.

(4-12) ʔa ʔe phrē dī
     3   eat fast   cooked.rice
     He eats quickly.

(4-13) nìdā jɛ̀
     listen difficult
     It's hard to listen to ≈ it sounds funny (said of unacceptable utterances).

4. Modal. The first verb denotes obligatoriness, or one of various other abstract conditions, pertaining to the action of the second verb.

(4-14) ʔa <u>be</u> <u>ʔe</u> dī
     3   must eat cooked.rice
     He must eat (rice).

(4-15) ʔírɛ nʌ ma vɛ̄ <u>kha</u> ʔírɛ dɯ   ʌ́

    work Nø be.so 1s promise work own.accord NS

As to work, I promise to work myself. (84.1)

We now turn to detailed discussions of the types of V-V. Each section begins with a list of the general characteristics of the type to be described, using the following terms:

Type of Characteristic	Possible Values
Mapping	none, Undergoer, Actor
Interpredicate Semantics	causation, sequence, modification
Openness	open, restricted

Recall that both Mapping and Openness refer to the first verb position.

4.2.2 Resultative Constructions

4.2.2.1 General

    Mapping: Undergoer (common); Actor (rare)

    Interpredicate: causation

    Openness: open

    In this type of V-V construction, the second V gives the result of some action described by the first. Examples:

(4-16) ʔū mɯ̄ sʌ̄ pe

    3:i beat die 1p

They beat us to death. (110.3)

(4-17) plò bū rʌ́ thwí

    smear white RØ lime

(They) paint (it) white with lime. (47.3)

(4-18) ce   li   bē?ū
     dye red cloth
[S/he] dyed the cloth red. (5/2)

(4-19) phō vā   thʌ̄ ku
     cook cooked water hot
[S/he] brewed the tea (till it was done). (5/3)

(4-20) ?a kló bí   dīpɔ
     3 cover closed pot
S/he covered the pot (with a lid).

(4-21) ?a jɔ́   kè   thɔ̄ khri tə-ki
     3 bend broken.off drum fragment one-C:bit
He broke off a few pieces of the drum. (329.6)

Note that, for the one-argument verbs denoting states (bū 'white') or processes (sʌ̄ 'die', kè 'break'), which are the most common fillers of the second position in Resultatives, appearance in that second position is the only way of giving them the causative meaning conveyed by the transitive versions of the English equivalents such as *break, shut, whiten*. All Kayah Li equivalents of such causatives are complex expressions, which name separately both the causing event and the result. In comparison, English causatives like *break* and *shut* are vague, since they name a result but do not name the causing event. Kayah Li can de-emphasize the causing event by using a Resultative with first verb me 'do, make', as in me sʌ̄ 'kill', me bī 'shut'; however this is not possible with all verbs. For instance with mo 'open', me mō sounds strange, the usual expression being bɔ́ mō, with first verb bɔ́ 'reach'.

Another point that should be made about the second verb in a Resultative (let us call the second verb the 'result expression'): result expressions describe intended or expected result, but do not predicate that result as actually happening to the Patient, although they may strongly imply it. Thus neither of the two following sentences is odd:

(4-22) ti   nō   ʔa nō   to
      stuff enter 3   enter NEG
(I tried to) stuff it in but it wouldn't go in. (5/15)

(4-23) ʔa chūū sⱥ̄ lū   né ʔīthoə ma   ʔa sⱥ̄ to   to
      3   stab die 3OBV OBL knife   be.so 3   die NEG RDP
They stabbed him to death with a knife, but he didn't die, either. (354.4)

The above clearly shows the adverbial quality of the Result construction (22 involves the Directional subtype of Resultative; see below). Therefore me sⱥ̄, the closest Kayah Li equivalent of 'kill', is more accurately translated as 'do something murderous'. The second V, the Result expression, may be thought of as specifying a direction of the action: concrete physical direction as in (22), or abstract direction towards a result as in (23). Statement of this directional specification may be used to imply arrival at the intended/expected result, but coming to pass of that result is not included in the literal meaning of the construction. With this understanding, I will normally gloss Result constructions as if the result were asserted: e.g. 'stab to death' rather than 'stab so as to tend to cause death'.

The second verb position in Resultatives is normally occupied by a one-argument verb.

The first verb may be either V_i or V_t, although the commonest pattern is for the first V to be a transitive action verb; let us call this the prototypic pattern. The two positions of this pattern are open to any pair of verbs that makes sense in a resultative relation. The first verb usually denotes an action that impinges on some entity, with the second verb naming a change of state undergone by that entity as a result. The second verb can be any one-argument V that can be construed as denoting a change of state; clear examples are sā 'die', bí 'closed', pjá 'broken, ruined', and the various verbs of breaking, cracking, shattering, etc.

In this prototypic pattern, with V_t followed by V_i, argument mapping is between the first verb's Undergoer and the second verb's sole argument, normally also Undergoer. Taking once again the example of (4-6) ʔū mū sā pe 'they beat us to death',

(4-24)   S   O

              | |

      mū [Ac Un]   sā [Un]

              └ _ _ _ _ ┘

This shows that the Subject (ʔū 'they') realizes the Actor role of mū 'beat', while the Object (pe 'us') realizes the Undergoer roles of both mū and sā 'die', as discussed above.

Second verbs whose single argument is Actor (Agent or Experiencer) appear also, if less frequently. Examples (second verb underlined):

(4-25) ʔa me ŋò̲   phúcè
      3   do laugh child
He made the children laugh.

(4-26) ʔa dɔ   mo du me <u>sí ʔichē</u> pè phúcè

     3   beat gong big do afraid   BEN child

He struck the big gong and frightened the children. (5/6)

(4-27) ʔa vī   <u>jo</u> cwá chā   mò bē   nʌ rʌ

     3   throw fly go   chicken female yellow NØ RØ

She threw the yellow hen so it flew away. (376.3)

(4-28) vē | phé <u>kəthɔ</u> cwà | ʔa

     1s   hug stand   help 3

I helped him stand (by putting my arms around him).

(In the last example cwà 'help' belongs to the Descriptive type of VPtc, see 4.3.6). The mapping in the last example is:

(4-29)   S   O

        | |

   phé [Ac   Un] kəthɔ [Ac]

         |_ _ _ _ _|

Nearly as common as the prototypic pattern is one with V_i as both first and second verb:

(4-30) ʔa dīpɔ tā   klɔ̄ títí

     3 pot fall spill constantly

His pot kept falling so it spilled. (397.2)

(4-31) sɔse khrā pjá ʎ

     fruit dry ruin NS

The fruit dried out and was no good. (10/31)

(4-32) hō   co pjá lɔ̄   ʎ

     h.rice wet ruin use.up NS

The rice got all wet and was ruined. (10/31)

The verbs appearing as second verb in (30–32) above all take Undergoer as their single argument. In such cases the single argument of the sentence realizes both Undergoers.

Finally, it is also possible to elicit acceptable examples with a transitive V as second V, but such constructions are rare in spontaneous speech:

(4-33) vḗ plí cwi pù
       1s whip pull ox
I whip the ox to make it pull (something).

(4-34) vḗ me cwi pùlò
       1s do pull oxcart
I made [stg] pull the oxcart. (28.v)

(4-35) ʔa ʔíjḗ cwi təchḗ
       3 jiggle pull elephant
He jiggled[1] to make the elephant pull (something).

In these last examples, the result of the action is a second action, performed by a second agent. These are very similar to the Directive V-V constructions (above, 4.2.1b, and below, 4.2.3, where the difference will be discussed).

Returning now to the prototypic V_t-V_i pattern, in the normal case the change of state named by the second verb is undergone by the first verb's Undergoer, i.e. the mapping is of the Undergoer type. But there are also instances of Actor mapping, in which the change of state applies rather to the first verb's Actor:

---

[1] ʔíjḗ means to jiggle one's body while remaining in place; it is the action performed by a rider to get an elephant to move, the equivalent of 'Giddyap'.

71

(4-36) ʔa ʔō   mɯ   thʌ̄ʔíphrɛ̀
    3 drink drunk whiskey
    S/he got drunk on whiskey. (common expression)

Here mɯ 'intoxicated' is what happens to the Subject (Actor) as a result of the action. Further examples are:

(4-37) vɛ̄ ʔīchi síphrá khru
    1s split tired firewood
    I got tired splitting firewood; I split firewood till I was tired. (8/9)

(4-38) ʔa dū   là   síphrá hi   dɔ́ kū
    3 sweep clear tired house wall inside
    He got tired sweeping the house; he swept until he was tired. (8/9)

(4-39) ne méthʌ mo   Phēlɯ́du me hú   ʔʌ̄ to
    2s see happy (name) do like this NEG
    You are unhappy seeing P. act like that; Seeing P. act like that makes you unhappy. (11/21)

(4-40) vɛ̄ mɛ́ mo   ne to
    1s look happy 2s NEG
    I feel sorry for you; I pity you; (literally:) I am unhappy seeing you [your condition]. (2/27)

Note especially (39) and (40, in which both Subject and Object NP's denote entities that could plausibly have mo 'happy, comfortable' predicated of them. But (40) does not mean 'It is not the case that I look at you with the result that you become happy', nor the more plausible 'I see that you are unhappy'.

The argument mapping pattern for (40) is:

(4-41)   S   O
            | |
      mɛ́ [Ac   Un] mo [Un]
            L _ _ _ _ _ _ _ _ ⌋

4.2.2.2 Directional Constructions

Mapping: Undergoer

Interpredicate: causation

Openness: restricted

In these, the second verb gives a directional specification to the action of the first V. Examples:

(4-42) jɛ́   cwá rɤ́ sínɛ
carry.on.shldr go RØ gun
[They] went carrying guns on their shoulders. (235.5)

(4-43) ʔa dɛ the   dɤ́ plò kū dɤ́ phrɛ̀ khu
3 put go.up at:U box in at:U shelf on
They put (it) up in a box on a shelf. (326.1)

(4-44) təlʌbóvī rɤ́ cɔ̄ the   nì lū   hi
whirlwind   PTC lift ascend get 3:OBV house
The whirlwind lifted up their house. (42.7)

Directional constructions can be considered to be a special type of Result construction. Semantically the direction can usually be understood as resulting from the action of the first V, as in (43) and (44), although in many cases it is not so clear that there is a true causal relation, as in (42) (jɛ́ cwá 'go carrying') and such expressions as dɛ́ thɛ 'ride (vehicle, animal) up', and lo hɛ̄ 'float away, go floating'. Syntactically, Directional expressions can

73

co-occur with (other, non-Directional) Result expressions, usually preceding them, as in the first two of the following examples,
but sometimes following, as in the third:

     V   Dr   R

(4-45) ne cwi the thū ʔacʌ   nʌ

       2s pull go.out long ITS-wick NØ

     (If) you pull the wick out long. (341.6)

     V Dr   R

(4-46) ʔe nō jē

       eat enter deep

     Eat deep into [it]. (468.5)

     V   R   Dr

(4-47) bɔ́   mō the

       reach open go.out

     Open (stg) outwards.

Directional constructions are also like Result constructions in
that both may be embedded in a Sequence construction (4.2.2).

    Note also that there are cases of apparent Directional
V-V's in which the direction is metaphorical, as in:

(4-48) ʔase khrā the   ʎ́

       fruit dry go.out NS

     The fruit got drier. (92.6)

(4-49) ʔa bɛ́ thɛ   ʔíkhu nʌ

       3 mold ascend earth   NØ

     He [God] molded up the earth. (337.3)

Clearly no concrete object emerges in (48). In (49) likewise thɛ
does not mean that the earth moves upwards: the sentence is from

74

a creation myth, and describes God creating the earth (bé means to mold something formless, as mud or concrete, into a form). thε then in this sentence is better translated as 'coming into existence'. Since there is no syntactic realization of any argument of the second verb, these are considered to be not Resultative but Descriptive V-V's, for which see below (4.2.4).

Directional constructions differ from Result constructions in that the V's appearing in the second position, the 'Directional' V's, form a closed class with two subtypes, called simply Type A and B.

Type A Directionals

cwá	go
hē	move away from home ('go:FH' in glosses)
ka	move towards home ('go:TH' in glosses)

None of these has the same deictic orientation as English 'come' and 'go', namely 'motion towards/away from the speaker or other center of interest'. ka and hē usually refer to motion towards or away from the home of the speaker or other protagonist, whether the speaker/protagonist is at home or not. These two have complementary semantics somewhat like more familiar verbs 'come' and 'go'; for instance, they are paired in elaborate expressions such as vúvὲ ka vúvὲ hē 'wave-come-wave-go: wave back and forth'. As for cwá, as main V it usually has no deictic connotation at all; as Directional it may (but does not necessarily) mean 'away', as in kō cwá 'blow stg away' (of wind).

ka is a very common second V, meaning 'successfully get stg and bring it home': pὺ ka tachē 'catch elephants (and bring them home)', ʔīphri ka 'buy stg (and bring it home)'.

75

Type B Directionals

thɛ	go up
lɛ	go down (voluntarily)
tā	go down (involuntarily), fall
the	go out
nō	go in
thō	go to someplace near, 'go over' (as colloquial English go over to sbdy's house)
tò	arrive
rē	go across
təka	curved, hooked, winding

Most type B's may take the prefixes kə- 'moving Subject' and pə- 'orientation (no transit of space)'; cf. 3.3.2.2.6. The kə-prefixed forms are verbs, but do not belong to the Type B class, while the pə- prefixed forms are not full verbs; see (4.3.7) below.

For examples of Type B Directionals as second verb in V-V, see examples (43–47) above; also kəthɔ thɛ 'stand up' (kəthɔ 'be standing'), me tā 'drop stg (on purpose)' (me 'do'), phjá the 'take stg out' (phjá 'take'), sɤ́ nō 'put stg in' (sɤ́ 'insert'), cwá təka klɛ́ '(1) go around a curve; (2) go on a winding road' (cwá 'go', klɛ́ 'road'). For təka, cf. also kəjɛ̄ təka 'dishonest ('crooked') person').

Type B Directionals may be second verb with a Type A as first verb: cwá thɛ 'go up'. The reverse is not necessarily true: the cwá (471.5), with Type B the 'emerge' + Type A cwá 'go', is 'emerge and then go away', not 'emerge away from speaker'; that is, it is a Sequential V-V (4.2.2).

Argument mapping in Directionals is of the Undergoer type. There is one minor difference, in that directional verbs must be assumed to specify two roles: a moving Actor, and an Undergoer that is the goal (or, less commonly, source) of the motion. This contrasts with the typical general Resultative, whose second verb is a one-argument verb. However, the goal/source (or inner Locative) argument of directional verbs makes little difference in argument realization, since it is always realized as a PP and is not mapped onto any argument of V_1. It is the directional verb's moving-entity Actor that is mapped, to the single argument of a one-argument first verb, as in:

(4-50) pípὲ   jo cwá rʌ
       butterfly fly go   RØ
       They [butterflies] flew away. (358.3)

or to the Undergoer of a two-argument first verb, as in (43–44), and:

(4-51) ʔū pha tā dī   ʔiswí
       3:i drop fall cooked.rice curry
       They drop in food [into a pond, as an offering]. (207.2)

In (51) the food moves downwards, while the Agents 'they' do not; the derived argument structure would be:

(4-52)   S   O   Obl (PP)

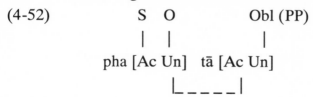

(The Oblique relation, realizing the goal argument of 'fall', is omitted in (51), since it is clear from the immediate context.)

It is not difficult to find sentences with Directional V-V's that are understood as having both arguments of the first verb designate moving entities, as in (42) above and:

(4-53) ʔa dɛ́ thɛ   təsí dɤ̀ cho   khʌ̄

    3   ride ascend horse at:U mountain top.of

He rode the horse up the mountain.

Here both the rider and the horse move upwards. But we do not need to have the Actor (moving-entity) argument of thɛ 'ascend' map to both Actor and Undergoer arguments of dɛ́ 'ride'; the fact that the Actor moves can be left up to inference. Part of the lexical meaning of this verb, along with vī 'drive' and klɛ̄ 'paddle', is the notion of action performed on some conveyance while located on or in that conveyance; it would then follow that any motion attributed to the conveyance would apply to the rider as well.

4.2.3 Sequential Constructions

Mapping: Actor

Interpredicate: sequence/purpose

Openness: open

These consist of several V's (usually two, but occasionally more) that describe a sequence of actions linked by temporal order and/or purpose, usually paraphrasable as 'V_1 and then V_2' or 'V_1 in order to V_2'. Examples:

(4-54) ʔa | ka   dɛ́hʌ̄ rʌ́ | ʔa phʌ̄

    3   return ask   RØ 3   grandmother

He went back and asked his grandmother. (93.6)

78

(4-55) hē ʔomʌ̄ klɛ̀ tənʌ̄ nʌ
    go sleep cut one-two day
[We] go and sleep (in the fields) and cut (brush) for one or two days. (177.2)

(4-56) ne hē nìdā mɛ́ kʌ̄ mʌ
    2s come listen look COM IMP
Come listen and look! (93.6)

(4-57) thwi mɛ́thʌ ʔe ʌ́ li phá nʌ
    dog see eat NS book skin NØ
The dog saw the hide book and ate it. (103.4)

(4-58) ʔonē ʔíbe chúi lū ma mo mo ʌ́
    sit speak confronting each.other be.so fun RDP NS
Sitting and talking together is fun, too. (180.4)

Notice that (55) and (56) contain three verbs in the Sequential construction; note also that the relation between the actions named by the second and third verbs in (55) is better described as 'alternating action' rather than 'sequential action': it is not the case that all instances of sleeping will precede all instances of cutting; rather, they will alternate. (58) is different again: sitting and speaking are simultaneous. The informant pointed out that the sentence (55) could also have the (nonsensical) reading of simultaneous action, 'sleep while cutting'. The same range of meanings is described for the Chinese 'serial Verb' by Li and Thompson (1989, 595); their terms are purpose, consecutive action, alternating actions, and circumstance of event (closest to my 'simultaneous' above).

The sequential units may themselves be Resultative constructions:

(4-59) vē pừ me sā̱ jòkhró

    1s catch do die rat

I caught and killed a rat. (10/8)

(4-60) ʔa cwá kəthɛ phjá kwa

    3   go   go.up take axe

He went up and took the axe.

In (59) the first verb is the single morpheme pừ 'catch' while the second verbal expression consists of the Resultative V-V me sā̱ '(do+die:) kill'. This complex V-V may be diagrammed as [pừ]$_{V1}$ [me sā̱]$_{V2}$. The sequenced element may be a Directional construction, as in the following:

(4-61) ʔa thɛ phjá tā

    3 ascend take fall

They went up and took [it] down. (326.4)

which is analyzed as [thɛ]$_{V1}$ [phjá tā]$_{V2}$, in which the second verbal expression is itself a Resultative (Directional) V-V. For a more complete discussion of complex V-V's, see section (4.4).

Since these, like all V-V's, are components of a single, non-complex clause, the Sequential V-V unit may take only one Object NP. If both verbs in the construction are transitive, a single Object NP may realize the Undergoer arguments of both, as in:

(4-62) təplu kū̱ rᴧ́ hᴧca nᴧ

    search wear RØ clothes NØ

[They] looked for their clothes to put on. (405.4)

Here the Object hᴧca 'clothes' is both the thing searched for and the thing to be worn. Notice incidentally that this is a clear case

80

of the relation between the two actions being purpose alone. Only the first action, that of searching, is asserted as actually happening; this is clear because one of the searchers cannot find his clothes, which the protagonist of the story has hidden. Thus we cannot gloss the sentence as 'looked for their clothes and put them on' (we also cannot gloss it as 'looked for clothes to wear', since it is clear that a specific set of clothes is at issue).

If a Sequential contains two V_t that can be interpreted as taking different Undergoers, the Object NP must realize the Undergoer argument of the second verb:

(4-63) ʔū | bɔ́mō mɛ́ ho   lū
      3:i   open   look secretly 3:OBV
      Secretly they opened it (mosquito net) and peeked at him. (41.6)

(4-64) *ʔū | bɔ́ mō mɛ́ ho | ʔikēthɔ̄
                               mosquito.net
      Secretly they opened the mosquito net and peeked (at him).

(4-65) vē chijá plwā   thɛ́
      1s untie   release pig
      I untied it (rope) and released the pig. (3/3)

(4-66) *vē | chi já plwā | súplʌ
                       rope
      I untied the rope and released it (pig).

Note also in (63–64) that ho 'secretly' (a Descriptive Particle, see 4.3.6 below) modifies bɔ́ mō mɛ́ 'open and look' as a unit, as is clear from the context.

Argument Mapping. The essential feature of Sequential V-V's is the mapping of the Actor argument of V_1. As always, V_2 maps its Actor if it has one, otherwise the Undergoer is mapped.

Consider (54), repeated below:

(4-67) ?a | ka déhā́ rá | ?a phā́
     3   go:TH ask   RØ   3   grandmother

He went back and asked his grandmother. (93.6)

This is perhaps the most typical sort of Sequential V-V, in which the first verb is a verb of motion. The argument mapping may be displayed as follows (I suppress the Locative argument that may be assumed to be a property of the first verb, since as explained previously this argument is unproblematic in its consistent realization as PP):

(4-68)

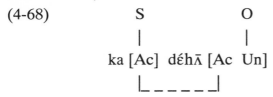

As to the question of which verbs may appear in a Sequential V-V, probably the most common first verbs are verbs of motion and posture, as in (54–56, 58). cwá 'go' is very common; in fact it has a related form já, a Verb Particle that precedes a verb in a construction that is analogous to a Sequential V-V (see 4.3.2.3 below). Also common is the verb lɯ 'go after, follow to overtake, go to get (usually to get some person)'. However, many other verbs may appear as first verb, and the second verb position is even less restricted. In terms of number of arguments, combinations V_i-V_i and V_i-V_t are fairly common, while V_t-V_t is perhaps somewhat less frequent. V_t-V_i is also possible, as this example shows:

(4-69) ʔa phjá kəthɛ Phētuɨəʔaphē hʌ   təpɯ

    3   take go.up [name]   pants one-C:cloth

He took a pair of P's pants and went up [with them]. (313.5)

Note that the second verb, with prefix kə-, specifically means that the Agent went up, and that this is the reason for analyzing (69) as containing a Sequential V-V rather than a Directional V-V. The equivalent Directional construction would be phjá thɛ, with unprefixed second verb, and would mean that the Agent takes something which moves upwards as a result.

The constructions in (59-61), in which V-V's themselves consist of V-V's, can be given an argument-mapping representation as follows, for (61) thɛ phjá tā 'go up and take down' (still omitting the Locative arguments):

(4-70)

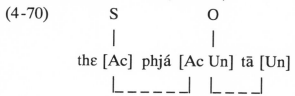

4.2.4 Directive V-V's

Mapping: Undergoer

Interpredicate: causation

Openness: restricted

In these, the first is one of a relatively small set of verbs having to do with commanding or permitting; what Searle (1975) classifies as the 'directive' type of illocutionary acts. These verbs denote situations in which one person gets another person to do something, whether the second person doesn't especially want to do it (as in commanding), or whether s/he does (as in permitting). Thus both verbs must include human participants (or participants treated as human, as in stories involving conversations among people, dogs, rats and the like). Examples:

(4-71) ʔa nɔ̄   pā phúcè mɛ̄klúí

      3   command cut child   rhythm.pipe

      She told the children to cut rhythm-pipes. (42.5)

(4-72) vɛ̄ dʌ́ cwá ne to

      1s let go 2s NEG

      I won't let you go. (3/31)

(4-73) ʔa phɛ̄ nʌ ʔé cwá vɛ̄ lū   jò du

      3 father NØ call go   dig 3OBV rat big

      Her father called to her to go dig out a big rat. (36.3)

The class of Directive Verbs includes the following:

nɔ̄	tell to V, get sbdy to V; (as main V) use (cf. Thai cháj, with the same range of meaning)
dʌ́	let V; (as main V) give
jo~jonɔ̄	forbid
ʔe~ʔénɔ̄	call to V
jū	point, order by pointing
dɛke	hire to V, employ
ʔiswá	teach to V

Notice that these all involve acts of communication, usually verbal.

These Directive Verbs have Indirect Object specification, meaning (briefly) that at least one NP immediately after the VC is licensed. Thus when a Directive Verb forms a V-V with a V_i, the VC takes a single following NP, as in (72). When the second verb is a V_t, there are two NPs after the VC, as in (71) and (73); in (71), they are phúcè 'child' and mēklúi 'rhythm-pipes' (a bamboo percussion instrument). The first of these is the Indirect Object licensed by the Directive Verb; it represents the causee, the participant that receives the command or permission to perform the action named by the second verb. It realizes the Undergoer of the first verb (in terms of role-types, probably a Recipient or Dative), to which is also mapped the Actor of the second verb. The second post-VC NP is the Direct Object, licensed by the second verb and realizing its Undergoer. Notice that in Kayah Indirect Object specification is not dependent on co-occurrence with Direct Object specification, and that a single post-VC NP argument may be licensed by the VC having either Direct Object or Indirect Object specification; see 5.4 for amplification.

As in General Resultatives, argument mapping is to the Undergoer argument of the first verb. E.g. the VC of (71) above, nɔ̄ pā 'tell to cut' can be diagrammed as:

(4-74)   S   IO   DO
           | | |
        nɔ̄ [Ac Un] pā [Ac Un]
           |_ _ _ _|

where S=ʔa 'he/she/it', IO=phúcè 'child', and DO=mēklúi 'rhythm-pipes'.

85

As with other V-V's, the structure of clauses with Directives is fundamentally identical to that of clauses with simple predicators. There is no evidence of embedding or any other sort of multi-clause structure. The grammatical relations taken by a VC including [Directive + V_i] are no different from those to a VC with a simple V_t, and the same identity holds between [Directive + V_t] and simple V_d, as can be seen be comparing the following with (71) above:

(4-75) vē | dʌ́ | ʔa ǂ rūū

    1s   give   3   money

I gave him money.

In both (71) and (75) the first NP is Subject realizing Agent, the first post-VC NP is Indirect Object realizing Recipient (of goods, of causation), and the second post-VC NP is Direct Object realizing Patient. Further discussion on this point can be found in (5.4) below.

In both the preceding cases there is an apparent additive relation between the syntactic valences of the two verbs: Directive Verb + V_i = two-argument VC, Directive Verb + V_t = three-argument VC. When the second verb is a V_d, the Indirect Object still realizes causee-Recipient and the Direct Object realizes Patient, but the Recipient argument of the second verb, which would appear as Indirect Object if that verb were head, must be realized in an Oblique PP with né:

(4-76) vē nɔ̄   dʌ́ Phāʌ rūū né ʔapò

    1s command give [name] silver OBL younger.sibling

I told P. to give money to [his] younger sibling.

Here Phāʌ is the Recipient specified by the Directive verb nɔ̄ 'command' as well as the Agent of dʌ́ 'give'; rūu 'money' is the Patient of dʌ́; and ʔapò 'his sibling' is the Recipient specified by dʌ́. Or rather, it would have been the Recipient specified by dʌ́: it is precisely the function of né to indicate participants that are peripheralized (5.5); in this case ʔapò has been pre-empted for the role of Recipient and the position of Indirect Object by the Causee Phāʌ.

Although it is not crucial to the understanding of V-V's, it may be worth mentioning here that the function of né is such that it would not be accurate to say that this VC nɔ̄ dʌ́ actully specifies the né-PP as one of four syntactic arguments. PP's with né are possible co-constituents of a wide variety of VC's; it is accidental that this né-PP corresponds to something that in another setting would be a licensed syntactic argument. See 5.5 for discussion of this point.

At this point we can return to the marginal type of Resultative V-V whose second verb is V_t. Recall (33) and (35), repeated below:

(4-77) vɛ̄ plí cwi pù

    1s whip pull ox

I whip the ox to make it pull (something).

(4-78) ʔa ʔíjɛ̄ cwi təchɛ̄

    3 jiggle pull elephant

He jogged to make the elephant pull (something).

In meaning these are very close to Directive constructions: V_1 names an action that causes a sentient being, denoted by a postverbal NP, to perform the action denoted by V_2. But these Resul-

tative V-V's are distinguised from Directives by the fact that their
first verbs are ordinary V_t, which do not have Indirect Object
specification. Therefore their VC's can take at most one post-VC
grammatical relation, which must realize the two mapped arguments, Undergoer of V_1 and Actor of V_2. This means that there is
no licensed syntactic slot that could realize the second argument
of V_2, its Undergoer. Thus these Resultatives contrast with Directives, which allow grammatical relations that realize both arguments of V_2.

If one insists on getting the Undergoer of a nonhead V_t
into sentences with Resultatives, it is sometimes possible to construct an acceptable equivalent with a né-PP. The following corresponds to (78) above:

(4-79) ʔa ʔíjē̄ cwi təchē̄ né sɔ

    3 jiggle pull elephant OBL tree

He jogged the elephant into pulling the log.

But corresponding to (77) above is the following, completely
recast with a new main verb and no second verb:

(4-80) vē̄ thá pənè né phré

    1s plow buffalo OBL swidden

I plow the field with a buffalo.

These examples belong to a much larger class of sentences
denoting three-participant events, which have various grammatical structures that display a high degree of sensitivity to semantic and pragmatic variables. These three-participant sentences are
examined more fully in (5.5.2) below.

The differences between the three types of V-V described so far can be summed up as follows. 'Special' general resultative is the 'drink-drunk' type, with the result applying to the first verb's Actor rather than its Undergoer:

Type	Mapping	Interpredicate	Openness
Resultative:			
general (normal)	Undergoer	causation	open
directional	Undergoer	causation	restricted
general (special)	Actor	causation	open
Sequential	Actor	sequence/purpose	open
Directive	Undergoer	causation	restricted

As (73) shows, the second position in a Directive V-V may be occupied by another V-V: a Sequential as in (73) (cwá vē 'go and dig'), or a Resultative as in:

(4-81) ʔa nɔ̄   kúvē the   lū   heso
 3   command dig   go.out 3OBV dust
 He told her to dig out the dust. (36.4)

Here the Directive Verb nɔ̄ is followed by the Resultative V-V kú ve the 'dig out', yielding a complex V-V of the form [nɔ̄]$_{V1}$ [kúvē the]$_{V2}$.

It may be recalled that Sequential V-V's may also be complex; Sequentials and Directives co-occur in various ways, but not all conceivable combinations are found. This matter is described fully in (4.4) below, but the reader may find the following sketch useful at this point.

A Directive may have a Sequential as its second element, as in:

(4-82) nɔ̄   kəlɛ   dɛ́   thā

command descend dip.up water

Tell sbdy to do down and draw water.

And a Sequential may have a Directive as its second element, as:

(4-83) hɛ̄ nɔ̄   dɛ́   thā

go   command dip.up   water

Go tell sbdy to draw water.

What is not possible is a Sequential V-V with the V_1 constituent made up of a Drv-V, as:

(4-84) *vɛ̄ | nɔ̄   cwá mū | ʔa

1s   command go   hit   3

*I told him$_i$ to go and (I) hit him$_i$.

which has the structure [nɔ̄ cwá]V_1 [mū]V_2. With a different structure (844) probably would be acceptable as 'I told him to go and (to) hit sbdy', i.e. [nɔ̄]V_1 [cwá mū]V_2.

4.2.5 Descriptive V-V's

Mapping: none

Interpredicate: modification

Openness: open

The remaining two types of V-V, Descriptive and Modal (following section) both lack argument mapping. Each is also closely related to a class of non-verbs with similar semantic function (Modal Particles, 4.3.3, and Descriptive Particles, 4.3.6). The first position in Modal V-V's is restricted to a small class of Modal Verbs, while Descriptives are relatively open in both Verb

90

slots. Although the latter is also true of Resultatives, in practice there is little overlap between those verbs that occur as V_2 in Descriptives and those that occur in that position in Resultatives.

Examples of Descriptive V-V's:

(4-85) ʔa ʔe phrē dī

3   eat fast cooked.rice

He eats quickly.

(4-86) ʔa me ré   rʎ lū

3   do good RØ 3OBV

They were good to them. (235.7)

(4-87) ma ʔe súi   ʔa che ke

be.so eat wrong 3 food perhaps

It may be that he ate something bad. (309.1)

(4-88) nìdā jè

listen difficult

It's hard to listen to ≈ it sounds funny.

Here there is no argument mapping. For example, in (85) ʔa ʔe phrē dī 'he eats (rice) fast', there is no NP constituent of which phrē 'fast' is predicated. If phrē is a predicate, it predicates quickness, not of any participant in the action, but of the action as a whole. One might speculate that phrē takes as argument either the whole proposition 'he eats (rice)' or perhaps just the verb 'eat'; but we will not pursue this line of inquiry.

Descriptive and Resultative can be contrasted in the following examples involving ré 'good', one of the few verbs that easily occurs as second verb in both Resultative and Descriptive V-V's:

(4-89) vē me ré twà   kā̄ rʌ́ vē hi (Resultative)

    1s do good beautiful COM RØ 1s house

I (would) improve (make good and beautiful) my house. (181.3)

(4-90) ʔa me ré   rʌ́ lū   (Descriptive)

    3 do good RØ 3OBV

They were good to (did well towards) them. (235.7)

In (89), ré 'good' describes the result of the action of me 'do, make', the result applying to the Object hi 'house'. In (90), ré describes a quality of the action of me, and it does not apply to lū: 'they' did not become good as a result of the action.[2] The V-V me ré is therefore ambiguous.

Ambiguous in the same way is ʔíbe jè 'speak + difficult', which may mean either 'speak difficulties > make trouble [by speaking]' (Resultative) or 'speak with difficulty, hard to say' (Descriptive). The 'metaphoric' use of the Directional verbs the 'go out; increasingly' and the 'go up; coming into existence', discussed in (4.2.2.2), qualifies them as further examples of verbs that can occur in Descriptive V-V's as well as Resultatives. An example is (49), repeated below:

(4-91) ʔa bé   the   ʔíkhu nʌ

    3   mold ascend earth   NØ

He [God] molded up the earth. (337.3)

---

[2] Here me might be better translated as 'do (stg) to (sbdy)'; cf.

ʔa me nɔ́ lū   təcɤ̀   to

3 do at.all 3OBV one-CLF NEG

He didn't do a thing to her. (78.2)

Below is a representative list of verbs appearing as V_2 in Descriptives:

súi	wrongly, to V the wrong one
phrē	fast, quickly
jɔ̄	slow to cover distance (cf. pəjè 'slow to accomplish')
thō	finish, finish V-ing
sē	new, anew, over again
rɛ́	good, well, carefully
mo	enjoyably, enjoy V-ing; (as main V) feel good, healthy, have fun
ŋjā	for a long time, last a long time
təmō	constantly
lɔ̄	exhaustively, including all of a set; (as main V) use up, spend; similar to Thai mòt
ro	early in the morning
plē	late in the morning
cha phoə	early in the evening, before dusk
hɛ́	in the evening, late (as compared to afternoon)
ʔɛ́	many, affecting many things; (as main V) be many, much
rò	many (people) V, plural action by humans
bɛ́	have the wherewithal to V; (as main V) be rich, well-endowed
khó	separately; (as main V) different, strange; this and the following are typically followed by the VPtc dɯ 'own.accord'
khɔ	separately; (as main V) different, apart

təple	over again, a turn; (as main V) be reversed, turned around; e.g. s$\bar{\text{ɛ}}$ <u>təple</u> hʌ ca 'change one's clothes' (contrast s$\bar{\text{ɛ}}$ khjā sɛ́ hʌca 'put on clothes again', with VPtc's khjā sɛ́)
jɛ̀	difficult
jū	easy
the	increasingly; (as main verb) go out
thɛ	coming into existence; (as main verb) go up

The foregoing list is representative only; the single clear restriction on the second verb in a Descriptive V-V is that it be a one-argument verb whose single argument is not at the Actor end of the Actor-Undergoer scale. For example, the single argument of mo 'enjoy V-ing' has the Actor properties of being human and sentient, but it lacks the properties of being purposeful and of causing.

However, in practice the set of verbs occurring as second verb in the Descriptives seem to be largely disjoint from that occurring in Resultatives. One way to characterize the difference is based on the observation that the V_i's that appear as second constituents in Resultative V-V's tend to denote processes, or states that result from processes; e.g. phé could be rendered either as 'to crack' (process of cracking) or as 'be cracked' (result of process of cracking). Those V_i that appear as second constituents of Descriptives, in contrast, tend to denote states only, or rather states that are typically not thought of as resulting from processes; e.g. phr$\bar{\text{e}}$ would more typically be interpreted as 'fast' (state) rather than 'become fast, speed up' (result of process). This is essentially the distinction drawn by Chafe (1970, 124) between intrinsic processes ('break' cited as example) and intrinsic states ('wide' and 'be open' cited as examples). It remains possible for certain verbs to be neutral between state and result-of-process; ré 'good', which appears naturally as both Descriptive and Result expression (89–90 above), would be an example.

4.2.6 Modal V-V's

Mapping: none

Interpredicate: modification?

Openness: restricted

In these the first verb has a meaning relating either to modality, in the sense of obligation, or to various notions having to do with the emotional setting of the action, often in terms of the mental attitude of the Agent participant. The term 'modal' is thus used as a convenient label rather than in the more usual technical sense.

The first verb is one of a closed class, known as Modal verbs; some of these have little meaning shift from their single-predicator use:

síplɔ tō	like; like to V
dɛ́ síplɔ	decide; decide to V
tɘne	think; think to V, intend to V
kha	promise
do	abstain, swear off
je	make as if to V, threaten to V
ʔɛ́cúí	pretend to V
ko	be unwilling to V
càphrʌ̄	endure; keep on V-ing

The first two are compounds, containing síplɔ 'heart', tō 'strike a target' (cf. Thai thùuk caj), and dé 'put'.

Others have notable shift (single-predicator meaning in parentheses):

me (do, make) try to do something undesirable or prohibited

be (impinge, affect, become manifest) must, should (cf. also 5.4.1)

tō (be correct, strike accurately) should, time is right to V

ré (good) should be the case that, you'd have thought that, counterfactual

Note that all but the last three are restricted to animate (usually human) Subject NP.

Examples:

(4-92) ʔírɛ nʌ ma vē kha ʔírɛ dɯ ʎ
work NØ be.so 1s promise work own.accord NS
As to work, I promise to work myself. (84.1)

(4-93) ʔa do ʔō thʎ̄ʔiphrè
3 abstain drink whiskey
He gave up drinking. (10/13)

The following has do as single predicator:

(4-94) bó ré to ma ʔū do
rice good NEG be.so 3:i abstain
Because the rice [crop] isn't good, I'm abstaining. (175.1)

(Note use of remote third-person pronoun ʔū for humilific self-reference.) kha as single predicator may be found in kha no 'go into debt', but the category of no is uncertain. Also possible as single predicator is tō:

(4-95) ʔa <u>tō</u> kʌ̄ sɛ́ rʌ́ li kulā
    3   COM same RØ writing European
    It should be like the European script. (221.4)

Although these verbs have the semantics of modality, they are not like modal auxiliaries in taking a following VP as co-constituent. Kayah Li Modal V-V's, like other V-V's, form the core of the VC, which interacts as a unit with the rest of the clause. Evidence of the unitary character of Modal V-V's can be found in certain morphemes (both verbs and VPtc) that, although not adjacent to the Modal, have scope over it. Consider:

(4-96) do   cwá beche ʌ́
    abstain go   bored   NS
    be tired of abstaining from going. (10/13)

Here bəche 'bored' relates to do cwá 'abstain from going' as a unit; semantically it has scope over it, which indicates a structure [[do cwá] beché]. If the Modal do were in construction with the entire remainder of the sentence (or at least with the remainder of the VP), the structure would be [do[cwá bəche . . .]], which should mean 'abstain from being tired of going'. A similar example is:

(4-97) ʔa ʔɛ́cɯ́ sɪ́pləducɛ̀
    3 pretend angry   know.how
    He's good at pretending to be angry. (13.v)

Here the structure must be [[ʔɛ́cɯ́ sɪ́plədu] cɛ̀]; if ʔɛ́cɯ́ 'pretend' were in construction with the following items as a unit, as [ʔɛ́cɯ́ [sɪ́pləducɛ̀]], one would expect the meaning to be 'pretend to be able to be angry'. Again we see that the Kayah Li VC is a close-knit unit, in which verbs interact first with each other and then, as a unit, with the rest of the clause.

There are a few verbs, distinct from the Modal Verbs listed here, that do take clausal Objects; see 9.3.1.

As with Descriptives, argument mapping is not applicable to Modals. Modal V-V's are also difficult to fit in with other V-V features, namely interpredicate semantics and headedness. The semantic relation between the Modal V and the second V is perhaps more like modification than like causation or sequence, but it is not entirely clear which verb modifies which. One might say that the modal modifies the more concrete semantics of the second verb, which is certainly what must be said of the Modal VPtc (4.3.3). On the other hand taking the Modal V as head is consistent with the otherwise exceptionless rule that verbal modifiers follow their heads. Moreover, of the two verbs it is the modal, not the second verb, that is asserted, as in the following:

(4-98) chápā ʔū jừʔe vē to he vē ʔo kē   dɯə   ʌ

soon 3:i believe 1s NEG LEST 1s exist NEW.LOC own.accord PTC

ʔa ré   ne kʌ̄ nʌ

3   should think COM NØ

He should think, 'Soon nobody will trust me and I'll be an outcast,' (but he probably won't). (313.2)

Here the Modal ré 'should (counterfactual)' is asserted and the second verb ne 'think' is not.

4.2.7 Summary of V-V's

The differences between the types of V-V can be summed up as follows. Mapping lists which argument of V_1 is mapped (V_2

always maps Actor); 'restricted' types are further specified as to which slot is restricted; special general resultative is the 'drink-drunk' type:

Type	Mapping	Interpredicate	Openness
Resultative:			
General (usual)	Un	causation	open
Directional	Un	causation	restricted V_2
General (special)	Ac	causation	open
Sequential	Ac	sequence/purpose	open
Directive	Un	causation	restricted V_1
Descriptive	none	modification	open
Modal	none	?	restricted V_1

4.3 Ptc/V Constructions

4.3.1 Introduction: Types of Verb Particle

We distinguish verbs, which may function as unitary predicator, from Verb Particles, which appear in the VC but cannot function as unitary predicator. The two categories are distinct enough to be useful, but they blur at the edges in certain ways. For instance, there are two classes of particles that are semantically quite similar to types of V-V. Compare the following:

(4-99)   with verb cwá 'go'
          Modal V-V ʔa be cwá   he must go
          Ptc + V   ʔa lò cwá   he ought to go; it's his duty to go

(4-100)   with verb ʔíbe 'speak'
          Descriptive V-V   ʔa ʔíbe jὲ   it's hard for him to speak
          V + Ptc   ʔa ʔíbe cὲ   he's good at speaking

99

In such cases we will take advantage of the resemblance by naming the class of particles after the similar verbal construction
type: thus lò is a Modal Particle (4.3.3), and cè is a Descriptive
Particle (4.3.7).

There are also some borderline cases: non-verbs that
function like second verbs in Resultative V-V's, of various types.
These are described separately (4.5).

Other classes of particles have neither an obviously associated type of full-verb construction nor a plausible common
semantic value that could serve as a name for the class. In such
cases I fall back on naming the classes after an arbitrarily chosen
class member: the khwe-class particles, the rʌ-class particles
(4.3.2, 4.3.6).

Verb Particles may be divided into pre-verbal particles,
which precede verbs and V-V constructions; and post-verbal particles, which follow.

4.3.2 Pre-Verbal Particles: khwe-class Particles

These express aspect and aspect-like notions.

tərē	almost V'd
lèklō	have ever V'd, experiential
khwe	in the midst of V-ing, continuous
tè	about to V, incipient
tənē ~ kənē	about to V, incipient
túi	just now V'd

Both túi and khwe usually co-occur with the rʌ-class
Post-Verbal Particle pa 'durative, etc.' (4.3.6). lèklō may possi-

bly consist of lè 'purpose nominalizer, thing for V-ing'(6.7) and klō 'speech, language': place for speaking, occasion for language; i.e. one has done something and hence knows enough to speak about it. Examples:

(4-101) ʔʌ̄ tərō   tɛ̀ já lù   kʌ̄ rʌ́ ʔū ʔa hé nʌ
        this one-morning go.and make.merit COM RØ 3i 3 say NØ
He said he was going to make merit with them this morning. (290.4)

(4-102) sí ʔe dī ní // khwe phō ʔe pa, ʔe chá pā ní
        want eat c.rice EMPH cook   exploit DUR eat upcoming IRR EMPH
I'm hungry! // I'm cooking right now, we'll eat in a minute! (24.v)

There is a symmetry between the khwe-class particles, which appear first in the VC, and the rʌ́-class particles, which come last in the VC. Neither relates to any V-V construction type, and both have meanings relating to aspect, although the rʌ́-class, much more numerous, includes many with non-aspectual meanings.

4.3.3 Modal and Quasi-modal Particles

Like the Modal verbs, these include some meanings that are truly modal in referring to obligation or probability, and some meanings having to do with attitude of the Agent.

Modal Particles

lò   ought (by duty)

klé   should be the case (epistemic); possibly related to a word meaning 'to require as ingredients'

thú   probably is the case [analysis uncertain]

Quasi-modal Particles

sí   want to V

tərú   go ahead and V, feel free to V

lā   V intrusively, rashly

For examples of the last, cf. lā hé to interrupt (hé 'say'); lā kə?ɔ̄ hé to guess; and

(4-103)   phrè nʌ <u>lā</u> limē nʌ

            Shan NØ   smart   NØ

            The Shans were smart [to our detriment].

4.3.4 já, a 'Sequential' Particle

     já is like a worn-down, grammaticalized first verb in a Sequential V-V. It has lost the literal sense of motion, perhaps similar to *go* in colloquial English *Now you've gone and done it.* For example:

(4-104)   vē ke <u>já</u> sā̄ bōʌ ‖ ka   lō bɤ́ ?ʌ̄

            1s if   die and.then   go:TH bury at:V this

            If I ('go and') die, come bury me here. (217.5)

It is most likely cognate to the full verb cwá 'go', but is distinct enough grammatically that the two may co-occur:

(4-105)   ?a <u>já</u> cwá təpavā

            3   go   EXCL

            He (went ahead and) went (even though I told him not to)! (10/29)

4.3.5 Post-verbal Particles: rʌ́-class

     These VPtc's occupy the final positions in the VC, and have quite a variety of meanings. Some have to do with aspect or aspect-like notions, some relate to the presence of certain participant roles in the clause (e.g. an NP with a Benefactive role), but many have meanings that cannot be easily gathered under a single rubric. This class resembles the khwe-class Particles in its inclusion of aspectual meanings.

In the list that follows, the rÁ-class Particles are listed in the general order in which they occur. At the end of the list we group them into order-classes; members of an order-class are either mutually exclusive in that position or may occur in any order with respect to each other.

khjā   back again, over again; commonly occurs together with sɛ́ (listed below). E.g. dʌ́ k̲h̲j̲ā̲ sɛ́ 'give stg back'. Related morphemes: Localizer noun khjā 'back' (6.5), kəkhjā 'backwards' (Bound Directional).

kóʌ   temporarily, V instead for a bit. This is obviously related to the Descriptive Particle kó 'temporarily' (4.3.6); but both may occur in a single VC: ʔo kó rʌ̀ k̲ó̲ʌ̲ luɪ rest a bit first (for rʌ̀ see Descriptive Ptc, 4.3.6; for luɪ see below, this section).

pò   additionally. Tends not to occur with V$_i$'s denoting states; compare pa below. Examples: ʔe p̲ò̲ dī eat more rice; ʔo p̲ò̲ sɛ́ tənʌ̄ pa stay one more day.

pé   new negative situation, not after all, will turn out that not X; 'turn.out' in glosses. Must co-occur with the negative Clause Ptc to. E.g. ʔa | pùɪ cɛ̀ pé | to it turned out that he didn't know how to catch (fish) after all (pùɪ 'catch', cɛ̀ 'know how to V');

(4-106) ne mò   décho sínjē <u>pé</u> pa cè   pā
       2s mother tell   know   DUR maybe.not IRR

Your mother told you but you don't seem to understand. (137.5)

sé   again, in reaction, completing one half of a cycle;
'in.reaction' in glosses. Often with khjā 'back again', pò
'additionally' (both listed above). Examples: ʔū | síplɔ
du <u>sé</u> | pe they'll get mad back at us (if they hear you
talking that way about them); hɛ̄ pò <u>sé</u> | kúklē, |ka tò <u>sé</u>
went to work the swidden (again), and returned again (tò
'arrive');

(4-107) cwá ma lɔ̄   rūū, ʔe pò   <u>sé sé</u>, ʔomā pò <u>sé sé</u>
       go be.so exhaust silver eat additionally   sleep   additionally

Going takes money, and there's food and lodging on
top of that. (for reduplication cf. 3.4.3)

nɔ́   emphatic or unexpected negative; 'at.all' in glosses. Must
co-occur with negative to. E.g. nō <u>nɔ́</u> | hóhé | to ɛ̄ aren't
you going to school? (130.4); vɛ̄ | cwá <u>nɔ́</u> | to I'm NOT going.

lā~lʌ each other, reciprocally, in exchange. Similar in function
to the more common lū (below).

kā   comitative participant involved, situation is relevant to
more than one participant, interested person involved
(COM in glosses). Has the effect of adding an argument,
specified as Indirect Object. Examples:

(4-108) cwá <u>kā</u> vɛ̄
       go   1s

Go with me.

(4-109) sɔtɔ là   <u>kʌ̄</u> pe pe
        weed sparse   1p RDP
        Weeds are sparse with us, too. (31.2)

(4-110) vē hē   ʔíchi <u>kʌ̄</u> lāí phē khru   to
        1s go:FH chop   yet father   firewood NEG
        I haven't yet gone out with Father to cut firewood. (5/7)

The extra argument does not have a direct syntactic relation to kʌ̄; i.e. kʌ̄ is not a preposition taking the extra argument as its object. Evidence is provided by numerous examples such as (iii) above, with items intervening between the two; in this case the intervening material is the VPtc lāí 'yet'. Very often kʌ̄ seems to add virtually nothing to the meaning of the sentence, either because (i) the additional argument has already been licensed by some other valence-increaser such as the Descriptive Particles cwà 'help' and bébū̄ 'show the way to', or (ii) kʌ̄ only indicates a vague relevance of the event to either some NP participant in the discourse or to some human participant in the speech event. As an example of the latter sort, cf. the common utterance (in my presence, at least!) síŋē <u>kʌ̄</u> to '(you) don't understand ("with" us)'. This and the following morpheme are extremely common, usually omissible, and particularly difficult to pin down semantically.

rʌ́   participant obliquely involved. Indicates that a following NP argument has a role such as instrument, object of emotional-state verb, or some other oblique relation, often difficult to identify. Similar to kʌ̄ but seems not to be restricted to allusion to human participants; also like kʌ̄ it

105

may either add an argument (ii-iv below) or redundantly echo an argument already licensed (v-vi below). Very common, often optional, further analysis needed. Examples:

(i) ʔase dɛ r̠ʌ ʔaklwī kɔ	save the fruit for seeds (91.1)
(ii) bɛ́swá r̠ʌ pənè	be companions with a buffalo (19.3)
(iii) síplɔ du r̠ʌ ʔamòʔaphē	be angry with his parents
(iv) ʔo r̠ʌ lè donē	to be a matter for legend (51.6)
(v) ʔʌ̄ ma nɔ̄ ʔe r̠ʌ ʔitē	what's this used for?
(vi) chū̄ sʌ̄ r̠ʌ lū né ʔithoə	stab him to death with a knife

dītùì   keep on V-ing, undesirable event/action continues:

(4-111) kè   lɛsé   pī   dītùì mi
         AMB wind.blows go.out   fire
         The wind keeps blowing out the fire. (1/24)

(4-112) bɔ́   kʌ̄ dītùì bja |thé ǂ hú   ʔʌ̄ nʌ ‖ma hé | hú tē
         weave COM   PTC cloth like this NØ be.so say like what
         [If she] went on weaving like this what would he say?
         (286.2) (of a woman whose husband had told her not to
         work too hard)

mʌ̄   mild imperative, suggestion:
         thō̄ mʌ̄ tɛ kle   come over, Kle! (14.4)

(4-113) já   me mʌ̄ khē̄ Klémè lè   mʌ̄ nʌ ho
         go.and look PL.AC [name] place.for sleep NØ as.for
         phákɔ́ ʔo phɛ́ təkwa too
         pallet exist simply one-half only
         [They should] go look at Klemeh's bed; she has only
         half a sleeping-pad. (268.3)

phɛ́   simply, only, just; 'simply' in glosses:

    vē ʔo <u>phɛ́</u> tɤ́ ʔʌ̄ ŋē ba to: I have only (as much as) five baht.

    vē cwá nɔ́ to, vē ʔo <u>phɛ́</u> ʔa bʌ̄ I didn't go here, I live here! (169.10)

    phɛ́ may be repeated later in the clause:

    ʔe <u>phɛ́</u> təklɛ́ <u>phɛ́</u> ate only half.

    The status of the second phɛ́ is not clear; it may be func-
    tioning as a sentence particle (7.2). See also the Descrip-
    tive Ptc bja(phɛ́) 'ordinary' (4.3.6).

chílū ~ sílū too, excessively, very:

    kɛ́ ku təlwá <u>chílū</u> phɛ́ It's just too hot! (129.5) təlwá is a
    Bound Directional (4.3.7). The alternation of [s] with [ch]
    is a Western Kayah characteristic.

lēkhē also khē. Plural action; 'PL.AC' in glosses. Often used in
    imperatives (second example):

(4-114) ʔa ka   kəthɛ tò   <u>lēkhē</u> bɤ́ ʔʌ̄ ǂ nʌ hō

      3   go:FH ascend arrive   at:V this NØ as.for

      They all came back up here, and . . . (247.3)

(4-115) cwá mɛ́ <u>lēkhē</u> tɛ̀   me ní

      go   look   don't don't EMPH

      Don't you (pl.) go look at it, now! (326.2)

khrɛ́ plural questioned entity, 'what-all':

    ʔʌ̄ tənʌ̄ |me <u>khrɛ́</u> |ʔitē What [various things] did you do today?

bja V because of a feeling of obligation:

    cū kʌ̄ <u>bja</u> | lū te accord with his (things=) words —> heed him [as you
    ought]. Possibly related to the first syllable of the Descrip-
    tive Particle bja phɛ́ 'ordinary, simply, gratis' (4.3.6).

láte on the other hand

láteá instead:

(4-116) síŋē ʔé ʌ ‖ pe | síŋē kʌ̄ <u>láte</u> |
       know   much NS 1p   know COM

kulā   ŋò ǂ təphré´ ǂ to
European language one-C:hum   NEG

You understand a lot, on the other hand not one of us understands English. (220.6)

(4-117) ʔa dʌ́ pa li   thē to, ʔa dʌ́ <u>láteá</u> li   phá
       3 give DUR book gold NEG 3 give   book skin

He didn't give a gold book, he gave a hide book instead. (100.4)

jʌ́   emphatic or exclamatory. Often in the expression cè jʌ́ pa ... to 'very, really', with cè 'maybe not', pa 'durative', to 'negative', evidently a kind of double negative: 'not the case that maybe not' — > 'definitely the case':

(4-118) vē ʔomʌ̄ mè já   méthʌ ʔé cè   <u>jʌ́</u> pa rū to
       1s sleep dream go.and see much maybe.not DUR silver NEG

I dreamed [that I] went and saw a great deal of money. (121.2)

(4-119) ké ro cè   <u>jʌ́</u> pa to
       AMB cold maybe.not DUR   NEG

It's *really* cold! (257.3)

(4-120) pe cwá ja nɛne <u>jʌ́</u> cwá tò <u>jʌ́</u> mú nó khu
       1p go far really   go arrive at:l swamp on

Ah! This time we've gone a long way; we've gone all the way into a swampy place. (458.4, Kekhu) dɯ   on one's own, of one's own accord; 'own.accord' in glosses. Adds Direct Object argument coreferential with Subject, as in first example below:

ʔa | hɔ́ lɔ́ d<u>ɯ</u> |ʔa te   She is pregnant on her own. (i.e. immaculate conception) (78.3)

chā| ʔe <u>dɯ</u>   The chicken ate it of its own accord (i.e. it's not my fault). (104.3)

súplʌ cɔ̄ <u>dɯ</u>   a self-tying [magical] rope (360.1)

..ma <u>dɯ</u> | pe phú   . . . is still our own child. (52.6)

Note: reflexive meaning is usually indicated by the NP X nè 'X's body', occurrence of which as Direct Object may be licensed by either dɯ or rʌ́. The two latter items often co-occur: mé rʌ́ dɯ ʔa nè looks at himself in it [a mirror]. vē hé <u>rʌ́</u> <u>dɯ</u> vē̄ nè I say to myself. (8.xi)

ʌ́   new situation (NS in glosses). Note that although ʌ́ very often occurs with the verb thō 'finish', the two are distinct in meaning. Compare:

ké cɯ <u>ʌ́</u>   It's raining. (said on noticing the rain, whether or not it has been raining prior to the time of noticing).

ké cɯ thō <u>ʌ́</u>   The rain has stopped ('it's finished raining').

lāí   (not) yet. Must co-occur with the clause Particle to 'negative'. vē̄ | ʔe <u>lāí</u> | dī ǂ to I haven't eaten yet.

lɯ   just, a bit. Often occurs following kɔ́ʌ 'temporarily' (see above) and/or preceding the ClfP təki 'a little': nì dā kɔ́ʌ <u>lɯ</u> təki Listen a bit; i.e. Wait a minute (to one's partner in conversation). ʔo kó kɔ́ʌ <u>lɯ</u> pò sɛ́ Rest for a while again.

pa   durative, still (DUR in glosses):

mɛ́ thʌ nɔ́ kā̄ | ʔa ǂ to ‖ ʔa | ka <u>pa</u> | dɤ́ khjā [I] haven't seen him, he's coming along behind. (197.2)

ké | cɯ <u>pa</u> | to   Rain is no longer falling.

thwā NP <u>pa</u>   (still is an NP=)NP is alive. Note: thwā is an 'incorporating' verb (see 4.5). The construction V pa . . . to, literally 'not V any more', can have the force of 'don't have to V'. The gloss 'durative' is only part of the story, as shown by the fact that pa co-occurs frequently with the preverbal Ptc tɯ́ 'just now V'd'. Note also the following:

ʔa | ʔo <u>pa</u>   (1) there's more; (2) it's still there

du lɤ́ <u>pa</u> <u>pa</u>   still bigger=even bigger

The details of the semantics of this morpheme remain to be explored.

nɛ̄   high time to V, must V because hasn't V'd in so long. Often with Modal Ptc klé 'should be the case' and rʌ́-class VPtc phɛ́ 'simply' (above), as in second and third examples below:

(4-121)   párò   ma   ké   cɯ <u>nɛ̄</u> dɯ   ʌ́
            tomorrow   be.so AMB rain   own.acccord NS
            Tomorrow it's just got to rain. (9/29)

(4-122)   ʔa dʌ́ khjā lāí to   ŋjā   lō   ʌ́,
            3   give back   yet   NEG long.time INT NS

            párò   ʔa klé   dʌ́ khjā sɛ́   <u>nɛ̄</u> tɛ   phɛ́
            tomorrow 3   should give back   in.reaction   on.time simply
            He hasn't paid [me] back for ages, tomorrow he's got to. (9/29)

(4-123) na be   ma ʔa klé mo lɤ́ nē chá
     year manifest be.so 3   should happy more   when:F

    hē   ŋē pā təki phɛ́
    go:FH front IRR a-bit simply

    Next year it's just got to be more pleasant up ahead.
    (183.2)

tɛ̀   shouldn't; strengthens negative imperative, often with
    Sentence Particle me 'don't' (section 8.2): chá tɛ̀ lū me
    Don't fight! (9/22)

(4-124) cwá mɛ́ lɛ̄khē tɛ̀ |me ní
     go   look PL.AC   don't EMPH

    Don't you (pl.) go look at it, now! (326.2)

(4-125) vē lɛkhúi tədɤ́ ma sī hē   lɔ́plú tɛ̀ vē me ní:
     1s fall   although be.so 2p go:FH across   1s don't EMPH

    Even if I fall, don't go across [=step over] me! (382.4)

cɛ̀   maybe not, tentative negative:

(4-126) cwá pé   pa cɛ̀ pā
     go   after.all DUR   IRR

    May not go after all.

(4-127) ʔa se ʔo pa cɛ̀ pe ʔe nɔ́ pa   cɛ̀
     3   fruit exist DUR   1p eat at.all DUR

    [If] perhaps it [rice plant] has no fruit, we may not eat
    at all. (32.6)

Note that this negative, like all other rʌ́- class Particles,
has a fixed position following the last verb in the VC, and

so cannot be used to pick out the main verb (or any particular member of a V-V), resembling in this respect the Clause Particle to.

lū   each other, together. Distinct from the homophonous obviative pronoun, but probably related; cf. pe me cwà <u>lū</u> We help each other ('we help him' would be pe me cwà ʔa, with unmarked pronoun ʔa). Often in sɛə lū the same ('same as each other'), V rò lū many things V, to V together.

nɛkū~nɛ́kū   when . . . then.

(4-128)   ʔa thō mé súí <u>nɛkū</u> rʌ hé tò jʌ́   pe mē ɔ̄
        3 go.over look wrong   RØ: say arrive EMPH 1p EXCL EXCL
        When he went over and couldn't find it, then he went and (talked=) complained to us! (251.4)

(4-129)   ʔū chá <u>nɛ́kū</u> lū   ma thɛ   khé lū   bɤ̀ nʌ
        3i fight   each.other be.so ascend shoot each.other at:V that
        When they were fighting they went up and shot at each other right there. (226.3)

pè   benefactive/malefactive, dative of interest, to sbdy's
~pjà   benefit or detriment (cf. 3.3), BEN in glosses; adds an argument specified as Indirect Object.

       ché <u>pè</u> phúcè ca to sew clothes for children

       me bī <u>pè</u> ʔa kədā Shut the door to keep him out. (9/26)

       ʔa sɔ̄ lɔ̄ <u>pè</u> lū It all rotted on them, to their detriment. (155.6)

Contrast the (probably related) Bound Directional pè 'transfer of possession' (4.3.7). The difference between the two forms pè and pjà seems to be that pjà is confined to contexts in which the Recipient is third-person. Note the possible contrast with mὲ 'older sibling': ʔa me pὲ mὲ He did it for you, OS (mὲ as a term of address); ʔa me pjà mὲ He did it for OS (mὲ as a term of reference). pjà may be a fusion of pὲ and the third person pronoun ʔa.

The foregoing lists the rʌ́-class particles roughly according to the order they appear in with respect to each other. Particles that are either mutually exclusive or that may occur in any order with respect to each other can be assigned to a single order class. These order classes are listed below:

khjā	sɛ́	phɛ́	ʌ́	tὲ	pὲ
kóʌ	nɔ́	tamō	lāí	cὲ	pjà
		chílūɯ	lɯ	təpa	
		lēkhē	pa		
		khrɛ́			
		bjá			
		láte			
		rʌ			

4.3.6 Descriptive Particles

This is a fairly large and in some ways problematic class. Its unifying characteristics are the broad syntactic features of a) following co-occurring verbs; and b) preceding the rʌ́- class particles. The class of Descriptives is more heterogeneous than the other Verb particles, with meanings ranging from quite concrete to fairly abstract. Also, the class contains a great many members, although not so many as to make an unlistable number (i.e. it is

113

probably a closed class); and the members show hard-to-discern properties of ordering, both with respect to each other and with respect to other classes.

It can be divided into two subclasses.

4.3.6.1 Movable Descriptive Particles

These may permute with each other, with other Descriptive particles, or with V_2's in Descriptive V-V's, often with corresponding shifts in meaning. The first four in the following list share a common semantic element of potentiality:

cè   able, know how to V, good at V-ing

pè   physically able, strong enough to V; possibly related to full V pè 'win'

bé   have the wherewithal to V (money, raw materials)

bɯ   dare to V

cɔ́   insist on V-ing, stubbornly V

kho   V as cover for stg else

lɤ̌   more, -er (comparative degree), very, than; 'CMP' in glosses

khrɯ   equally, as (much) as

hā   often

tɛ   V on time

rλ   beforehand (this and the following have some verblike features, such as the ability to modify nouns; see below)

no   afterward

Examples of permutation:

ʔíbe cè phrē   learn rapidly to speak, e.g. a precocious child

ʔíbe phrē cè   good at speaking fast.

cwá rʌ̀ jὲ	going beforehand is hard
cwá jὲ rʌ̀	going was hard before
ʔírē phrē lɤ́ jὲ	hard to work faster
ʔírē phrē jὲ lɤ́	harder to work fast
me thō bɯ	dare to finish
me bɯ thō ʌ́	become fully brave enough to do
cwá jὲ hā	often hard to go
cwá hā jε	hard to go often

These are subtle distinctions, at least when deprived of context. In the last pair, cwá jὲ hā might be said in reference to a road that is frequently washed out, while cwá hā jὲ could contrast with 'but to go once or twice would be easy'.

4.3.6.2 General Descriptive Particles

Again, there is little in the way of a semantic common denominator to this class; like the second verb in a Descriptive V-V, the sense is vaguely 'adverbial'.

ho   secretly, sneakily.

kó   temporarily, for a while; e.g. ʔo kó 'to rest' (ʔo 'be at, dwell), phjá kó 'borrow' (phjá 'take').

cwà   help to V; adds an Indirect Object argument. E.g. ʔa me cwà Mīʌ Thīm hi 'He helps Mia build Tim's house'.

bébɯ̄   show the way to V, take sbdy V-ing; e.g. cwá bébɯ̄ 'lead sbdy'. Adds an Indirect Object argument.

115

phe   supplanting, appropriating; e.g. Phrè ka ʔo <u>phe</u> 'the Shans came and lived (on our land, supplanting us). (200.1)

re   unrestrainedly, often connoting an undesirable extent; e.g. cwá re 'go all over, go just anywhere', ʔíbe re 'talk loosely, talk wildly'; ʔa cwá re dɤ́ mi kḷē 'it [path] goes on into the forest' (21.v); perhaps related to the following.

tərecū̄   regularly, all the time.

tὲ   wrongly, V the wrong one; cf. ʔíbe ta tὲ 'make a slip of the tongue', also the Elaborate Expression (9.2.2) ta tī ta té 'unclear, halting' (of speech).

ʔone   against, defensively; usually co-occurs with VPtc pὲ benefactive/malefactive, dative of interest; e.g. me bī ʔone pὲ kəjē kədā 'close the door (kədā) against people, close the door so no one gets in'.

lé   keep up with, to V overtaking somebody.

lὲ   hurry and V.

bja(phé) just V, ordinary; gratis. phé 'simply' is a rʌ́-class VPtc (previous section). This bja occurs so often in conjuction with phé that the combination can be treated as a single item. In the VC it means 'just V, usually V, V in an ordinary way': ʔo <u>bjaphé</u> 'just sit around', cwá rò lū <u>bjaphé</u> 'they usually go in a group, usually many of them go'. It can also modify nouns (see below). Possibly related is dʌ́ bjaphé 'give for free, gratis', with the

116

idea being 'to just give' with nothing else involved, not even a price.

Both types of Descriptive particles can intervene in Descriptive V-V's:

cwá ho jὲ	hard to go secretly
me cwà lō	all help to do
kōthɔ tərecūī rò	get up early regularly

In particular cases it may be that there is only one possible order; in others there are several possibilities.

It was mentioned above (4.3.2) that there is a kind of symmetry between the khwe-class and rʌ́-class particles, consisting of peripheral position in the VC (initial and final respectively) and inclusion of aspect-like meanings. Likewise a symmetry can be seen between the Modal class of preverbal particles and the Descriptive class of postverbal particles. Positionally each is adjacent to one of the peripheral classes just mentioned; that is, the relative ordering is:

khwe-class   Modal   V   Descriptive   rʌ́-class

Another resemblance lies in their closeness to verbhood. The Modal particles are like Modal verbs both semantically and syntactically (preverbal position), the sole but decisive difference being their inability to stand as unitary predicate of a clause. The Descriptive particles, for their part, are semantically and syntactically like second verbs in a Descriptive V-V, with the same vital distinction that the particles cannot be unitary predicates.

Another verb-like property of Descriptive particles is the ability of some of them to modify a preceding noun, post-nominal modifiers being normally verbs. This can be conveniently

117

demonstrated with rλ 'beforehand' and no 'afterward'. They appear in the examples of permutation above; cf. also:

(4-130) ʔíbe cὲ   rλ,   cwá cὲ no
         speak know.how beforehand go   able afterwards

[Child] is able to talk first, able to walk later. (c)

They may modify a preceding noun: phú rλ 'previous child' (i.e. child by a previous marriage) phú no 'later child' (i.e. child by a later marriage). E.g. ʔa phú rλ ʔo sí nā 's/he has two previous children'. This function is not restricted to occurrence with phú 'child', cf. Mĩʌ phē rλ ʔa mi Chwephō 'Mia's previous father's name is Chwepho', where phē rλ 'previous father' refers to Mia's blood father in contrast to his step-father.

In addition to rλ and no, the General Descriptive Particle bjaphέ may also modify a noun: kəjē bjaphέ 'ordinary person'. rλ and no may also appear embedded as nominalized objects of Prepositions. Cf. the two very common expressions dɤ́ ʔa rλ 'recently', with the general-purpose Preposition dɤ́, and chá no pā 'later on', with the future-time Preposition chá and the Sentence Ptc pā 'unrealized situation'. It is of course true that the object of a preposition may be a lexical noun as well as a nominalized verb (clause); the occurrence of the Sentence Particle pā confirms that the latter expression at least has no in a verblike function.

4.4 Interactions

Thus far we have described the VC in terms of binary combinations of morphemes; these may be called simple V-V's. This section will consider some of the ways in which constructions of more than two members are formed in the VC. A division is made between constructions involving verbs only and constructions involving both verbs and particles.

4.4.1 V-V and V-V

Constructions of more than two verbs are formed in two ways. First, one type of V-V construction may have more than two members; this may be called a compound V-V. We have already seen examples of this for Resultatives and Sequentials; cf., respectively, (22) and (42), repeated below:

(4-111) ne cwi the   thū ʔacʌ nʌ
2s pull emerge long ITS-wick NØ
(If) you pull the wick out long . . . (341.6)

Here both the and thū describe results of the action.

(4-112) hē̄   ʔomʌ̄ klè tənʌ̄   nʌ̄
go:FH sleep   cut one-two day(C:)
(We) go and sleep (in the fields) and cut (brush) for one or two days (177.2)

Here hē̄, ʔomʌ̄, and klè describe sequential and alternating actions.

For an example of a compound Descriptive V-V, cf:

(4-113) síŋē jè   lɔ̄   ʌ́
know difficult exhaust NS
It's all hard to understand. (11.4)

Secondly, different types of V-V construction may combine; that is, in many cases one or both 'V's' may themselves be V-V's. This can be called a complex V-V.

119

To facilitate discussion of complex V-V's, let us adopt a type of constituent-structure notation in which nodes or brackets are labeled with the name of the V-V construction type; thus a Sequential V-V could be:

[$_{Seq}$ V V]   or

Similarly, a Sequential V-V whose second member is a Resultative V-V, like:

(4-114) vɛ̄ pù̀ me sʌ̄ jòkhró
      1s catch do die rat
      I caught and killed a rat. (10/8)

would be represented as [$_{Seq}$ pù̀ [$_{Res}$ me sʌ̄]], or more abstractly [$_{Seq}$ V [$_{Res}$ V V]], or in tree form:

The abbreviated node labels are Mod = Modal, Dsc = Descriptive, Drv = Directive, Seq = Sequential, and Res = Resultative.

For a complex V-V made up of Directive and Sequential, cf.:

(4-115)=(4-82) [$_{Drv}$ V [$_{Seq}$ V V]
      nɔ̄   kəlɛ dɛ́ thʌ̄
      command go.down dip.up water
      tell sbdy to do down and draw water

Not every type of V-V can expand both of its V constituents as any other type of V-V. For instance, Modal and Directive V-V's

120

are defined by having first verbs that belong to certain closed classes; since most individual verbs are barred from acting as that first constituent, *a fortiori* V-V's are also barred from so acting. This still leaves a great many possible combinations, not all of which actually occur. For instance, $[_{Drv} V [_{Seq} V V]]$ is common, as in (64) above, and:

(4-116) nɔ̄   cwá ʔílò
       command go   plant
       tell sbdy to go plant (from 20.8)

but $[_{Res} V [_{Mod} V V]]$ seems to be impossible:
(4-117) *mū̄ sí   ŋò
       beat   want weep
       beat sbdy so that they want to weep

The sum of possible combinations in complex V-V's can be displayed as follows, using a tree diagram with two possible forms:
(4-118)   (a)   (b)

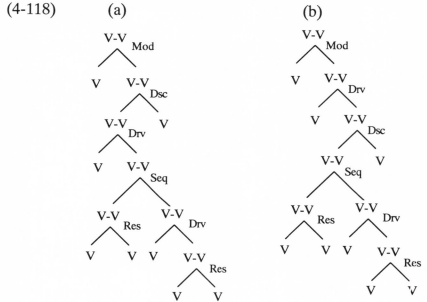

Notice that the structure below the Seq node is the same in both (118a) and (118b). The two differ only in the relations between the upper Drv node and the Dsc node: in (118a), Dsc dominates Drv, while in (118b) Drv dominates Dsc.

These two displays do not represent maximal possible complex V-V's. I have no example of either of the above patterns with all slots filled, although I would not wish to rule out the possibility of such an example in principle. The displays sum up co-occurrence facts about V-V types. For example, the position of Modal at the top of both patterns indicates that in a complex V-V any Modal V-V must come first, and that it must have semantic scope over all following V-V's.

Examples of various complex V-V's follow; they illustrate the scope relations that are the evidence for the constituent structure I have posited. This semantic scope has already been cited in 4.2.6 above; for an additional example, (127) below is nɔ̄ ʔírɛ phrɛ̄ 'tell somebody to work fast'. In other words 'fast' is part of the content of the command, which is taken to indicate that the structure is [nɔ̄ [ʔírɛ phrɛ̄]]. If the structure were [[nɔ̄ ʔírɛ] phrɛ̄] we would expect it to mean rather 'quickly tell somebody to work'.

Examples of complex V-V's:

Sequential with Resultative

(4-119)	pṳ̀ [me sʌ̄]	catch and kill stg
(4-120)	thɛ [phjá tā]	go up and get down
(4-121)	[cɔ̄ ma] mū̄	tie up and beat stg
(4-122)	[bɔ́ mō] mɛ́	open ('reach'+'be-open') stg and look

Sequential with Directive

(4-123) hɛ̄ [nɔ̄ dɛ́]   go and tell to draw [water] (Seq+Drv)

(4-124) nɔ̄ [kəlɛ dɛ́]   tell to go and draw [water] (Drv+Seq)

Directive with Resultative

(4-125) nɔ̄ [kúvē the]   tell to dig out

Directive with Descriptive

(4-126) [nɔ̄ ʔírɛ] jɛ   have difficulty telling sbdy to work=sbdy is hard to get to work (10/11)

(4-127) nɔ̄ [ʔírɛ phrɛ̄]   tell sbdy to work fast

(4-128) [nɔ̄ʔírɛ] rɛ́   tell sbdy nicely to work

(4-129) nɔ̄ [ʔírɛ rɛ́]   tell sbdy to work well

Descriptive with Resultative

(4-130) [me pjá] ho   ruin stg secretly

(4-131) [təkɔ̄ mɯ] lɔ̄   chop stg all up fine

Descriptive with Sequential

(4-132) [kèkjá kəthɛ] nʌ̀   manage to fold up stg and go up, fold up stg and go up taking it (317.3)

Modal with Descriptive

(4-133) tɔ̄ [cwá jɛ̀]   should go with difficulty

(4-134) sí [cwá hā]   want to go often (10/15)

Note: the examples cited in 4.2.5, such as (84) [[do cwá] beche ʌ́] 'tired of abstaining from going', involve Descriptive Particles rather than verbs.

Modal with Directive

(4-135) tɔ̄ [dʌ́ cwá]   should let sbdy go (5/26)

(4-136) sí [nɔ̄ʔírɛ]   want to tell sbdy to work (10/15)

Multiple: Modal, Sequential, Directive

(4-137) ?a kha cwá nɔ̄   hē   vē̄ pò kúklē

      3   promise go   command go:FH 1s YS field

He promised to go tell my younger brother to go out to [work] the field. (10/13)

Multiple: Compound Sequential with Resultative

(4-137a) hē ?e tɯ   ka ?ɔ̄ plɔ́ lēkhē̄ lū   bʌ̄

      go:FH eat together go:TH drink piled.up PL.AC   each.other here

They went and ate in groups and came and drank in crowds here. (178.6)

The structures of the last two examples are given below:

(137)   (137a)

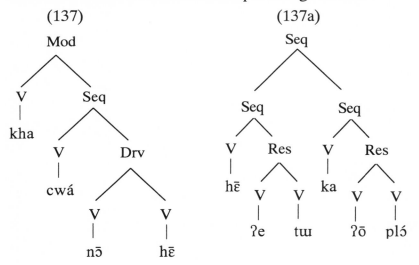

4.4.2 Particles

The khwe-class and rʌ́-class particles are unproblematic in their interactions with verbs and with other particles: they are always the outermost constituents, occupying first and last positions respectively in the VC, and they seem to have the whole of their co-constituent in their semantic scope. For example:

(4-138) tərē cwá jὲ ʎ

  almost go difficult NS

  almost hard to go (10/15) (not 'hard to almost go')

It is consistent with this that a particle may apply semantically to one part of its co-constituent rather than to another:

(4-139) nɔ̄ cwá pɔ̀ sɛ́

  command go additionally in.reaction

  again order him to go *or* order him to go again (10/13)

I do not take the second reading as evidence for a structure like [nɔ̄ [cwá pɔ̀ sɛ́]], the primary reason being that [cwá pɔ̀ sɛ́] does not otherwise act like a constituent in V-V constructions. In (127) above 'tell somebody to work fast' is analyzed as [nɔ̄ [ʔírɛ phrē]] both because of its meaning and because [ʔírɛ phrē] can act as a constituent of a V-V in other contexts; e.g. ʔírɛ phrē jὲ 'hard to work fast', be ʔírɛ phrē 'must work fast'. But *cwá pɔ̀ sɛ́ jὲ is impossible (the correct version is cwá jὲ pɔ̀ sɛ́).

Descriptive Particles. The variable positioning of these and its semantic effects, which come under the heading of interaction with V-V's, have already been described (4.3.6.2). There are also some noteworthy examples of interaction with Modal verbs:

(4-140) [do cwá] bəche ʎ

  abstain go bored NS

  be tired of abstaining from going (10/13)

(4-141)   [dɛsíplɔ cwá] cè   to
          decide   go   know.how NEG
          be unable to decide to go (10/20)

Worthy of note here is the fact that these Descriptive particles have scope over the modal verbs, while second verbs in Descriptive V-V's usually have lower scope than Modal verbs, as shown by (133–134) above. This is interesting because in other respects the Descriptive particles are like second verbs in Descriptive V-V's.

Modal Particles. There are hints that the Modal Particles have lower scope than at least some V-V types, as in the following example including a Descriptive:

(4-142)   [lā cwá] jè   be hard to plunge-in and go (see 4.3.3 for lā)

4.4.3 Excursus: Noun-incorporating Verbs and Particles
A few morphemes have the property of incorporating classifiers or nouns into the VC. Note that this phenomenon differs in various ways from constructions known as noun incorporation in other languages.

Examples:

1. Classifier-incorporator pé 'by the ___ unit, so as to be ___ units'

(4-143)   ʔíchē pé kīlō lāí to
          sell   kilo yet NEG
          They don't yet sell it by the kilo. (10/29)

(4-144)   dɛ pé plu thō ʌ́
          put pile finish NS
          They finished piling it up ('putting it in piles'). (10/29)

(4-145) vḗ me tā phé <u>pé</u> khri belɔ̀

    1s do fall crack shard drinking.glass

    I dropped the glass and it broke to bits. (10/29)

  2. Noun-incorporating Verb thwā 'be, become'

(4-146) tēú nʌ lɛ thwā tēú sɛ́   nʌ

    fish NØ descend be fish in.reaction NØ

    The fish went down and came back to life.

    (Cf. ʔa thwā N pa 'N is still alive', literally 'it is still an N')

(4-147) sílù   thwā kúpɛ̀ lāí to

    caterpillar be butterfly yet NEG

    The caterpillar hasn't yet become a butterfly. (10/29)

(4-148) təré cu thwā thʌ̄ lɔ̄ ʌ́

    wax melt be water exhaust NS

    The wax has all melted into liquid. (10/29)

The preceding examples have been chosen to demonstrate the VC-internal position of these incorporating constructions. In (143–144), [pé+classifier] precedes rʌ-class particles, as does [thwā +noun] in (146–147). In (148) [thwā+noun] intervenes between the two verbs of a Descriptive V-V, cf. the additional possibilities təré cu thwā thʌ̄ jū 'the wax melts easily' (jū 'easy'), təré cu thwā thʌ̄ rʌ̀ 'the wax melted beforehand' (for rʌ̀ see 4.2.5).

  Note also the two possible orders:

(4-149) ʔa ʔíchē sʉ́ <u>pé</u> kīlō

    3 sell wrong by.the kilo

    He sold it by the kilo, incorrectly [e.g. it should be sold by the piece].

(4-150)   Ɂa Ɂíchē <u>pé</u> kīlō súi

      id

Since Ɂíchē súi 'sell wrongly' is a Descriptive V-V, the permutability of pé kīlō with súi indicates that pé, which occurs only in this classifer-incorporating construction, is a Descriptive Particle. It is probably a loan from Thai/Shan pen, a copula that includes a similar semantic function, cf. Thai man khǎaj pen kiloo 'it sells by the kilo'.

      thwā 'be, become' is a verb, as is the only other known incorporating morpheme, chī 'as a _, the whole _', which incorporates classifiers. Examples:

(4-151)   Ɂa tā <u>chī</u> mē   lɔ̄   nʌ

      3   fall   C:large exhaust NØ

      The whole thing fell. (330.3)

(4-152)   Ɂō   <u>chī</u> sē   thʌ̄Ɂíphrè

      drink   night whiskey

      drink whiskey all night (18.v)

As main verb:

(4-153)   Ɂa <u>chī</u> pɯ   hú Ɂʌ̄ nʌ Ɂa twà to

      3   C:cloth like this NØ 3 pretty NEG

      For the whole thing [cloth] to be like this wouldn't be pretty. (277.4)

4.5 Borderline Cases between Verb and Particle

    In this section we discuss various items that do not categorize easily as either verb or verb particle.

4.5.1 Bound Result Expressions

There are various morphemes that combine with a preceding verb to form constructions closely resembling Resultative V-V's, while at the same time showing features that prevent classing them as full verbs. In many cases the feature is simply failure to occur as unitary predicator; in others it is a specific effect on argument mapping and syntactic valence. These morphemes are labeled Bound Result Expressions (BRE), and they fall into three listable classes.

4.5.1.1 Special

These items take two arguments as main verb, but they are more common as apparent V_2 in V-V's. In the latter function their special feature is to contribute the semantics of their Undergoer argument, either by imposing it on the Direct Object of a V_i or by adding an Object argument to a V_t. For this reason, and because their Actor arguments are suppressed, they are considered to be independent lexical items, related to but distinct from the full verbs.

The semantics added can be glossed as:

be~bja   with drastic, often destructive effect (cf. also the homophonous Modal Verb 'must', 4.2.6)

tō   with precise, wished-for effect

nì   manage to, V_1 and get

The following includes examples of both full verb and BRE.

be   strike, affect adversely, impinge—

As main verb:

(4-154) lɔ̀ <u>be</u> ʔa kuklɔ́

     rock   3 head

     A rock struck his head. (2/7)

(4-155) thⱭ̄ <u>be</u> hⱯca

     water   clothes

     Water affects the clothes. (2/7)

As BRE:

(4-156) thé   <u>be</u> kūʔu phá

     to.chisel   mouth skin

     [it] cut [his] lips. (25.3)

(4-157) plὲ <u>be</u> bése

     slap   face

     slap [sbdy's] face. (8/3)

(4-158) vē̄ khéthuú khé <u>be</u> nⱭ̄ be

     1s   shoot bird shoot   2 C:flat

     I shot at some birds, and hit two.

(4-159) vē̄ ʔonē̄ <u>be</u> nālī

     1s   sit   watch

     I sat on and damaged the watch.

(4-160) vē̄ khē <u>bja</u> pjá   nālī

     1s   step   ruined watch

     I sat on and damaged the watch.

(4-161) lɔ̀ tā <u>be</u> hi

     rock fall   house

     A rock fell on and damaged the house.

(4-162) kè lɛsé <u>be</u> pe mi rʌ
AMB blow   1p fire RØ:
The wind blows on [fans] our fire (30.7)

(4-163) ké cɯ <u>be</u> phrā   hikhu
AMB to.rain   to.sound roof
The rain falls noisily on the roof. (2/22)

(4-164) sī pā <u>be</u> ʔídɯ né lɔ̀
2p cut   knife OBL rock
You cut and hit a stone with your knife. (157.4)

tō impinge accurately, affect in just the right way, hit a target—

As main verb:

(4-165) ʔʌ̄hō <u>tō</u> vē síplɔ
this   1s heart
This one strikes my fancy, I like this one. (c)

As BRE:

(4-166) ʔa phjá <u>tō</u> khɛphá
3 take   shoe
He took the right shoes.

(4-167) kəjē̄ li phú ke hē   pè lū   nʌíma, ʔa the <u>tō</u> nʌ
Kayah red child if   go:FH BEN 3:OBV as.for   3 emerge   NØ
If the Kayah Li went for it, it would come out right to
them. (331.3)

131

(4-168) Motaəphē hē   nō tō̲ lū   ʔa plú chɯ   lū
[name]   go:FH enter 3:OBV 3 punch confronting 3:OBV

Motaphe went right in between them, and they hit him.
(242.2)

nì get, obtain; able, possible—

As main verb:

(4-169) nì̲ rɯ

to get money

(4-170) ʔa nì̲ kA̅ ʔamē təphre rʌ
3   COM ITS-wife one-C:hum PTC

He got a wife, and . . . (414.3)

As BRE (a) 'V and get, get by V-ing':

(4-171) vē ʔīchi nì̲ lāí sō   khrì   to
I   cut   get yet three packbasket NEG

I haven't cut three packbaskets-full [of firewood] yet.
(5/14)

(4-172) ʔa dɛ́hA̅ nì̲ kA̅   lū   ʔikē du ɔ
3 ask   COM 3.OBV blanket big   huh?

He got [by asking] a blanket from them, huh? (290.6)

(4-173) ʔé nì̲ lɔ̄   rʌ́ ʔa swá ʔa khō   nʌ
call use.up RØ 3 friend 3 companion NØ

He called (and got) all his friends. (477.5)

As BRE (b) 'able to V, V and accomplish:

(4-174) kɯ̄ sɛ́   nì̲ lɔ̄   dɯ   ʌ́
wear in.reaction use.up own.accord NS

They all managed to get their clothes back on (405.5)

132

(4-175) ʔa ʔírɛ <u>nì</u> sō nʌ̄

        he work   three days

        He worked [as much as] three days. (5/14)

(4-176) ʔíbe <u>nì</u> vā

        speak   sure!

        Sure you can say [it]! (in conversation)

All three of these take two arguments as main verbs. be and tō are quite similar: the Actor is a moving entity, not necessarily animate, that has an effect on a stationary Undergoer. nì also takes two arguments, the Actor (usually) animate, the Undergoer being the thing obtained.

As BRE, these morphemes form constructions very similar to V-V's with the causation type of interpredicate semantics. But these constructions are unlike either Resultatives or Directives, the two V-V types with causation semantics. Resultatives typically have a one-argument V_2, but these morphemes take two arguments as verbs. Directives can easily include two-argument V_2's, but their V_1 position is restricted to Directive Verbs, whereas the constructions displayed above have an open V_1 position. Also unusual is the argument mapping, which is not to the second element's Actor, as in all V-V's, but rather to the second element's Undergoer. As an example, the mapping for (156) above is as follows:

$$\text{S} \qquad \text{O}$$
$$| \qquad |$$

(4-177)   thé 'to chisel' [Ac Un]   be [(Ac) Un]

$$|\_ \_ \_ \_ \_ \_ \_ \_|$$

(S unexpressed; O = kūʔu phá 'lips')

When the first verb is a V_i, the second morpheme's Undergoer is simply added, as in (161):

$$S \qquad\qquad O$$
$$| \qquad\qquad\quad |$$

(4-178)　　　lɛsé 'blow'　　[Ac] be [(Ac) Un]
(S = kè 'Ambient', O = mi 'fire')

In fact it seems likely that these BRE's do not specify an Actor at all. It is true that in some sentences the BRE can be interpreted as having an Actor which is identified with the main verb's Actor. An example is (173) above, in which 'he' is both the caller and the getter of his friends. But this cannot be the result of any consistent argument mapping, since many other sentences lack such an interpretation. Consider (158), with khé be 'shoot and hit', in which it is not the Subject vē 'I' that hits the birds; or (164), with pā be 'cut and strike', where sī 'you' is not the participant that strikes the rock.

　　　Thus the special feature of these BRE's is that of specifying a single Undergoer argument, which takes precedence, as described above, over any other Undergoer in the VC.

　　　Possibly also to be listed here is ʔe 'use, to V for a purpose'.

　　　As main verb:

(4-179)　rūū ma ʔūū ʔe　　dɯ　　rūū be　　hú ʔʌ nʌ
　　　　　silver be.so 3i　exploit own.accord silver flat.thing like this NØ
　　　　　As for money, they used silver coins like this [one].
　　　　　(201.7)

It may occur as first verb in the compound ʔe ho 'to steal', with Descriptive VPtc ho 'secretly, sneakily' (4.3.6.2), as if literally 'use sneakily'.

As second verb:

nɔ̄ ʔe	use
jɯ ʔe	believe
cū ʔe	obey, go along with
jɛ̀ ʔe	rob sbdy

(4-180) phrɛ̀jwi hɛ̄ kwī ʔe kè
Tai.Yuan go:FH beg country
The Tai Yuan came asking for land. (201.7)

This ʔe occurs most often after another (head) verb. Many cases are indeterminate between this morpheme and the homophonous verb 'to eat'. For instance 'to cook rice' is usually phō ʔe dī, with phō 'cook in water' and dī 'cooked rice'; is it 'cook rice to eat' or 'cook rice for use'? Similarly tho ʔe təkhése 'gather mangoes to eat/for use', and the compound noun bó ʔe 'unhusked rice' (rice that has been threshed and winnowed but not yet husked) as if meaning 'rice for eating/for use', although oddly bó ʔe must first undergo husking to become hō, then cooking, before it becomes dī, which can be eaten. It is not inconceivable that these two ʔe are related; cf. Thompson's (1965, 336–7) remarks on the analogous Vietnamese verb ăn.

Finally, mention should be made of another verb be, possibly related to the be just discussed, a one-argument verb meaning 'become manifest, be the time for, be plentiful'. Examples as main verb are sɔle be 'the leaves come out (in the Spring)'; di be 'frogs are plentiful, it's frog season'; na be pā 'next year' (i.e. 'when the year comes forth'). It also occurs as second verb in V-V's: ʔe be dī 'to have plenty of food'; phú lɛ be 'have plenty of children' (literally 'children descend in plenty').

135

4.5.1.2 Bound Directionals

These are quite similar to the verbs that appear as V₂ in Directional V-V's, and many are in fact derived from Directional verbs by prefixation. They form a closed class of fairly versatile morphemes, of which two subtypes can be distinguished.

(A) Orientational Directionals.

This class is made up of forms derived from Type B Directional verbs (4.2.2 above) by prefixation with pə-, plus several forms with other prefixes. The semantic function is to describe the orientation of some participant in the action, usually that denoted by the Object NP, if present. Semantically these differ from the Directional verbs in two ways. First, the oriented participant does not necessarily move; e.g. mɛ́ pəhɛ̄ 'look ahead' (mɛ́ 'look'), jɔ̀ pəthɛ khɛ 'have the leg raised' (jɔ̀ 'extend, hold extended'). It is also possible for the oriented participant to move: jɔ̀ pəthɛ khɛ may also mean 'raise one's leg'. Second, if the situation does involve motion, the Orientational Directionals give the orientation of the moving entity, while the Directional verbs refer to the path it describes through space.

pə-prefixed Directionals:

pəhɛ̄	ahead, forward
kəkhja	backwards
pəthɛ	upwards
tālɛ̄	downwards
pəthe	outwards
pənō	inwards
pərɛ̄	across

Like the Directional verbs, the pə-prefixed Directionals include at least one member that may refer to non-literal direction:

(4-181) phúcè limē̄ pəhē̄ ʌ́

       child   smart   ahead NS

      Children are getting smarter (these days). (15.6)

(B) təlwá-class Directionals.

vɔ	around a obstacle, circumventing
təlwá	past
phā~təphā	out of the way
bé~kəbé	across, crossing, omitting
rwá	along
Cf. also təka	around, in a curving path (full verb)

These have several special characteristics: (a) they consistently follow Directional verbs; in fact they favor an intervening Directional verb if the first verb is not a Directional; (b) they add a Direct Object argument to the clause, the added argument denoting the entity serving as reference point for the spatial configuration (i.e. having the same semantic function as the object of a preposition in English). The full verb təka 'around, in a curving path' is also listed here because it shares these two characteristics, another example of the closeness of these Bound Result Expressions to verbs.

To illustrate the argument-adding property, consider the verb cwá 'go', which is a V_i, taking no Object NP. The combination cwá təlwá 'go past' becomes a V_t: ʔa cwá təlwá vē̄ hi 'he went past my house'.

4.5.1.3 General

This group does not have such a clear semantic common denominator as the preceding two, although it still deals with results of events named by a preceding verb. It differs from the Special BRE's (4.5.1.1) in that its members have no related full verbs, and that they cannot be interpreted as taking more than one argument.

To demonstrate the verblike semantics of these morphemes, consider the following examples featuring the semantically complementary chwí 'cool' (verb) and le 'warm' (nonverb). Each appears in four contexts: as unitary predicator, following the colorless verb me 'do, make', following a verb with more semantic color (dɛ 'put' and thɔ́ 'be covered, wrap oneself up'), and modifying a preceding noun:

(4-182) dī chwí ʌ́

rice cool   NS

The rice is cold.

(4-183) ʔa me chwí dī

3   do   cool   cooked.rice

He cools the rice.

(4-184) ʔa dɛ chwí dī

3   put cool   cooked.rice

He set out the rice to cool.

(4-185) [NP dī chwí]

cold [cooked] rice

(4-186a) *dī le   thō ʌ́

rice warm finish NS

The rice is warm.

138

(4-186b) √dí ku le
   rice hot warm
   The rice is warm.

(4-187) ʔa me le dī
    3 do warm rice
    He warms up the rice.

(4-188) ʔa thɔ́ le ʔikē
    3 cover warm blanket
    He wrapped himself up warm in a blanket.

(4-189) [NP dī le]
    warmed-up rice

Examples (182) and (186a) demonstrate that chwi is a verb while le is not. The sentence (186b) gives the grammatical equivalent of the ungrammatical (186a): as a predicator, le must be in construction with some preceding verb. Comparing (183) with (187) and (184) with (188) shows the close similarity of the two morphemes. The similarity is semantic, in that both relate to the preceding verb (and hence to the rest of the sentence) in the manner that we have discussed as the derived argument structure for Resultative V-V's: the participant bearing the Undergoer role of V_1 (in this case dī 'rice') is interpreted as being associated with the Patient role of the second morpheme: the rice becomes warm (for the concept of roles specified by a non-verb cf. 3.2.4). The similarity is also syntactic, in that nothing can intervene between the two morphemes in either case, and the two-morpheme constructions act as a unit in relation to other VC constituents; e.g. they may act as V_2 in a Directive construction:

(4-190) nɔ̄ me chwí   tell [somebody] to cool off [something]

(4-191) nɔ̄ me le   tell [somebody] to warm up [something]

Of secondary interest is the ability of both morphemes to modify a preceding noun, a feature that is shared with some Descriptive Particles (previous section) but not with all the morphemes being described in this section.

The following lists all additional known General BRE:

plúɪ́   to the end of an expanse, all the way through

dwá   away, available for future reference, possibly also occurs in the compound dwá sé 'thrifty'

kɛ̄   new location, to V so that something ends up in some place. E.g. dɛ kɛ̄ 'put down, put somewhere'; vī kɛ̄ 'throw away'; klɯ kɛ̄ 'shave off' (the beard ends up in a new location); ʔo kɛ̄ (1) 'stay, dwell temporarily', (2) 'separate, split up (as a couple)'. The same morpheme probably appears in the compound kɛ̄ dē 'go to waste, be wasted' (dē is a Descriptive Particle 'to V in vain').

pè   transfer of possession, abbreviated 'TRN'. E.g. ʔīche pè 'sell to'; dʌ́ pè 'give to'; khɛ̄ ʔo pè 'rent to'. In the last example pè follows a Resultative construction consisting of khɛ̄ 'rent' and ʔo 'be at, dwell', literally 'rent so that (sbdy) lives at'. Since it typically follows only three-argument verbs, it seems not to add an argument. This distinguishes it from the related rʌ́-class verb particle pè 'benefactive', which adds an Indirect Object Argument. Also 'benefactive' pè follows any co-occurring rʌ́-class particle while 'transfer' pè would precede any such particle.

140

ʔó   be hidden, into hiding, away. E.g. klɛ́ ʔó 'escape' (klɛ́ 'run'); dɛ ʔó 'hide stg' (dɛ 'put').

chɯ   confronting, facing, coming from opposite directions; often appears together with the rʌ́-class Particle lū 'mutually, each other'. E.g. cwá chɯ́ lū 'meet, approaching from opposite directions' (cwá 'go'); ʔíbe chɯ lū 'converse' (ʔíbe 'speak').

4.5.2 Bound Verbs?

If these borderline items are described as bound morphemes occurring in the VC, it must be recognized that the entire class of Verb Particles also fits that description. Recalling the use we have made of the Free/Bound feature in Nouns (3.2, also 6 passim), it is worth briefly considering here whether some or all of these bound morphemes should in fact be recognized as Bound Verbs.

All of the bound VC morphemes discussed in this chapter have some degree of versatility. The VPtc are highly versatile; in fact, co-occurrence with some of the rʌ́-class Particles can serve as a criterion for verbhood. The General BRE's are less so, but still may occur after a fair number of verbs. Contrasting with all of the foregoing are two types of highly restricted items.

The first is the class of Intensifiers. These only occur immediately following Verbs, where they serve to intensify the meaning of the Verb. Some examples are:

Verb	Intensifier
lɔ black	sɤ́rɤ́~sɤ́ŋjɤ́ very black, pitch-black
lɔ̄ use up	plīchaə~pīchaə with none remaining
phrɛ̄ fast	liə very fast *or perhaps* lightning-fast

141

The function of these Intensifiers is somewhat like that of the conventionalized metaphors in English expressions like *pitch-black, snow white, blood-red, soaking wet, freezing cold* (if used when the temperature is not actually below 32° Fahrenheit), and so on. But the Kayah Li Intensifiers lack the semantic specificity of *jet, snow, freezing* and the like. For example, lɔ sɤ́rɤ́ could be glossed 'pitch-black', but *pitch* denotes a class of thick dark sticky substances in addition to being conventionally used to mean 'very black', while sɤ́rɤ́ is not known to have any such concrete or specific meaning.

Many Verbs lack Intensifiers; for these Verbs the Intensifier function may be filled by expressions such as nɛnɛjʌ́ 'really, very' (cf. nínɛ 'true, real, for sure'), tədɯjʌ́ 'most, extremely', chílɯ̄ 'too, very'.

A second type of highly restricted bound verbal morpheme is exemplified by the second syllables of the following:

ʔo mʌ̄   lie down, sleep
ʔo nē   sit
ʔo lē   do for fun, visit

The first syllable of all three can be identified as ʔo 'exist, be at'. In each case, the second morpheme is not known to occur after any other verb, but it is reasonable to assign the bulk of the semantic content to it. These constructions are thus compounds, which can be construed as 'be located so that one sits/lies/enjoys'. Another set of examples involves the head verb no 'be odorous':

no mʉ́   fragrant
no mɛ̀   stink (cf. mʉ́mɛ̀ 'ugly')

142

no so	rotten, spoiled
no vi	sniff, smell at (cf. vi 'delicious')

With the indicated possible exceptions, these second syllables occur nowhere else in these meanings. An example with clearly resultative meaning is thʌ 'see', only after mɛ́ 'look' (mɛ́ thʌ 'look with the result that one sees').

Note that although items of this second type are highly restricted, their meanings are quite concrete. In this they resemble the Bound Result Expressions and contrast with largely grammatical meanings of the Verb Particles. As for the Intensifiers, their meanings are certainly not grammatical, although it is not so obvious whether they can be aptly described as concrete. Let us use 'content' as the opposite of 'grammatical' in this context; the features of versatility and semantic type may then be used to differentiate three classes of bound verbal morphemes as follows:

Versatility	Semantic Type	Class
high	content	Bound Result Expression
high	grammatical	Verb Particle
low	content	Intensifiers, other Bound Verbs

The logically-possible combination of low versatility with highly abstract meaning presents practical difficulties in identification (cf. the discussion in 3.2).

To sum up, all of the types of items listed in the preceding chart are bound verbal morphemes. Those with more specific features can be given more specific names: BRE, Verb Particle, Intensifier. The residue, the type of nɛ̄ in ʔonɛ̄ 'sit', can retain the more general term 'Bound Verb'.

Chapter 5

The Clause

5.1 Definition and Structure

The purpose of this chapter is to describe the structure of simple clauses; i.e. those without embedding, for which see Chapter 8. The description is mostly in terms of the various grammatical relations. The following chapter (6) will deal with the major lexical categories Noun (including Classifier) and Preposition, and with the internal structure of their phrasal projections NP and PP.

The clause is defined as any construction including a verb and terminable by to , the negative. The clause can also be delimited by the occurrence of the obviative third-person pronoun lū, which may occur only if preceded by a noncoreferential third-person NP within the same clause; see 5.3 below.

The linear order of elements in the clause can be represented as below:

(5-1)   (NP$_1$) VC (NP$_2$) (NP$_3$) (PP$_1$) (PP$_2$) (Clf') (SPtc)

VC is Verb Complex, PP is Prepositional Phrase. Clf' consists of Quantifier (usually a numeral) and Classifier. SPtc is Sentence

Particle. As for grammatical relations, NP_1 is Subject, NP_2 is Indirect Object, and NP_3 is Direct Object. The remaining phrasal categories represent various oblique relations, and may be labeled Oblique$_1$, Oblique$_2$ and so on. Since the clause-final Clf' is semantically fairly specific, I give its grammatical relation the more revealing name of Extent.

An artificial example with all elements represented is:

(5-2) Khōmὲ | ʔiswá pò | vē ǂ kəjē li ŋò ǂ dɤ́ ʔa hi
       Khomeh   teach   additionally 1s   Kayah red speech at:U 3 house
       sō   phō   ǂ bōʌ
       three C:times   and.then
       Khomeh taught me Kayah Li three more times at her house and then . . .

The configurational structure of the clause is represented as follows:

(5-3)

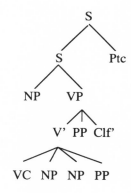

The SPtc is adjoined to the clause, consistent with its semantic relation to the entire proposition. For example, the SPtc to 'NEG' is a sentence-level negative.

145

The second break is between NP₁, the Subject, and VP. VP, besides its function as a clause constituent, also serves as the obligatory modifier of the abstract Noun lè 'place for V-ing' (see 6.7). The further division of VP into V' and V'-external elements is not of great consequence in the grammar, but there is one construction best described as a sequence of V'+V'. It is the only instance in Kayah Li grammar of serialization of intermediate-sized units that are neither single Verbs (as in the VC, 4.2) nor full clauses (9.4 Clause Sequences). Notice also that PP can appear both inside and outside V', reflecting a distinction between PP that are and are not lexically specified by the main Verb.

5.2 Source Expression: V'-V' Sequence

This construction involves a sequence of two V' within a single clause, having the general meaning 'V₂ from having V₁-ed'. When V₁ is ʔo 'exist', it is the most usual way to express the notion Source:

(5-4) ʔo dɤ́ sɔ kū tā the nɔ́ to,
      exist at:U tree inside fall go.out at.all NEG

      ʔo dɤ́ ve kū tā the nɔ́ to
      exist at:U bamboo inside fall go.out at.all NEG

      It didn't fall out of the trees; it didn't fall out of the bamboo. (8.4)

This example illustrates the monoclausal nature of the construction: the negative to has scope over both verbs in the sequence. In fact the main point of this particular utterance is to negate the first verb: the topic, previously mentioned, is jòse lɤ, meaning roughly ancient language or knowledge; having said that it doesn't grow on trees, the speaker goes on to tell where it does come from:

(5-5) ʔo dɤ́ hɔ́   kū tā the ʔo dɤ́ phrā kū   tā the
       exist at:U stomach inside fall go.out exist at:U intestine inside fall go.out
       It falls out of [our] stomach, it falls out of [our] guts

Since the first element, which includes the source NP (ʔo dɤ́ sɔ kū in the example) is V', it cannot include a Clf or SPtc. The latter especially would force interpretation as a sequence of clauses.

5.3 Subject and Topic

5.3.1 Subject versus Topic

Non-embedded clauses in Kayah may include two NP's preceding the verb:

(5-6) [bó]₁ nʌ [sɔtɔ̄]₂ khɛ́   kʌ̄ hú pwā na to mēɔ
       rice.plant NØ weed   overgrow COM like every year NEG CNC
       It is true that the weeds didn't overgrow the rice the way they do every year. (176.5)

(5-7) [he khrè]₁ [ʔa]₂ ʔe lū   nʌ
       earth bug   3   eat 3OBV NØ
       Earth bugs ate it. (84.4)

(5-8) [ʔʌ̄ təna]₁ [vɛ̄ lù vɛ̄ bwí vɛ̄ lùtərʌ̄]₂ tā pəhɛ̄ ŋɛ̄
       this one-year 1s   merit 1s fortune 1s luck   fall ahead front
       This year my luck, my fortune keeps on getting worse. (178–9)

Informally speaking, (6) has a 'fronted Object' followed by a Subject, (7) has a 'fronted Subject' followed by a 'resumptive pronoun', and (8) has a time expression followed by a Subject. In all three, the first NP is a Topic and the second is Subject.

It may be noted that the pattern exemplified in (7) is the favored form in some predications. E.g. chā bē nʌ sō be (ʔa) dʌ to 'those three yellow chickens don't lay eggs', where use of ʔa is optional but preferred, probably because of the complexity of the Subject NP, which contains both the Ordinary-headed NP chā bē 'yellow chicken' and the ClfP nʌ sō be 'those three CLF' (cf. 6.1 on these constructions).

Topics may also be PP's, most frequently time-when expressions referring to the past. An example is:

(5-9) d̰ɤ̀ [vē jì   bó nʌ] vē bá hē chā ‖ ʔa ri mē
     at:U 1s thresh rice NØ 1s   divine go:FH chicken 3 good PTC
     When I was threshing, I divined[1] about going [to work];
     [the indication] was auspicious! (183.6)

Note that the Topic we are describing here is a syntactic constituent. It is not the same as Topic in the sense of 'what the sentence is about', which is rather a discourse function: a sentence may well be 'about' something without containing a Topic constituent.

The difference between Subject and Topic (apart from the fact that Subjects cannot normally be PP's) is that the former is a clause constituent, while the latter is outside the clause proper and belongs to a larger unit.

The clause-internal position of the Kayah Li Subject has few of the morphosyntactic consequences typical of Subject

---

[1] bá chā is the practice of divining by inserting splinters of wood into holes in the leg-bones of a chicken.

cross-linguistically, since Kayah Li lacks such things as case marking, verb agreement or an active-passive voice distinction. There is, however, one minor but noteworthy syntactic phenomenon that is sensitive to the Subject constituent (but not to the Topic). This is an alternation between two of the third person pronouns.

Briefly, the third person pronouns are:

ʔa he/she/it/they; more specific, foregrounded

lū id.; also foregrounded; the other one

ʔū they, people, other people, someone; less specific, backgrounded; (also used in humilific self-reference)

The pronouns ʔa and lū alternate within a clause as a way of keeping track of two third-person protagonists. lū, which I will refer to as the obviative form (abbreviated OBV) can only be used if ʔa or some other non-coreferential third-person NP appears before it in the clause. Compare the following two examples:

(5-10) ʔa chū ʔa thwi
      3   stab 3 dog
He stabbed his (own) dog. (4/19)

(5-11) ʔa chū lū thwi
      3   stab   3OBV dog
He$_i$ stabbed his$_j$ dog. (4/19)

More generally, successive (foregrounded) non-coreferential third-person NP's require an alternation between ʔa (or other third-person NP) and lū. Note that since lū must follow another clause-mate third-person NP, it follows that lū can never occupy Subject position. The following includes an example of more than one turn of alternation:

(5-12) ʔa ʔé ka   lū   dɤ́ ʔa kè
    3   call go:TH 3OBV at:l 3 country

They$_i$ called to them$_j$ to return [with them$_i$] to their$_i$ country. (233.4)

The successive third-person NP's need not both be pronouns:

(5-13) təmɔ̀ chá ʔé   lū
    sun   shine much 3OBV

The sun shone strongly on it. (161.1)

The point to stress here is that this alternation operates only within the clause, thus providing a means of determining the boundaries of the clause. With the beginning of a new clause, the alternation must begin again. In the following example, note also that the third-person NP triggering the alternation may be realized as zero (here symbolized ø):

(5-14) ʔa | ʔé ʔojwā | lū ǂ bɤ́ tē ‖ ø | ʔojwā kʌ̄ |
    3$_i$ call wait   3OBV$_j$ at what (3$_j$) wait   COM

lū ǂ to ǂ bō̄ʌ ‖ ʔa | khrwā ʔíchɔ̄ kʌ | lū ‖
3OBV$_i$ NEG then 3$_i$ follow curse COM 3OBV$_j$

Whenever he called to them to wait they didn't wait for him; then he followed cursing them. (157.1)

Here the three occurrences of lū show that there are three clauses, each of them containing a third person Subject NP that triggers the appearance of lū as the Object. The third-person NP triggering the alternation need not be a Subject, although it often is, as in all three clauses in (14). It is also possible for a non-Subject to be the trigger:

(5-15) vɛ̄ dʌ́ pè kó   kʌ̄ ʔa lūte
     1s give TRN temporarily COM 3ᵢ   3OBVj-thing
I lent himᵢ hisⱼ. (10/8)

The alternation is not triggered by Topics, as is shown by the following examples in which a Topic is followed by a non-coreferential Subject:

(5-16) [ʔa dō lɤ̀ təpɯ]ₜₒₚ ja [ʔa]ₛᵦⱼphjá ʔomʌ̄ thɔ́ phe
     3 thick CMP one-clf PTC 3   take lie.down cover supplanting
The thicker one [blanket], he took to sleep under. (273.2)

(5-17) [hʌca pəkū]ₜₒₚ [ʔa]ₛᵦⱼ síjɯ bɔ́ mɛ́
clothes Sgaw   3   want weave look
Sgaw Karen clothes, [if] he wants some [I'll] weave some and see. (319.5)

In each example the Topic is not coreferential with the following third-person Subject NP, but it does not trigger the alternant lū for the latter. This of course follows from the clause-external position of the Topic.

Several other characteristics of Topic in Kayah should be mentioned. One is that, although examples like (16–17) in which Subject directly follows Topic, are not uncommon, very frequently there is something setting off the Topic from the following clause, such as the particle nʌ (see 8.3). There is also a common pattern X ma Y, with the verb ma 'be so', in which X relates to Y in the same way as a Topic to a following clause, which could be considered an expansion of the Topic+clause pattern; see (9.4). Secondly, sentences beginning with only one NP could conceivably represent a) Subject and no Topic; b) Topic and no Subject; c) a conflation of Subject and Topic. One type of sentence with this pattern deserves some comment, as in the following examples:

(5-18) khrɯ   ʔīchi lɔ̄   ʎ́
firewood chop use-up NS
The firewood is all chopped. (3/3)

(5-19) phúcè dʎ́ cwá lɔ̄   ʎ́
child let go use.up NS
The children have all been allowed to go. (2/20)

(5-20) ʔʎ̄ təmē bɔ́ sō nʎ̄ jʎ́ ʌ
this one-clf weave three day PTC PTC
This loom-set [I've] been weaving three days. (306.2)

In these a two-argument verb is preceded by an NP that could in other circumstances appear as its Object. If this preverbal NP is the Subject, the verbs could then be treated like the English verbs *open, break, drop* and so on (*The book dropped / John dropped the book*, etc.), as in Chao's (1968, 72) analysis of similar phenomena in Chinese. There is one bit of evidence that the Kayah sentences are rather to be analyzed as having Topic but no Subject. Consider:

(5-21) pe phú pe pò kənɛə X síjɔ lʎ̌ rʎ́ ʔa
1s child 1s YS youngest   care.for more RØ 3
Our child, our youngest brother, [we] care for him the most. (97.2)

Here if the NP pe phú pe pò kənɛə were Subject the meaning would be something like 'our youngest brother is cared for', and there would be no need for the Object pronoun ʔa. Note that if the meaning were 'our youngest brother cares for himself' the

Object expression would be more likely to be ʔanè 'himself', and the VC would probably also include the Verb Particle dɯ 'own.accord' (this nè is an Ordinary Bound Noun, not a pronoun; cf. also 6.2.1).

5.3.2 'Inverted Subjects'

There is a class of verbs denoting bodily sensations or emotions, whose single participant (the Experiencer of the state) most typically is realized post-verbally. Subject position may be empty, or may be occupied by the pronoun ʔa. Examples:

(5-22) kēsé lɔ̄   vɛ̄ nè
    itch use.up 1s body
    I itch all over. (127.2)

(5-23) ʔa mo   pa lū   síplɔ to
    3 happy DUR 3OBV heart NEG
    Their hearts weren't happy. (89.5)

(5-24) no   vɛ̄ to
    smell 1s NEG
    I don't smell anything. (29.iv)

Presumably these verbs specify in their lexical entries both the single argument and its realization as Object. That realization seems to be optional, given alternations such as the following:

(5-25) ʔa chē vɛ̄ kuklɔ́ ~ vɛ̄ kuklɔ́ chē
    3 hurt 1s head   1s head   hurt
    (both:) My head hurts. (29.iv)

5.4 Objects

A VC may be followed by zero, one or two unmarked NP's (i.e. without preposition). These post-VC NP's are Objects; when two of them are present the first is Indirect Object and the second Direct Object. As in English, with three-argument verbs the IO realizes the recipient or beneficiary and the DO realizes the thing transferred or other Patient. This similarity is reflected in the use of the familiar terms Direct and Indirect; there are of course substantial differences between the Kayah Li and English constructions, as will be evident.

In the discussion that follows, I will use the term 'root V_x' to refer to lexical verbs with a given syntactic valence, and likewise to VC's containing such verbs but no argument-adding morphemes. 'Compound V_x' will then be a VC including some argument-adding morpheme which interacts with the head verb's syntactic valence to produce a valence for the VC as a unit. For instance, a root V_t is a VC containing a V_t and no argument adding morpheme, while a compound V_t is a VC with a one-argument head verb plus some argument-adding morpheme that brings the total of licensed syntactic positions up to two.

In this connection, it is important to remember that argument-adding morphemes have both semantic and syntactic specifications. Semantic features specify the participant role of the added argument; syntactic features specify the syntactic realization of that argument, i.e. as Direct or Indirect Object.

5.4.1 Indirect Object

Root V_d's, which are not numerous, share meanings involving transfer of possession, whether literal or metaphorical.

They frequently occur with the Bound Result Expression (4.5.3) pè (glossed TRN for 'transfer'); recall that this item does not add an argument, so these VC's remain root V_d. The Direct Object is the thing transferred, and the Indirect Object has the role of the animate endpoint (recipient or goal) of the transfer; or, less commonly, that of animate starting point (source). Examples with IO as recipient:

(5-26) vē dʌ́ (pè) Khōmè rū

      1s give TRN (name) silver

      I give K. money.

(5-27) ʔa ʔíchē (pè) vē thɛ́ nʌ̄ dō

      3 sell TRN 1s pig two C:animal

      He sold me two pigs.

(5-28) ʔa bo ʔe (pè kʌ̄) thɛ́ che

      3 feed for.use TRN COM pig feed(n.)

      He feeds the pigs [their] feed. (10/29)

(5-29) sárá ʔiswá phúcè li

      teacher teach child writing

      The teacher teaches the children (their letters). (2/1)

(5-30) ʔa bulɛ vē hʌca

      3 exchange 1s clothes

      He exchanges clothes with me. (10/31)1

With kwī 'ask for, request', Indirect Object is source:

(5-31) já kwī títíˊ ʔū rū ma

      go.and ask.for constantly 1s silver PTC

      [You're] always asking me for money! (136.6)

      (humilific use of ʔū)

(5-32) vē | kwī khjā sɛ́   ʔa lòtɔthé
    1s   ask.for back   in.reaction 3   bicycle
I ask him for the bicycle back. (10/29)

Other V_d include déhʌ̄ 'ask' (IO=person, hearer; DO=subject matter) and tɔke 'begrudge' (IO=person, denied Recipient; DO=thing not transferred).

This structure, [VC IO DO], is the only way of casting these events in a single clause. There is no alternate form with the recipient in a PP, as in the English *give me money/give money to me*.

With compound V_d's, the DO often realizes the Undergoer participant specified by the head verb (which is a V_t), while the IO has a range of semantic roles, determined largely by the argument-adding morpheme that licenses it:

1. Comitative, with rʌ́-class Particle kʌ̄
(5-33) ʔō tɯ kʌ̄ | vē ǂ thʌ̄ʔíphrè
    drink PTC   COM   1s   whiskey
Drink (whiskey) with me. (10/20)

2. Standard, with rʌ́-class Particles lɤ̌ and khrɯ
(5-34) ʔa |ʔe ʔé lɤ̌ | vē ǂ dī
    3   eat much than   1s   cooked.rice
He eats more than me. (9/29)

3. Benefactive/Malefactive, with Descriptive Particles cwà 'help' and bébɯ 'show the way to', and rʌ́-class Particle pè 'to sbdy's benefit/detriment'
(5-35) ʔa |me cwà | Mīʌ ǂ Thīm hi
    3   do   help   (name) (name) house
He's helping M. build T's house. (10/20)

156

(5-36) ʔa vē pè lū   heso
      3   dig BEN 3OBV earth
      He dug out earth for her [i.e. doing her job]. (36.6)

Another frequently-encountered type of compound V_d results when a Directive verb combines with a V_t. In this case the IO is the Causee participant specified by the Directive verb, and the DO is the Undergoer of the second verb:

4. Causee, licensed by Directive head verb

(5-37) nɔ̄   já   dō   lū   thépənā
      command go.and forge   3OBV   chisel
      He told them to go forge a chisel. (94.1)

(5-38) ʔaphē | ʔiswá khē | ʔaphú ǂ sɔklʌ̄
      father   teach paddle 3-child   boat
      The father teaches his child to paddle a boat. (2/1)

5.4.2 Direct Object

With root V_t's, Object is a fairly typical Object relation in the semantic roles that it realizes: Patient with verbs specifying Agent and Patient; 'content' of perception with verbs like méthʌ 'see', nìdā 'hear'; Goal of verbs like síjùɪ 'want', ʔīphri 'buy', and mé 'look, look for'.

With compound V_t's, Object realizes various participant roles, some of them identifiable with those realized by the IO of compound V_d's:

1. Comitative

(5-39) ʔa cwá kʌ̄ vē
      3 go COM 1s
      He goes with me.

2. Standard

(5-40) ʔa ʔíbe cɛ̄ lɤ̌ vɛ̄
  3   speak able CMP 1s
  He can speak better than me. (9/29)

(5-41) vɛ̄ ʔírɛ phrɛ̄ khrɯ kʌ̄ ʔa to
  1s work fast   equal COM 3 NEG
  I can't work as fast as him. (10/31)

3. Benefactive/Malefactive

(5-42) ʔa sɔ̄ lɔ̄ pè lū
  3 rot use.up BEN 3OBV
  It all rotted 'on' them. (155.7)

(5-43) ʔa cwá bébɯ kulā dɤ̌ cho khʌ̄
  3 go   showway European at   mountain upper.surface
  He takes Europeans up the mountains. (6/25)

4. Causee

(5-44) vɛ̄ dʌ́ cwá ne to
  1s let go   2s NEG
  I won't let you go.

(5-45) ʔa nɔ̄ ʔonɛ̄ phúcè
  3 command sit   child
  He told the children to sit.

Plus the following, which have no equivalent IO realization:

5. 'Content' or 'goal' of emotional state, with Particle rʌ́

(5-46) ʔa síplɔ du rʌ́ ʔa phɛ̄
  3 heart big RØ 3 father
  He's mad at his father. (10/29)

(5-47) ʔa sínìso rʌ́ ʔa mē

    3   miss   RØ 3 wife

He misses his wife. (10/29)

(5-48) síjɔ̄   rʌ́ vē

    care.for RØ 1s

Have pity on me. (470.2)

(5-49) təphreʔukhré béswá rʌ́ pənè

    (name)   be.friend RØ buffalo

T. was friends with a buffalo. (19.3)

6. Point of orientation (Locative), with certain Directional morphemes

(5-50) ʔa cwá təlwá vē hi

    3   go   pass 1s house

He went past my house.

The reason that this last category does not appear with compound V_d's is that these particular Directional morphemes specify a DO argument. When one of these items, which include the təlwá-class Bound Directionals (4.5.2) plus a few full Verbs, follows a V_t, there are two different participants competing for the DO slot. Usually the Undergoer/DO argument specified by the head verb is realized as DO; while the Directional's argument is realized (if at all) as object of the Preposition né:

(5-51) ʔa | khē̄   təlwá | sɔklʌ̄ ǂ né sɔkhō

    3   paddle pass   boat   Né snag

He paddled the boat past the snag (fallen log).

(5-52) cɔ̄ təva lo   né cúkē

    tie encircle thread Né wrist

tie thread around wrist

For discussion of this function of né, see 6.5 below.

One last point concerns the name of the NP following a compound V_t: since some of these are licensed by argument-adding morphemes that specify IO, it would seem that it is possible for Kayah Li sentences to contain an IO with no DO, and that I am claiming that a single post-VC NP can bear one of two different grammatical relations. This is almost wholly a matter of non-substantive terminology. The facts are that items like kā, lɤ́ and pè have features specifying an unmarked NP that follows the VC, precedes any PP, and further may precede one other unmarked NP. When there is no second NP, we may call the argument added by kā et al. simply Object. It is true that single post-VC NP's can be divided into IO's and DO's, but that division is solely a matter of features of the VC consituent that licenses it. The only grammatical phenomenon that requires reference to the difference between IO and DO is their relative ordering when both are present.

5.5 Oblique Grammatical Relations

5.5.1 Clf'

Classifiers are a special type of Bound Noun, requiring modification by a Quantifier (the category including numerals). The resulting construction, known as Clf', is an intermediate-level category, an N' that, like any N', can function as NP, either on its own or with additional co-constituents. In the present section we discuss one special syntactic position that can be occupied by a Clf' but not by a full NP; i.e. it must be a Clf' with no additional elements. This position, which I term the Extent expression, is last in the clause except for the Sentence Particles. It is in fact the most common position for Clf' to occur in.

Examples:

(5-53)

(a) phúcè cwá dɤ́ hóhé sō nā̄   The children went to school for three days.

(b) phúcè cwá dɤ́ hóhé sō phó   The children went to school three times.

(c) phúcè cwá dɤ́ hóhé sí sō   Three children went to school.

Note that only in the last example does the Clf' 'count' partici-pants in the event; note also that (53c) is the normal way to con-vey this meaning. It is also possible to have the Clf' directly mod-ify the Noun that it 'counts' as a co-constituent of NP, as in:

(5-54) phúcè sí sō cwá dɤ́ hóhé   Three children went to school.

But (53c) is by far the more common pattern.

The syntactic division between the Clf' and the NP it 'counts' becomes unclear when the counted NP is an Object and there is no PP: the concatenated NP-Clf' might form an NP, or the two might be distinct. Since 'bare' Clf' are more common than those with additional modifiers, I assume that sequences V-NP-Clf' are Predicate-Object-Extent rather than Predicate-Object with the Object including a Clf'. See 6.1.2. for more discussion of this point.

The Extent expression may consist of more than one Clf', with a kind of distributive meaning. For example:

(5-55) ʔa sɛ́   nʌ   ma   təpɯ   təko   jʌ́   mē
      3   wear Nø   be.so one-C:cloth one-C:200B. EMPH Ptc
      What he wears [shirt] is two hundred baht apiece! (274.5)

161

(this Clf ko refers to quantities of two hundred baht; it may or may not be identifiable with the general Clf ko). The general pattern is Q_A-Clf$_B$ Q_C-Clf$_D$ 'C D's per A B's', but more usually A=1, i.e. tə-Clf$_B$ Q_C-Clf$_D$ 'C D's per B'. This type of multiple Clf' may even itself be repeated:

(5-56) ʔithɔ́ təphre   təpɯ   təphre   təpɯ

      cover   one-C:hum   one-C:cloth   one-C:hum   one-C:cloth

cover with one [blanket] per person. (272.5)

The Extent expression interacts with a subclass of the Sentence Particles (Subclass A in 8.2 below), consisting of pā 'irrealis', to 'negative', and too 'only'. Extent is in near-complementary distribution with the latter two; only the following patterns are found:

    A. Q-Clf-too 'only X Clfs', e.g:

kəjē ʔo sí sō too   there are only three people

    B. tə-[Clf+high tone]-to 'not a single Clf', e.g:

kəjē ʔo təphre˝ to   there's not a SINGLE person

    C. Ø-to 'not the case', e.g:

kəjē ʔo to   there are no people

One cannot say *kəjē ʔo sí sō to intending to mean 'there are not three people'; it is either unacceptable or interpreted as a (poorly pronounced?) version of kəjē ʔo sí sō too 'there are only three people'. To mean 'there are not three people' one would have to say kəjē sí sō ʔo to; i.e. for a negative assertion involving a quantity the Clf' cannot be in the Extent position, but must be part of the Subject NP.

The foregoing suggests that to itself has some character-

162

istics of a Clf', being perhaps a fusion of the numeral tə- 'one' with some other element (could it be the general classifier ko?). The original meaning 'not even one' has been bleached to simple negation, then re-created in the emphatic təClfˊˊ to. It is worth mentioning here that, in many conversational situations where I would be inclined to use the simple negative, Kayah Li speakers use the emphatic. E.g. cwá khé ʔitē? // khé təcɤˊ to 'what are you going to hunt? // Nothing' (actually khé is 'shoot'); vɛ̄ méthʌ təphoˊ: to 'I've never seen it'.

However, there are some special contexts in which Extent and to can co-occur. One is the type of contrastive statement exemplified below:

(5-57) ne təsá ʔo   ŋɛ̄ be, ma   ɛ̄? //
      2s duck exist five C:flat be.so QP

      ʔa ʔo ŋɛ̄ be, to, ʔo phɛ́ lwī be
      3   exist five C:flat NEG exist simply four C:flat
      You have five ducks, right? // I don't have five, I only have four. (4.vii)

(5-58) ʔa dʌ́ nɔ́ sō   cwe   to, ʔa dʌ́ lwī cwe   vā
      3   give at.all three hundred NEG 3   give four hundred PTC
      They didn't give (me) three hundred (baht), they gave four hundred! (4.vii)

Thus the interpretation of to as a fusion of tə- 'one' with something else is not quite valid as a synchronic analysis. It does, however, remain a likely hypothesis for the historical source of the interactions just described. Such an evolution would account for the relatively unusual state of affairs in Kayah Li having only a sentence-level negative: there probably was originally a verb-negating morpheme to which the ancestor of to was an emphatic partner, something like French *ne . . . pas* or Burmese mǎ . . . hpù.

5.5.2 Prepositional Phrase

5.5.2.1 General

The PP's occurring after the VC may be either inside or outside the V' constituent, the difference being that those inside are lexically specified by the head verb while those outside are not. Cf. the VP portion of the constituent-structure diagram (5-2), reproduced below:

(5-59) (=5-2)

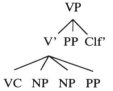

For example, PP is the normal realization of the Locative participant role. As in many other languages, Locative PP's may be specified by verbs like ?o 'exist, be located, dwell'; cwá 'go ; and dɛ 'put'; but they may also occur freely with a wide range of verbs. The former, sometimes called 'inner Locative' (considered to include Goal and Source), are realized by PP's that are daughters of V'; while the latter ('outer Locative') PP's are sisters of V' and daughters of VP. As has already been discussed, the first V' in the 'source', or serial V' construction may contain a PP, which

164

is restricted to a lexically-specified PP, like the inner-locative PP appearing with ʔo 'exist' in (4, 5).

In addition to (outer) Locative, V'-external PP's express a variety of 'adjunct' meanings. E.g. hú 'like, as, as if':

(5-60) ʔa | dʌ́ láteá |li   phá ǂ hú [phē ʔírō] ‖ hé nʌ
     3   give instead book skin like father sing   say NØ
He gave them a hide book instead, as Father sang, it's said. (100.4)

For an example with two PP's, cf:

(5-61) ʔa phʌ̄   nʌ ʔo dʌ́ hi   thuū hú pe ʔo ʔʌ̄ nʌ
     3 grandmother NØ exist at:l house edge like 1p exist this NØ
His grandmother lived at the edge of the village, as we do here. (204.4)

For a list of prepositions and some description of prepositions as a lexical system, see 6.6.

Although this chapter is concerned with simple clauses, it should be mentioned here that PP is the commonest location for embedded clauses (cf. 8.2). The two preceding examples contain embedded clauses functioning as object of the Preposition hú: phē ʔírō 'Father sang' in (60) and pe ʔo ʔʌ̄ 'we live here' in (61).

5.5.2.2 né-PP's

The preposition né has four functions.

1. Subcategorized. A few verbs require a né-PP as the following argument; the Object of né may be a NP or a clause. The following exemplify the verbs sɛə 'be the same', təkhrē 'be similar', and sɛtɛ̀ 'suppose wrongly':

165

(5-62) me sɛə <u>né</u> [ʔū pwe]   to
do same   3:i celebrate NEG
They don't do it like a festival.

(5-63) ʔa sɛə <u>né</u> vē te
3 same 1s thing
It's the same as mine.

(5-64) ʔa lā   təkhrē kʌ̄ <u>né</u> [ʔa ʔó pīló tīkwa
3 intrusively similar COM   3 blow flute flute

dɔ mēklúí nʌ] ke
beat drum   NØ PRH
It's as if he's blowing flutes and pipes and beating drums.
(59.2)

(5-65) vē sɛtɛ̀   ʎ ne <u>né</u> phrè
1s suppose NS 2s   Shan
I thought you were Shan. (31.x)

2. Ordinal numerals. né also appears in the pattern form-ing ordinal numerals: Num-Clf-né-ʔʎ̄; e.g. sō ʔú né ʔʎ̄ 'the third volume', ŋē be né ʔʎ̄ 'the fifth one [bird]'.

3. Backgrounded participant. Probably the majority of occurrences of né are as head of a PP that is not required by the main verb of the clause. Its grammatical meaning in this function is 'backgrounded participant': the NP object of né represents a participant that is semantically less salient than some other. In some cases that participant might otherwise have been realized as a Direct or Indirect Object, but has been pre-empted by some other participant. In other cases there is no other participant overtly present, but né still indicates something like lessened saliency.

Consider the following examples with verb chúɨ 'kindle, burn', which is a V_t taking as Direct Object either the thing burnt or mi 'fire'. With the thing burnt as Object we have:

(5-66) ʔa khī   chúɨ lū   kuklɔ́ kɔ̄

    3   in.law kindle 3:OBV head   shell

His brother-in-law burnt (up) his head-skin. (35.5)

And with mi 'fire' as Object:

(5-67) pe chúɨ   thō   mi pe do   sɛ́   ʔithā

    1p kindle   finish fire 1p chop.up in.reaction cut.brush

When we've finished burning (it) we chop up the brush again. (30.4)

Both the fire and the thing burnt may appear in the sentence, with one of them realized as object of né. In the following example, the thing burnt is Direct Object and 'fire' is the object of né:

(5-68) ʔa chúɨ ʔúɨ   lɔ́   pīchaə vēte né mi nʌ̄ pɯ

    3   burn   smolder use.up complete 1s-thing Né fire two C:cloth

She burned up two of mine [blankets]. (272.3)

Here mi 'fire', which in other contexts can be Direct Object, is 'demoted' to object of né. It has been pre-empted by vēte 'mine', referring to blankets, which are presented as more saliently affected by the action.

A similar situation that has already been mentioned is that of Directive V-V constructions in which the second verb is a V_d (4.2.4). The Directive head verb specifies Indirect Object as realization of its causee participant, preventing the second verb's Recipient argument from having that realization and relegating it to appearance as object of né:

(5-69) vē | nɔ̄   dʌ́ pè kʌ̄ | Phāʌ ǂ rūɯ ǂ <u>nɛ́</u> ʔa pò
1s   command give TRN COM (name)   money Né 3 YS
I told Pha'a to give his younger sibling money.

The object of né may often be interpreted as realizing a participant that has a recognized participant role type such as Goal or Instrument. Such interpretations must be seen as following from the semantics of the verbs involved, and not from the meaning of né.

The following examples show some of the range of occurrences of né.

(5-70)   ʔa |sɔ́ | phremɔ̀ hʌ   jē ǂ <u>nɛ́</u> sínɛ
3 ram.in woman   lower.garment old   gun
He loaded an old skirt into his gun. (228.6)

(5-71a)   phúcè vī thɛ   lɔ̀   <u>nɛ́</u> hi
child   throw ascend stone   house
The child threw a stone up at the house. (5/11)

(5-71b)   phú cè vī thɛ hi <u>nɛ́</u> lɔ̀
(same meaning as preceding)

(5-72)   ʔa | khē   təlwá | sɔklʌ̄ ǂ <u>nɛ́</u> sɔkhō
3   paddle pass   boat   snag
He paddled the boat past the snag [fallen log].

(5-73)   sī   pā be | ʔídɯ ǂ <u>nɛ́</u> lɔ̀
2p   chop strike   machete   stone
You chop striking your machete on a stone. (157.4)

(5-74)   ʔa chūɯ sʌ̄ lū   <u>nɛ́</u> ʔithoə
3   stab   die 3OBV   knife
They [tried to] stab him to death with a knife. (354.4)

168

(5-75) ʔa khé lū   né́ síne
        3   shoot 3OBV gun
        They shot him with a gun. (354.)

(5-76) ʔa phō né́ dīpɔ̀ du nʌ
        3   cook   pot big NØ
        They cooked [it] in a big pot. (356.4)

(5-77) [ʔū | kwā sʌ̄ | ʔūnè ǂ né́ sɔ] sī
        3   chop die 3:i-body Né tree those.who
        the ones who get killed chopping trees . . . (255.4)

(5-78) təphɔ̄ thē̄ | khɛle ǂ né́ līpəna
        stub   wound foot   nail
        [He] stubbed his toe and wounded it on a nail.

(5-79) vē̄ plí cwi pù né́ sɔ
        1s whip pull ox   tree
        I whipped the ox to make it pull the log
        = I got the ox to pull the log by whipping it.

(5-80) ʔa me ʔonē̄ bja   vē̄ né́ liú
        3 do sit   damage 1s   book
        He made me sit on and damage the book.

(5-81) ʔa bulɛ   vē̄ né́ hʌca
        3 exchange 1s   clothes.
        He gave me clothes in exchange. (10/31)

I think it will be fairly clear that in most of the preceding examples the participant with Direct Object realization is more saliently affected than the né́-PP participant. The saliency that is in question in this comparison of more and less salient participants is a many-factored notion.

I. Salience of effect. This is largely a matter of intrinsic properties of the event in question, which the speaker has little choice about presenting.

A. Event-dependent properties. The event named by the Verb or VC usually entails certain effects on its participants. E.g. in (73) an impact involving a knife and a rock will clearly affect the knife more, and in (69) causing person A to give something to person B involves a greater effect on A than on B.

B. The participants. There are two properties intrinsic to the participants, i.e. not dependent on the event they are involved in, that are relevant.

1. Animacy, meaning a scale human > animal > plant > inanimate. For instance, in (77) both the person and the tree end up dead, but human participants, being higher on the animacy scale than nonhumans, have an intrinsic importance such that virtually any effect on a human will be presented as more salient than any coincident effect on a nonhuman.

2. Relative size. The smaller participant is sometimes considered to undergo a more salient effect.

II. Pragmatic salience. If the preceding factors do not differentiate sufficiently among participants, the speaker may select either pattern, as in (71a-b). This type of reversable pattern will be described more fully immediately below.

The various factors will naturally often overlap; e.g. in (78) it is in the nature of the action of toe-stubbing that the toe will be affected more than the nail, but it is also true that the toe is animate and the nail is inanimate.

4. Quasi-coordination. When the difference in saliency

between the Direct Object and the né-PP is very small, né must often be translated as 'additionally' or 'and':

(5-82) təcù ‖ vɛ̄ sí ʔe kʌ̄ lừ né dʌ̄
        bland 1s want eat COM gourd   melon
        For blandness, I want to eat gourds and melon. (28.1)

(5-83) ʔa khé ka nì thuú sō be né təkhʌ tədō
        3   shoot come get bird three C:flat   muntjac one-clf
        He shot three birds and a muntjac. (2/22)

(5-84) vɛ̄ ʔomʌ̄ kʌ̄ Mòphrè né Pímò sī   klɛ̄mēkū
        1s lie.down COM [name]   Né [name] and.them between
        I slept between Mophre and Pimo. (257.6)

Often the Direct Object and object of né can be reversed with no discernible change in propositional meaning:

(5-85) vɛ̄ sɤ́ hō khʌ̄   né sɔklʌ̄ ~ . . . sɔklʌ̄ né hōkhʌ̄
        1s insert h.rice gunny.sack Né boat
        I put ricebags in the boat. (6.xii)

(5-86) vɛ̄ chūū dīcò né ʔíja ~ ... ʔíja né dīcò
        1s poke spoon Né flesh
        I poke a spoon into the meat ~ I poke the meat with a spoon. (6.xii)

Incidentally, although these reversable né constructions are structurally reminiscent of English pairs like *load hay onto the truck/load the truck with hay,* the Kayah Li sentences do not have the implications regarding completeness of effect found in the English *spray/load* sentences.

The reversability of these né constructions is due to the failure of any of the saliency-of-effect criteria to distinguish

171

sufficiently between the two participants. The speaker may then choose either order, based presumably on pragmatic factors such as emphasis, contrastiveness, information status and so on. I have not made a full study of the workings of these pragmatic factors, but it is noteworthy that speakers seem able to override the expected ordering even when there is a pronounced difference in saliency of effect between the two participants:

(5-87) ʔa chứ li mi né tɔthé
      3 kindle red fire Né iron
      They heated an iron red in the fire. (355.5)

Here the iron ought to be more salient: it is more saliently affected, becoming red hot, and it is more relevant to the discourse, since it is about to be used as a weapon. I can only speculate that the speaker wanted to emphasize that it is fire that is being used to heat the iron.

    Finally, it is not unusual for né to appear with no preceding Direct Object:

(5-88a) ʔū | təpló rʌ́ | <u>né</u> ʔa po
         3 put.on RØ 3 finial
         They also put on its[2] finial. (47.4)

(5-89) ʔe chā dʌ, ʔe pò <u>né</u> khɔ́mū
       eat chicken egg eat additionally bread
       (I) ate eggs, and I also ate bread.

---

[2] Describing construction of the ʔilū ritual post (see Lehman 1967). po, here rendered 'finial', is an elaborate structure of carved wood and bamboo that surmounts the ʔilū; the word also means 'pen, coop, corral'.

(5-90) nɔ̄   ʔeho khjā   sɛ́   <u>nɛ́</u> Pjājē
     command steal back.again in.reaction Né bag-(name)
He again told the Pyayei to steal something. (411.2)

Let us call these UNACCOMPANIED nɛ́-PP's. Notice that it is only in some instances that VC + unaccompanied nɛ́-PP can be interpreted as 'to V something and X', as in (89), which could be 'I ate them and/with bread'. In (90), the owner of the Pyayei (a magical sentient bag) is not addressing both the Pyayei and some unstated other thing; rather, he has previously told it to steal something, and now he is telling it to steal something else. Likewise (88a) cannot be interpreted as 'put on [something] and the finial', as is clear from the context (glosses simplified):

(5-88b) ʔū rō̄ʔe thō rʌ ‖ ʔū súplī phōchase ‖ súplī thō rʌ ‖
     3 hew finish   3:i wash soap.pod   wash finish

     plò bū rʌ́ thwí ‖ plò bū thō ʌ́ pā pɔ̄ rʌ ‖
     smear white RØ lime   smear white finish NS

     ʔū təpló rʌ́ nɛ́ ʔa po ‖ təplò thō ʔa po ʔʌ̄ nʌ ma . . .
     3:i put.on Rø 3 finial put.on finish 3 finial this NØ be.so

When they've finished hewing it, they wash it with soap-pod; when they're done washing it, they paint it white with lime; when they're done painting it white, they also put on the finial; when they've put on the finial, well then . . .

The point is that ʔū təpló rʌ́ nɛ́ ʔa po does not describe an additional instance of putting-on, since the finial is the first and last thing to be put on the ʔilū. Rather a meaning like 'additionally' is applied to the entire clause, putting it as an additional step in the procedure of preparing the ʔilū.

Since there is not necessarily any participant X, either overtly present in the clause or alluded to in surrounding context, such that the object of né is less salient than X, these unaccompanied né-PP's cannot be described in terms of relative saliency of participants. There is perhaps a kinship between the notion of relative saliency and the meaning of 'additionally, moreover' that I have assigned to the unaccompanied né-PP, having to do with priority: the object of the 'backgrounded participant' né-PP is pre-empted by another participant with priority in ranking of effect; with the unaccompanied né-PP, the entire clause represents an event that follows on some prior event—prior temporally, and perhaps in other ways as well.

Along with the complex semantic facts concerning né that we have been examining, it must be recognized that its syntactic behavior is not always as straightforward as has been presented in all of the preceding examples, in which it consistently occupies the post-DO Oblique position. There are in addition scattered examples of né-PP's in other grammatical functions. The following might be analyzed as simply containing two PP's following the VC, which must be allowed for anyway:

(5-91)　mo du dɛ dwá　dɤ́ vē　hi　né　Phāʌ hi
　　　　gong big put put-away at:U 1s house (name) house
　　　　The big gongs are kept at my house and Pha'a's house. (2/22)

But semantically it would make more sense to treat vē hi né Phāʌ hi 'my house and Pha'a's house' as a single unit functioning as the object of dɤ̄ 'at'. né would then be functioning as a coordinating conjuction, as it seems to in the next example:

(5-92) ʔa <u>né</u> ʔa phʌ̄ já   ʔo tɯə   léhē rè lē
       3   3   GMo go.and exist together pumpkin trellis base
      He and his grandmother went and lived at the base of a
      pumpkin trellis. (19.5)

Since there are no other cases of a clause beginning with a sequence NP-PP, it seems that the preceding must be analyzed with a Subject NP consisting of two NP's joined by né. Although such cases are definitely rarer than those with né in the Oblique position, it may be necessary to recognize a distinct but related né that is the sole member of a class of coordinating conjuctions. There are even examples where né is associated with no NP at all, as if it were some sort of adverbial:

(5-93) te | ʔo   kʌ̄ | <u>né</u> pā ke
      thing exist COM   IRR PRH
      [we] may soon be rich as well.

Finally, two relevant comparative points. First, né is not found in the nearby Upper (kè khu) dialect, which uses the Verb Particle rʌ́ in many of the contexts in which Lower né is found. Second, né is probably a loan from Burmese: Written Burmese nái, modern né (the acute accent indicates creaky tone). Okell gives this form two separate listings (Okell 1969, 120–1): subordinate marker 'and, both; by, with, from, to, *manner,* etc.'; and coordinate marker 'and, both'. These may well correspond to the prepositional and conjunction functions of Kayah Li né respectively.

5.5.3 Other Oblique Expressions

Apart from PP and Clf', there are a few expressions filling Oblique functions that fit neither of these grammatical categories well.

Some time expressions that occur sentence-initially can be considered to be NP's, like ʔʌ̄ tənʌ̄ 'today' (ClfP) pāro 'tomorrow', or PP's, like chá mɔ̀ hé pā 'this [coming] evening'. However, kúnɛ̀ 'now' pāhénɯ 'yesterday' would be labeled N(P) only with difficulty; e.g. neither can be counted by a Clf', and neither can function as Object.

Time expressions may, and some interrogative expressions must (7.4), come late or last in the sentence. Some of these are PP's, like chápā 'later on' and bá Clf tē, and so present no problems of analysis. But some these sentence-late expressions are not PP's, like tōútē, bɔ́kētē (required to come last or near-last in the sentence), and pāro 'tomorrow' (optionally occuring there).

These expressions that are neither NP's nor PP's can be recognized as a distinct grammatical category of Adverbs.

Chapter 6

The Noun Phrase

This chapter describes the internal syntax of the NP, as well as the lexical semantics of some special types of noun (pronouns, classifiers, localizers), quantifiers (including numerals) and prepositions. Quantifiers are not nouns, but are included here as prominent members of the NP. Prepositions are also not nouns, but are included in this chapter partly for convenience and partly because Kayah Li PP's are not very different from NP's; e.g. they may function as Direct Object.

NPs may contain clauses. The resultant structure of course remains an NP, but since the clausal constituent is of more interest than the NP containing it, extended discussion of such structures will be deferred to chapters 7 and especially 8, on non-autonomous clauses. In the present chapter briefer mention will be made of these attributive clauses, chiefly regarding their position relative to the nominal head.

6.1 Types of Noun and Types of NP

Several types of nouns may be distinguished:

1. Ordinary. Further divided into Common (e.g. thwi 'dog', sɔ 'tree', hi 'house', bwí 'fortune'), Name (e.g. personal

names Khōʌ, Sēthūphē, Pɤ̄mè; place names Mē Lē, Thʌ̄ Médɤ Lē Khʌ̄) and Pronoun (e.g. vē 'I/me', pe 'we/us', ne 'you (sg.)' ʔa 'he/she').

2. Classifier (e.g. dō 'Clf for animals', plɔ 'Clf for small round things', vē 'Clf for seasons'). Also with several subtypes.

3. Localizer (e.g. khʌ̄ 'upper surface', kū 'inside').

Pronouns and Localizers are listable classes, Common nouns make up an open class, and Classifiers probably do also (e.g. the name of any container can be a classifier). Names and pronouns are Free; Classifiers and Localizers are Bound, and common nouns include both Free and Bound types.

Since features of heads have a hand in determining the features of the phrase they head, we can speak of NP's headed by ordinary nouns as ordinary NP's (OrdNP); similarly classifer-headed (ClfP) and localizer-headed (LzP).

These major types can be characterized in terms of the type of modifiers they include (the head constituent is underlined in the following examples).

Ordinary nouns take other OrdNP's and reduced clauses: in vē <u>sínɛ</u> du 'my big gun', the head sínɛ 'gun' is preceded by an OrdNP consisting of the pronoun vē and followed by a reduced clause consisting of the verb du 'big'. Note that sínɛ is a Common noun; the other subtypes of Ordinary noun, Names and Pronouns, tend not to have modifiers of any kind except in restricted circumstances (see 6.2 below).

Localizers are obligatorily (because Bound) modified by OrdNP's, the resulting expression further requiring a preceding preposition. An example is dɤ́ khra du <u>kū</u> 'inside the big calabash', with the Localizer kū 'inside' modified by the OrdNP khra du 'big calabash' (itself consisting of head noun followed by reduced clause), and the whole OrdNP-Lz unit standing as object of the preposition dɤ́ 'at'.

Classifiers are obligatorily modified by Quantifiers (mostly numerals), and the resulting unit may be modified by a Demonstrative and/or a nominalized clause. An example is ʔa ʔe tēú tǝhe 'the ones who eat fish', in which the classifier for groups he is modified by the numeral tǝ- 'one' and the clause ʔa ʔe tēú 'they eat fish'. The unit Quantifier-Classifier has some importance on its own as the sole possible filler of the Extent position of the clause (5.5). Since it is an N' built on a Classifier, we will call it Clf'.

Beyond these co-occurrence facts, the three NP types do not often occur as constituents of each other; in particular, ClfP and the other types tend not to modify each other. Nevertheless it is possible to have a 'maximal' NP including both OrdNP and ClfP. The linear order is—

$$[NP \; N \; (S_1)]_{OrdNP} \; [[P \; S_2]_{PP} \; D \; Q \; Clf \; (S_1)]_{ClfP}$$

—where (S_1) is a reduced clause (postposed Attributive Clause, 8.2) and $[P \; S_2]$ is a prepositional phrase containing a nominalized full clause (preposed Attributive Clause, 8.1.2). (S_1) appears twice since its position depends on the type of Clf: if the Classifier head is a Measure Classifier, (S_1) may appear in the ClfP, otherwise it must be in the OrdNP. In the following examples, the maximal NP is enclosed in brackets, and the position of du 'big' illustrates the possible positions of (S_1):

(6-1) [ʔiswí théja dɤ̀ vē phōʔe pāhenɯ nʌ

      curry   pig-flesh at:U 1s cook   yesterday   that

təpɔ du] ʔo tōútē

one-pot big exist where?

Where is that big pot of pork curry that I cooked yesterday? (31.i)

(6-2) phjá [dīpɔ du dɤ̀ ʔa kɔdɔ́ kúdi ʔo to sō mē (*du)]

    take pot   big at:U 3 lid   handle exist NEG three C:large big

[I'll] take three pots with lids that don't have handles.
(31.i)

(6-3) ʔiswí nʌ̄   bēlɔ̀ du

    curry two   bowl big

two big bowls of curry

I assume the following structure, using (6-2) as example:

(6-4)

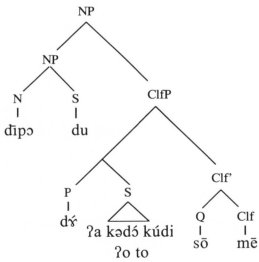

I take the OrdN dīpɔ 'pot' to be the head of the entire NP. Although this is the usual analysis, it is not fully obvious that such an NP is not headed by the ClfP instead. Consider (6-1), ʔiswí théja . . . nʌ təpɔ 'that pot of pork curry'; certainly in the English translation the head is 'pot' rather than 'curry'. And is it the ordinary N (dīpɔ 'pot' in the example) that determines which Clf(s) can occur, or vice versa? Also, if the OrdNP is head, the position of the modifying ClfP violates the default rule that nominal modifiers precede their heads (6.3 below). If the ClfP is head, the default pre-head position of nominal modifiers is preserved. Cf. Thompson's analysis of Vietnamese noun+classifier constructions: in such examples as một con chó 'one-CLF-dog' and ba cái ghế 'three-CLF-chairs', the classifier is considered to be the head, and the noun is analyzed as 'descriptive complement to [the] classifier' (Thompson 1965, 192–3).

Recall that when a ClfP and an associated OrdNP (i.e. the NP naming the thing that the ClfP counts) occur in a single clause, the two usually are syntactically independent, with the ClfP occupying the Extent position (5.5.1). When an OrdNP Object is directly followed by a ClfP, we have the appearance of single maximal NP, as phrekhū sí nā 'two men' in:

(6-5) phremɔ̀ méthʌ phrekhū sí   nā
       woman   look-see man   C:human two
       Some women saw two men. (4.xii)

But Object NP and the ClfP are actually separate constituents of the Verb Phrase; for example, Locative PP can always be inserted between the two, without affecting the semantic relations between them: phremɔ̀ méthʌ phrekhū dɤ́ klébe sí nʌ̄ 'Some women saw two men <u>at the market</u>'.

The rarity of maximal NP's in natural speech is undoubtedly not due to a rule of Kayah Li grammar, but is a consequence of facts about discourse and cognition, of the same order as the factors working against occurrence of full NP's in two or more major sentence constituents (the reasons that spoken English tends not to include sentences like *the farmer killed the duckling that had big feet for his daughter on Thursday*). One way of describing these factors is to recognize two different tasks for items in discourse: establishing a category, and individuating the category (I leave these terms undefined on purpose). The former is the job of OrdN's (and other things including the extralinguistic context); the latter is the job of Classifiers. Just as it is unusual to both establish a new topic and add information about it in a single clause, so it is unusual to both establish a category and individuate it in a single NP.

Where do such maximal NP's actually occur? A few answers are suggestive. One situation is in response to elicitation concerning the proper Clf to be associated with a given noun; thus dībē sɔ nʌ̄ be 'two wooden bowls', cited above. While this is at best a highly marked form of discourse, such expressions are probably legitimate nominal sentences (8.1).

One of the very few maximal NP's recorded in spontaneous, unelicited speech is the following sentence, which introduces a new discourse participant:

(6-6) ʔamòphrè phremɔ̀ təphre   ka   dɤ̀ khjā
old.person   woman   one-C:human go:TH at:U back

One old woman came behind. (167.5)

(the situation is of a woman watching a large number of villagers
returning, hoping to see her son among them; this old woman is
one of the returning group). It seems also possible to interpret
this relatively rare type of expression as something like apposition, or nonrestrictive modification: in the above example, *an old
woman, one of them,* or in example (1) above, *the pork curry, that
big potful I cooked yesterday.*

For convenience, I will divide the following discussion by
the subtypes OrdNP, ClfP and LzP. But first, some notes on two
special types of Ordinary N: pronouns and names.

6.2 Pronouns and Names

6.2.1 The Pronoun System

The pronouns are:

	Sg	Pl	Unmarked
1	vē	pe	
2	ne	sī	
3		jesī	ʔa, lū, ʔū

The third person plural form jesī is rare. The more common third
person pronouns ʔa, lū, and ʔū, are unmarked for number.
Briefly (see also 5.3 above), the two alternate within a clause as
a way of keeping track of two third-person protagonists. lū
appears only if ʔa or some other non-coreferential third-person
NP appears before it in the clause. More generally, successive

non-coreferential third-person NP's require an alternation between ʔa and lū.

ʔū is indefinite, backgrounded, often to be translated as 'other people' or 'they' as in 'they say' (ʔū hé nʌ, standard expression in legendary narratives; see 8.3.3). It means 'who?' when the sentence ends in the particle pē (cf. 7.2, 7.3). It may also be used as a humilific first-person pronoun: this is the only instance I know of in which Kayah has linguistic marking of status, something that is usually not found in the languages of the hill cultures in Southeast Asia (compare the elaborate status-marking apparatus of Thai).

sī, besides being the second-person plural pronoun, is also a bound noun meaning roughly 'and the rest, and things like that', e.g. ʔamɔ sī 'Amaw and that group' (similar to Mandarin Zhāngsān tāmen 'Zhangsan and his group, Zhangsan and that lot'), thwí kɔ̄ sī 'the lime-box and all that sort of thing', and:

(6-7) sʌ̄ ré to   ma hú ʔū tā sʌ̄ thʌ̄ <u>sī</u>
       die good NEG be.so like 3i fall die water
       Dying badly is like those who are drowned and so on. (255.3)

Here sī is modified by the preceding clause ʔū tā sʌ̄ thʌ̄ (which must be considered to be nominalized; see 9.2), forming an NP that then acts as object of the preposition hú.

Pronouns usually do not take modifiers. One exception is the appeerence of ʔū in ʔū du 'adults', ʔū mòphrè 'old people', and ʔū ro 'other people', with Verbs du 'big' and mòphrè 'old (of humans)' and ro 'other', of uncertain category (acts like a verb in dɣ̀ ʔaro tə-CLF 'another one'). Another is expressions like pe kəjē lihú (33.4) 'we Kayah Li', although here it is unclear whether pe is modified by kəjē lihú or the reverse (or neither, if we allow a relation of apposition).

Kayah Li has no reflexive or reciprocal pronouns. These meanings are covered by the following morphemes:

Reciprocal. lū, a rʌ-class Verb Particle, for which see 4.3.5.

Reflexive. nè, a Bound OrdN meaning 'body'. It is generally modified by a pronoun, as in vē mɛthʌ vē nè 'I see myself'. There is no particular required semantic relation between the NP headed by nè and other NP's in the same clause, as shown by the following:

(6-8) vē təri vē nè
      1s dress 1s body
      I get dressed (=dress myself). (16.xi)

(6-9) vē təri vē phú nè
      1s dress 1s child body
      I dress my child. (16.xi)

6.2.2 Names

Kayah Li personal names fall into two common patterns, both of which indicate gender.

	female	male
Pattern A	X + mè	X + ʌ
Pattern B	Y + mò	Y + phē

Each pattern has its own repertoire of initial elements, not differentiated by gender (X and Y in the list); thus Khōmè is a woman's name, Khōʌ a man's. Pattern A seems more common, at least in the Mae Hong Son area. The X elements in Pattern A are without known meanings; some are: khō, phre, sē, ŋā, klē, pɤ, do, sō, lē, plúɪ, mī. The Y elements of Pattern B may be meaningful, as in the female name Thérúmò, in which thérú is an ethnic designation for a Western Kayah State group (cf. Western Kayah thiá rú lia khiē 'Zayein Karen', cf. Lehman 1976b, 69). Others are not meaningful: sēthūphē, bámò.

The above lists are not exhaustive, but the X elements of Pattern A at least seem not very numerous, inasmuch as the same names recur frequently. There is even a single lexical item mwī 'to have the same name as'. Names from the basic patterns may have other elements added, serving to distinguish people with otherwise identical names. Some of these added elements are meaningful, as in Luɪə pé 'mute Luɪ', poká Phāʌ 'Headman Pha'a'; others are not, as in Phāʌ Bómò.

Kayah Li do not use personal names as readily as Westerners. They are often reluctant to tell a stranger their own names. People may be referred to as 'X's parent', i.e. if a couple has a son named Doʌ, the spouses will call each other Doʌ phē 'Do'a's father' and Doʌ mò. This pattern is different from Pattern B above, in which mò and phē combine with elements that are not themselves names.

6.3 Ordinary-headed NP's

6.3.1 The General Pattern of NP Modification

The order of constituents in the NP can be described in terms of a default rule and specific exceptions to it. The default rule is that nominal modifiers precede the head, and verbal mod-

186

ifiers follow. This goes for all NP types; we will first illustrate with ordNP's (head constituent underlined):

nominal+head	head+verbal
ne <u>mò</u>	<u>rù</u> du
2s mother: your mother	snake big: big snake
chā <u>dʌ</u>	<u>phre</u> bɔ́mō
chicken egg	person open: the person
	[who] opened [it]
	<u>kəjɛ̄</u> pā tha
	person cut sesame: people
	[to] cut sesame

A combination of the two is seen in:

> phremɔ̀   <u>hʌ</u> je
> woman   skirt tattered: tattered woman's skirt

The postposed verbal modifier is in fact a clause, of the postposed Attributive type (8.2), hence in addition to the verb it may contain other constituents; e.g., kəjɛ̄ pā tha includes, besides the head kəjɛ̄ and the verb pā, the NP tha functioning as Object in relation to pā.

With nominal modifiers, the default modifier+head order signifies possession, as in:

> ne mò   your mother
> Phāʌ hi   Pha'a's house
> ʔūro kè   other people's country

or some more general meanings that may be seen as extensions of the possessive meaning, as:

cha̅ dʌ   chicken+egg

thɛ́ ja   pig+meat

cho kha̅   mountain+apex: on top of the mountain

bése tha̅   face+water: tears

khɛ bó   leg+long.thing: leg-rings (an item of costume)

Localizer-headed NP's follow the default pattern, as in cho kha̅ 'on top of the mountain' above; cf. also dɤ́ khra̅ ku̅ 'inside the bottle-gourd', more literally 'at the bottle-gourd's inside', with khra̅ modifying ku̅. In other words the Localizers are not equivalent to English prepositions, except semantically: ku̅ here is the head of an NP which in turn functions as the object of the Preposition dɤ́. For a complete listing of Localizers see 7.1.4.

6.3.2 Exceptions to the General Pattern

Exceptions to the default structure have head-modifier order, and fall into three semantic types:

1. Artifact-material. Examples:

di̅pɔ tɔthɛ́   pot+iron: iron pot

di̅bē sɔ   pot+tree: wooden bowl

bē̅ʔu̅ təphɛ́   cloth+cotton: cotton cloth

ʔiswí thɛ́ ja   curry+pig+flesh: pork curry

dɔ́ sɔba   wall+board: wall of boards

dɔ́ twa   wall+split.flattened.bamboo: split-bamboo wall

(examples all 5/2)

Note also təkī sɔle 'leaf insect' ('grasshopper, beetle' plus 'leaf'), in which the insect *looks as if* it were made from a leaf. That these are head-first is confirmed by the fact that the classifier used with the whole expression is the same as that used with the first constituent. For example, dībē sɔ takes the Classifier be, as in dībē sɔ nʌ be 'two wooden bowls', which as the same Classifier as is taken by dībē alone (dībē nʌ be 'two bowls'); sɔ, however, takes a different set of Classifiers, e.g. sɔ nʌ bō 'two trees'. Here the choice of classifier is one of the features of the larger expression that is determined by its head.

Examples like sɔ ba 'wooden flat-thing: board' may seem to have the opposite order, material+artifact, but ba is not in fact an artifact. It is a classifier for thin flat objects (mats, pages, hats, paper money) which also appears as the head of compound nouns like ce ba 'paper', tēú ba 'fish scale', and kū ba 'dandruff' (for kū see 2.4), of which the last two are definitely not artifacts. ba belongs to the class of Configurational Classifiers, which are characterized by this kind of overlap between classifier and Bound Noun; see 6.4.3.2.2 below.

2. Generic-specific. Names of plants and animals often begin with the general term for the kind, such as sɔ for plants, thu for birds, tē for fish, and so on. It is not entirely clear how to analyze this type. On one hand, it is often said that the expression and its head exhibit an 'is-a' relation (a blackberry 'is-a' berry, and so on). The 'is-a' relation indicates that the general term is the head: a tē lɔ 'rock-fish' 'is-a' fish (tē), not a rock (lɔ). On the other hand the specific (second) member of the compound often has no identifiable use outside the compound: the second element

189

of tē phjá 'a kind of large-headed fish' is surely not to be identified with the verb phjá 'take'; tē phjá must be simply 'phjá-fish'.
For a different case, consider tē thó 'a kind of eel-like fish'. This
thó might be identified with sɔ thó 'oar', as if tē thó were 'oar-
fish'; another way to look at it is to say that both sɔ and thó function as disambiguating prefixes ('the thó that is wood', 'the thó
that is a fish'). The same point can be made about thu khwi 'parrot' and sɔ khwi 'vine'.

3. Ethnic designations. These may either precede or follow the head. Preceding they are possessive modifiers; following
the meaning is 'characteristic of, X-style'. Thus phrè hʌca 'a
Shan's clothes', meaning any clothes that a Shan might happen
to have, versus hʌca phrè 'Shan-style clothes', which need not
belong to a Shan. This is evidence that ethnic designations have
dual class membership, in both nouns and verbs: as nouns they
precede the head, with possessive meaning, while as verbs they
follow the head.

It may even be that all three of these exceptional head-
modifier patterns actually have the postposed modifier functioning as a verb rather than a noun. Thus in the generic-specific tē
thó 'oar-fish: eel', thó would not be the Noun 'oar' but a Verb 'to
be oar-like'. Or in the artifact-material type bē?ū təphɛ́ 'cotton
cloth', təphɛ́ would be 'to consist of cotton' rather than the Noun
'cotton'.

However the ethnic designations have one further verbal
characteristic not known to apply to the other two: the ability to
occur inside the Verb Complex, as in ?íbe phrè cè 'know how to
speak Shan', in which ?íbe . . . cè is a Verb+Descriptive-Ptc
construction (4.3.6).

6.4 Clf-headed NP's

6.4.1 General Structure of the ClfP

Classifiers are a type of noun. Their special grammatical feature is the requirement that they occur with a Quantifier (they are thus bound morphemes) to form a Clf'. The usual order is Q-Clf; see 6.4.4 for expressions with the order Clf-Q.

The Clf' may be modified by a preceding Demonstrative, a nominalized clause, or occasionally both. The Demonstratives are:

ʔλ̄	this
nʌ	that

Example of a ClfP containing a modifying clause (bracketed; this example has no overt marker of nominalization, see 9.1):

(6-10) [ʔa ʔe tēú] təhe

    3   eat fish   one-C:group

the ones who were eating fish (198.6)

A Clf' may not, however, be modified by a postposed clause. If a Clf' is to receive verbal modification the verb must be in a preposed (nominalized) Attributive Clause (8.1), as in (10) above. Thus we get ʔa ré to təhe 'the group that's not good' (271.2); a construction with ré 'good' after the Clf', e.g. təhe ré to would have to be a clause, 'one group is not good'. Note that preposed Attributive Clauses heavily favor the presence of a Subject constituent. Thus in speaking of e.g. animals, 'the white one' would be ʔa bū tədō, literally 'it is-white one-CLF', not *dō bū, *tədō bū or *ʔadō bū. Cf. also ʔa sōlē təpɯ 'a green one [blanket]' (271.4). In a few occurrences ʔa+V seems to stand alone

191

with no following ClfP, giving the impression of a nominalizing function of ?a, as in ?a bū ?íchē lɔʌ 'the white ones have all been sold' [27.xi]. But the ClfP may also be present as in the alternative and synonymous ?a bū <u>nʌ</u> təhe ?íchē lɔʌ (ClfP underlined, he Clf for groups of animates).

In the latter type of construction, ?a- must be considered referential, since there is always an object or category established in preceding discourse to which ?a- can refer: in the above examples, the categories are animals, textiles, and buffalo respectively (although there is no overt linguistic element in the last example to indicate that it is animals that are under discussion). It may also be mentioned that the preposed Attributive Clause favors referential transparency over opacity (8.2), i.e. ?a sōlē təpɯ 'green one(s)' is not likely to be used in contexts like *He wants to buy a green one* or *I can't find any green ones*. However, this referentiality is like that of the classifiers in these examples, which by their semantics require that some category be previously established (cf. 6.1).

There are two exceptions to this generalization.

The first exception, described in 6.1 above (examples 1–3), is that measure Classifiers can have a posposed verbal modifier. The second involves the morpheme lɤ, a Descriptive VPtc 'more, than'. Numx+Clf+lɤ means 'over x Clf's'; for example:

hō ?o ŋē khwē lɤ   there's over 5 baskets of rice (2/1)

síne ?o khu nʌ je lɤ   there's over 200 guns

mɯ̄ sō swá lɤ   after 6 o'clock

Note the minimal pair:

ʔo sō swá təmū lɤ̌   be there over 7 hours

ʔo lɤ̌ só swá təmū   there's 7 hours remaining

Thus lɤ̌ can be considered a postposed modifier, although since it is not otherwise a verb this construction is exceptional. It is undoubtedly a loan from Shan, the Thai cognate being the verb ly̌a 'be left over, remaining, in excess of what is needed' (Haas).

6.4.2 Grammatical Functions of ClfP's

ClfP's can be found in all functions open to NP's in general, including Topic:

(6-11) nā̄ mjō ʔa rέ   ʔέ to
    two C:sort 3 good so NEG
    Neither kind is very good (both kinds are not so good).
    9/22

(6-12) təhe   ʔa khέ rʌ́ klʌ ‖ təhe   ʔa khέ rʌ́ sínɛ
    one-C:group 3 shoot RØ bow one-C:group 3 shoot RØ gun
    One group shot (with) bows, one group shot (with) guns.
    (226.7)

Athough there are problems in identifying Clf' in Direct Object function (cf. above, 6.1 and 5.5.1) full ClfP's are less doubtful:

(6-13) bɔ́   pjà təloə   tí   ʔʌ̄   təmē
    weave BEN medium.sized X.much this one-C:large
    Weave a medium-sized one like this. [more strictly, 'medium-sized to this extent'] (305.1)

(13) is to be analyzed with təloə tí ʔʌ̄ təmē as an NP, functioning as Direct Object, and consisting of the Clf' təmē, modified by

the clause təloə tí ʔʌ̄ modifying, itself consisting of the verb təloə and the PP tí ʔʌ̄.

Clf''s with modifiers can also be the object of a Preposition, e.g:

(6-14) də́ thɛ   təkjā
      at ascend one-C:side
      above, up there (see 9.1.2)

The above examples have presented a mixture of Clf' and ClfP. Clf' alone is required in the Extent position, penultimate in the clause, as has been discussed in 5.5.1 above.

6.4.3 Classifiers as a Lexical System

The choice of classifier relates in various ways to what is being counted. In the case that is perhaps prototypical (or most familiar to students of classifier languages), Common Nouns are associated lexically with one or more General classifiers:

Noun	Classifier
təple 'cabbage'	to
ʔaple 'crack', kədā 'door'	kū
thuú 'bird', bē lɔ̀ 'cup'	be
sɔ 'plant'	mɔ̀ (smaller plants)
"	bō (trees)

Other Classifier types and other countable 'things' relate in other ways, to be described momentarily. Here recall that although there is a lexical association between the noun and classifier, in the sentence there is often no direct syntactic relation between the NP and the Clf' (3.3, 6.2.2, 7.1.3).

6.4.3.1 Types of Classifier

Classifiers can be divided into the following types:

A. Time. Includes:

1. Units of time such as nā 'day', na 'year', vē 'Clf for seasons'.

2. Classifiers counting instances of an action, e.g. phó 'a time' (the general Clf for instances of action), mū 'Clf for strokes, blows, utterances' (related to homophonous verb; cf. below).

B. Measure. Mostly names of containers, plus a few conventional units of length, volume, etc. Examples: pē 'bottle, Clf for liquids', khrì 'packbasket; Clf for anything carried in a packbasket', plè 'cubit (length from elbow to fingertip)', tha 'measure of volume (about 20 liters) for husked rice'.

C. General, further divided into:

1. Animate, with only two members: dō 'Clf for animals', phre~sí 'Clf for humans' (suppletive, see 6.4.4).

2. Configurational. Include some notion of the shape or other physical characteristics of the thing counted. E.g. plɔ 'Clf for small round things', bō 'Clf for lengths', ba 'Clf for sheet-like objects'.

3. Miscellaneous. Something of a leftovers category. Examples: cɤ 'Clf for kinds, types', mē 'Clf for larger semiregular shapes', ko 'general Clf'.

The rationale for the grouping into types comes first from the 'counting' relationship with other nouns. A time Classifier does not count anything denotable by a noun (I know of no noun meaning 'time' in the abstract); a measure Classifier can count

195

anything, with only real-world constraints (e.g. for animates, one can easily imagine one basketful of frogs di təkhrì, but not one basketful of buffalo *pənè təkhrì); a general Classifier counts only certain things denoted by nouns that are lexically associated with that Classifier.

The subdivision of the General Classifiers is only partly on semantic grounds. For instance, while both Animate General Classifiers count animate nouns, there are many animate nouns counted by other Classifier types, especially Configurational. For example, snakes, worms and lizards are counted by bō 'Clf for lengths', which also counts ropes, intestines, tongues, cigarettes etc. Similarly birds, fish and pangolins join with dishes, axes, doors, boats and many other objects in being counted with be 'Clf for winged and winglike things'.

Thus only the general Classifiers have lexical links to certain nouns. Often the link from common noun to Classifier is one-to-many, sometimes with much semantic differentiation, as bó təmɔ̀ 'one rice plant' vs. bó təplē 'one ear of rice'; or dī 'cooked rice', counted as təplɔ 'one grain', təpɔ 'one pot', or tətà 'one meal'. Sometimes there is much less such differentiation, as with thʌ̄ klō 'ditch', counted either with its own constituent klō or with bō 'Clf for lengths'.

Another difference: Measure Classifiers may have postposed verbal (clausal) modifiers, as in ʔiswí nʌ̄ bēlɔ̀ du 'two big bowls of curry'; if the Clf' is headed by any other Classifier type, any verbal modifier must appear in the preceding OrdNP: chādʌ du ʔʌ̄ təplɔ 'this big chicken-egg'.

6.4.3.2 Overlaps

There are various patterns of overlap between Classifiers and other syntactic categories, both verbs and nouns. Some of these are idiosyncratic, involving only one or two sets of items, some fairly general involving a dozen or more sets. Some of the latter are as follows (using <> for 'overlaps with'):

1. Clf_{misc} <> $OrdN(F)$ i.e. 'self-classifiers'
2. V <> Clf_{cnf}
3. Clf_{cnf} <> $OrdN(B)$
4. $Clf_{measure}$ <> $OrdN(F)$: names of containers

Patterns 1 and 3 are quite similar; for example, both exhibit a general rule that the related OrdN (and compounds headed by it) are counted by the related Classifier, although exceptions exist. This contrasts with pattern 4; see below. The difference between 1 and 3 hinges on the Free/Bound status of the related OrdN. Perhaps the apparently greater frequency of prefix ʔa- with pattern 3 (Clf_{cnf}) is a consequence: the pattern 1 nouns, being (F), do not need a coconstituent to occur on their own, while the pattern 3 nouns do, being (B).

Worthy of separate mention at this point are plant names, which are generally Bound, and must be compounded with a plant-component term like mɔ̀ 'trunk, plant', le 'leaf', se 'fruit', or phō 'flower'. Of these phō and mɔ̀ overlap with Classifiers, but le and se do not. Note also that most Localizer nouns have an overlap like pattern 3 above, in which they function as Bound heads of compound Ordinary Nouns; cf. 6.5 below.

6.4.3.2.1 Containers and Measure Classifiers

Nouns involved in this pattern of overlap are not counted with the related Classifier; most take mē. Such is the case for pē 'bottle', khrì 'packbasket', pɔ 'pot', bēlɔ̀ 'drinking glass' (latter also takes be, kɔ̄). A similar pattern is found in hi 'house', counted with mē, but itself a classifier for humans, meaning 'household'. Perhaps a house is construed as a container for people.

6.4.3.2.2 Configurational

Configurational Classifiers include most of those associated with a characteristic shape: ba flat sheets, bō flexible lengths, plɔ small round things. They are also, by class overlap, ordinary Bound nouns which appear as heads of ordinary noun compounds: sɔ ba 'board' (sɔ 'wood'), khē bō 'neck', ʔaplɔ 'a seed'. In this they contrast with the two Animate Classifiers: *ʔadō is not possible, although semantically conceivable as 'a head' of cattle or the like. As the examples show, the nonhead constitutent may be an ordinary Free noun like sɔ 'wood', an ordinary Bound noun like khē 'neck', or ʔa- (see 3.2). A compound headed by a CC-related OrdN is, in the default case, counted by the related CC, as in tɔré bō ŋē bō 'five candles', in which the two co-occurring morphemes bō are separate but homophonous lexical items. There are exceptions, such as the self-classifier lò 'vehicle' (see list below).

The following lists selected Configurational Classifiers, some compounds they occur in, and information on their function as Classifiers, other overlaps, and so on. In this list the CC counts nouns formed on its derived OrdN(B), unless otherwise stated:

198

ba   ce ba paper; sɔ ba board, tēú ba fish scale, kūba 'dandruff'; also Clf for sheets, e.g. mats, money, umbrellas,
towels, pictures, hats, the earth

be   rū be silver coin, bī sɔ be 'fermented bean paste', ʔabe
'a round flat thing (of coin or dried fermented bean only);
otherwise Clf for winged or winglike things, which can't
be referred to by ʔabe

bō   khē bō 'neck', təré bō 'candle', dīklɛ bō 'sugarcane', mi
mɔ bō 'electric light'; dībō 'navel' takes ko; perhaps in
khɛ bō 'ladder', but that takes Clf ko for the whole, sū for
rungs; Clf for cigarettes, sprouts, intestines, worms,
tongues, vines, snakes, roads, etc.

dā   phē dā 'crotch of tree', sɔ khɛ dā 'crotch in tree roots,
cho dā ravine between mountains'; also Clf for təré
'fence'

kɔ   mi khwí kɔ̄ 'lamp', thwí kɔ̄ 'betel cud', but bése kɔ̄
'facemask, glasses' takes ko~kɔ̄; khɛ kɔ̄ 'socks'; also Clf
for tɤ́ta 'can'; ʔakɔ̄ 'small box'

phē   sɔ phē 'branch', khru phē 'small firewood'; ʔaphē
'branch'

plɔ   bése plɔ 'eye' (Clf also kjā,'side, Clf for one of a pair), li
plɔ 'letter of the alphabet', təkhése plɔ 'mango seed', ké
plɔ 'eggplant seed', sínɛ plɔ 'bullet', mi plɔ 'light bulb'
(mi 'fire'), phátha plɔ 'battery (drycell)[1]'; also Clf for
small fruit, eggs, stars, kidneys, etc.; <u>not</u> Clf for síplɔ
'heart', Clf mē; ʔaplɔ 'its seed, a seed'

---

[1] phátha 'flashlight' is probably from Shan phái thāat 'electric light'.

6.4.3.2.3 Self-Classifiers

Below are listed selected self-classifiers, with some additional information to suggest the complexity of relations among Classifiers and related OrdN's:

bē   Clf for id. 'unit of thatch consisting of pole with thatch attached'

lē   Clf for id. 'stream, ravine'

khɔ   Clf for id. 'dam'

klō   Clf for thʌ klō 'ditch', which may also take bō 'Clf for lengths'

klō   Clf for id. 'language', thāī klō 'Thai'

mi   Clf for mi 'name', which also takes cɤ 'kind, type'

lò   Clf for id. 'vehicle', for pù lò 'oxcart', but lò tɔthé 'bicycle' takes phu 'Clf for pairs' (tɔthé 'iron'); occurs also in lò se 'wheel' (Clf mē; se 'fruit')

plè   Clf for plè~ʔaplè~klʌ plè 'arrow', which also takes ko 'general Clf'; plè is also Clf for mi phō 'match' (mi 'fire', phō 'flower'?)

dɔ̄   Clf for id. 'village', also Clf for kəjē 'person, Kayah'

pja   Clf for tənī pja 'beehive', plūū pja 'wasp nest', tənī 'bees', which may also take be 'Clf for winged and winglike things'

mɤ̄   Clf for id. 'town', mɤ̄ du 'city'

pwi   Clf for thu pwi 'bird nest'

Note that the last four share the feature of being dwellings.

200

6.4.3.2.4 Verb-related Classifiers

Several types of semantic relation between verbs and related Classifiers may be distinguished:

1. Instances of an action:

	as verb	as Clf
muū	hit	strokes, blows
khē	to step	steps

2. Entities resulting from an action or embodying a state:

	as verb	as Clf
tuū	sever	stumps
khri	be in bits	bits, shards, hills
cɔ	wrap	packages
phō	to flower	flowers
plu	be in a pile	piles

3. Entities characteristically involved in the action (instruments):

nɔ	to butt, gore	horns
ʔíkhu	to wind	khu spools of thread, guns

Most of the Classifiers in the preceding lists are Configurational; muū is not, but is a Time Classifier.

6.4.3.3 List of Some Common Classifiers

General Classifiers:

mɔ̀	smaller plants
dō	nonhuman animals
phre~sí	humans (see 7.3.2.2)

201

mē   larger semi regular shapes: houses, drums, heads, stomachs, livers, larger fruits, hammers, hills, wheels, etc.

bō   lengths: ropes, snakes, intestines, worms, tongues, trees, vines, lizards, cigarettes, sprouts etc.

ko   the general classifier; also: beds, sticks, ridges, stoppers, splinters, pincers, noses, certain bones

plɔ   small round things: smaller fruits, stars, buttons, eggs, cakes of soap, scabs, grains of sand, etc. (cf. Thai lûuk)

be   winged, flat-faced and flakelike things: birds, leaves, fish, dishes, cups, spiders, sickles, drinking glasses, axes, saws, moon, sun, doors, hoes, boats, teeth, paddles, etc. etc. (cf. Thai baj)

ba   sheet-like things: mats, paper objects (money, cards, pages, pictures), cloth, mosquito nets, umbrellas, hats, the earth, etc.

pɯ   clothing: shirts, towels, shawls

Measure Classifiers:

thē   span (the distance between outspread thumb and middle finger)

plè   cubit (from elbow to fingertip)

klī   fathom (distance of spread arms)

cɯ   handful

khwē   the volume of a packbasket

dɛ   eight khwē

and the name of any basket (khrì, dī phɔ́, phɔ́ mó, su du , etc.)

202

6.4.4 Quantifiers and Counting

Quantifiers are discussed here for two reasons. First, any time a Classifier occurs it must be accompanied by a Quantifier. Second, the choice of Quantifier effects the syntax of the ClfP, in that it determines the relative position of Quantifier and Classifier. For example, in counting houses, five of them is Nḗ mē, Q+Clf, but six of them is mē sōswá, Clf+Q.

Quantifiers include the numerals plus the following morphemes:

pwā   every

chī   whole, the entire

bá   how many? (also an Extentive Preposition, 6.6)

təklēmē half (general)

təkwa   half (of stg long)

E.g. pwā phre 'every person', pwā cɤ 'every sort', chī hi 'the whole household'. The last two Quantifiers are compounds whose base elements klē and kwa are probably verbal in origin, 'to be in half'. E.g. cwá klēmē ʌ́ klɛ́ 'go only part of the way, only half way' (klɛ́ 'road') has klēmē inside the VC, between the head Verb cwá and the Postverbal Particle ʌ́. But when combined with tə- they behave as Quantifiers, as in təkwa na 'half a year' təkwa nʌ̄ 'half a day' (notice that spans of time are grouped with long objects, i.e. objects longer than they are wide).

The remainder of this section will be devoted to a description of the numeral system and how numerals combine with classifiers.

The basic numerals are:

1	tə- (prefix)
2	nʌ̄
3	sō
4	lwī
5	ŋɛ̄
6	sō swá
7	sō swá tə-
8	lwī swá
9	lwī swá tə-
10	chʌ́ (basic form) ~ chʌ̄ (in 20–90)
100	(tə)je
1000	(tə)rí
10,000	(tə)sɔ́

The last three forms are always accompanied by a 'multi-plying' digit: təje 'one hundred', nʌ̄ je 'two hundred', and so on (the proper translation for je or rí on its own would be 'hundred' and 'thousand').

The Kayah numerals are emphatically bound morphemes, to the extent that if a speaker is asked to recite them, he or she will usually recite numeral-classifier constructions, using the classifier for small round objects plɔ, thus: təplɔ, nʌ̄ plɔ, sō plɔ, lwī plɔ and so on. (Does this indicate that numbers in the abstract are thought of as small round lumps, like counters?)

The morpheme swá also appears in bɛ́ swá rʌ́ 'be com-panions with' and khō bɛ́ swá 'friend'. It is evidently verb-related, as shown by its occurrence in the verb 'be companions with' ('friend' presumably has the verb modifying a noun khō), and can be glossed 'to double, make a pair'.

204

Thus 'six' is literally 'three doubled', 'seven' is 'three doubled plus one', and so on. These 'analytic' numerals appear to be a recent innovation: other Kayah dialects preserve the monomorphemic forms of 6-9. Below are listed these numerals in the Western Kayah dialect of Ma Khraw Shie (see 9.3.1 below), along with the forms they would probably have if preserved in Eastern Kayah:

	Western	Eastern (hypothetical)
6	shɯ́ə	*chó
7	núo~dá	*nwá~dá
8	θíu	*swá
9	nɯ́ə	*nó

The numbers 11–19 (the teens) are formed by chʌ́ followed by the units numeral: chʌ́ lwī '14', chʌ́ sō swá '16', and so on. The numbers above 19 are formed by chʌ̄ plus a 'multiplier' unit. The relative ordering of numeral and classifier varies, and can be described by a series of rules.

Rule 1: Numerals that end with swá, chʌ̄~chʌ́ or je follow their classifier; all others precede the classifier. Thus the recitation above would continue ŋē plɔ, plɔ sō swá, sō swá təplɔ, plɔ lwī swá, lwī swá təplɔ, plɔ chʌ́.

Rule 2: chʌ̄ in the numerals 20–90 acts like a classifier, preceding multipliers that end in swá, thus:

20	nʌ̄ chʌ̄
30	sō chʌ̄
60	chʌ̄ sō swá
70	sō swá təchʌ̄

The function of the tonal allomorphy of 'ten' can now be seen: those tens whose multiplier follows 'ten' would otherwise be indistinguishable from the teens, which all consist of 'ten'+ 'unit'. Minimal pairs are:

chʌ́ sō swá	16	chʌ́ lwī swá	18
chʌ̄ sō swá	60	chʌ̄ lwī swá	80

chʌ́ sō swá tə-	17
chʌ̄ sō swá tə-	61

The significance of the mid tone of 'ten' in 20–90 can thus be seen as that of signaling a multiplicative (rather than additive) relationship with the adjoining numeral. For example, the difference between '17' and '61' can be symbolized algebraically as:

$$10+(3\text{x}2)+1=17$$
$$(10\text{x}(3\text{x}2))+1=61$$

Notice that while expressions like sō swá tə- are probably best considered compounds, tə- 'one' is phonologically dependent on an element outside the expression, the following morpheme chʌ̄ 'ten', deriving its vowel color from it. Although I have treated tə- as a prefix, no other prefix has this sort of dual dependence; recall that tə- also stands out as the only prefix having full productivity.

Rule 3: When the classifier refers to humans, it has the following three allomorphs:

phre   following pwā 'every', and numerals ending in tə-

zero   when the numeral ends in swá or chʌ̄

sí   otherwise, preceding the numeral

206

Thus:

təphre	1 person
sí nʌ̄	2 people
sí sō	3 people
sí lwī	4 people
sí ŋē	5 people
sō swá	6 people
sō swá təphre	7 people
lwī swá	8 people
lwī swá təphre	9 people

This may be a factor in the required use of the classifier plɔ in 'abstract' counting as mentioned above: if no classifier were supplied, sō swá and lwī swá would not mean 'six' and 'eight' in the abstract, but 'six people' and 'eight people'.

Apart from the cases covered by Rule 3, the placement of the classifier follows Rule 1 regardless of the internal structure of the numeral. Thus even though the numeral 'ten' precedes its multiplier in 'sixty' chʌ̄ sō swá and follows it in 'seventy' sō swá təchʌ̄, the classifier precedes both, since both end in a numeral that requires the classifier to precede. To illustrate (classifier underlined):

20	<u>plɔ</u> nʌ̄ chʌ̄
21	nʌ̄ chʌ̄ tə<u>plɔ</u>
22	nʌ̄ chʌ̄ nʌ̄ <u>plɔ</u>
26	<u>plɔ</u> nʌ̄ chʌ̄ sō swá
27	nʌ̄ chʌ̄ sō swá tə<u>plɔ</u>
30	<u>plɔ</u> sō chʌ̄

31   sō chā̄ təp̲l̲ɔ

60   p̲l̲ɔ chā̄ sō swá

70   p̲l̲ɔ sō swá təchā̄

Further complications arise above one hundred. The classifier is often repeated, once with the hundreds and a second time with the tens, as in the following examples with na 'year':

na təje nʌ na   102 years

na təje chʎ́ təna   111 years

The first occurrence of the classifier may be omitted; thus '111 years' may also be təje chʎ́ təna. The classifier follows Rule 1 even to the extent of appearing 'inside' the construction:

(na) təje na lwī swá   108 years

(na) təje na chʎ́   110 years

This suggests that the construction is not unitary, but perhaps coordinate, as if it were to be glossed e.g. 'one hundred years and ten years'. A similar impression is given by the possible occurrence of ʎ́, presumably the rʎ́-class Particle 'new situation', after the hundreds expression:

təje ʎ́ na sō swá   106 years

na nʌ, je ʎ́ ŋē̄ chʌ, sō swá   256 years

But ʎ́ appears to be optional:

(6-15) na sō je   sō swá təchā̄ lwī swá təna

        year three hundred three double one-ten four double one-year

379 years (3/21)

Here je is not followed by ʎ́.

6.5 Localizers

Localizers form a closed class of nouns that cover much of the semantic territory of English prepositions. The Kayah Li construction [noun+localizer] is usually to be translated as an English [preposition+noun], but the localizers are not structurally equivalent to prepositions; they are not postpositions. In the Kayah Li construction, the localizer is the head and the noun is its modifier, thus dɤ́ khrā kū 'inside the bottle-gourd', cited above, is 'at (dɤ́) the bottle-gourd's (khrā) inside (kū)' dɤ́ toə khu 'on the table' is 'at (dɤ́) the table's (toə) upper surface (khu)', and so on.

This follows Chao's analysis of the corrresponding Chinese category, and borrows his term for it; cf. also Thompson's similar analysis of Vietnamese 'Relator Nouns'. Most of the Kayah Li Localizers may also form ordinary compound nouns, as can be seen in the following list. For each Localizer I give a general gloss, examples (A) as Localizer, and (B) in other functions, mostly as head of compound Ordinary Nouns. Note that the general gloss applies only to use as Localizer (e.g. the first item kū could be given a general gloss 'hole' in its non-Localizer functions).

kū inside

A. dɤ́ lē̄ kū   in the ravine

   dɤ́ pjā kū   in the bag

B. ʔakū   hole

   thʌ̄ kū   spring, well

   kədā kū   window

   kū   Classifier for holes, springs, windows, etc.

klɔ̄ outside

A. dɤ̀ hi klɔ̄   outside the house
B. li klɔ̄   book cover

khu on (the upper surface of), above

A. he khu   on the ground
   hi khu   (1) on the house
B. kɔ̄ khu   upper end of a swidden
   plā khu   shoulder
   twa khu   floor
   hi khu   (2) roof
   ʔíkhu   land, earth, world
   ʔakhu   main root of a plant

kɛ̄~kɛ̄dē down inside, at the bottom inner surface

A. pe jʌ́ ʔo tā dɤ̀: khrā du kɛ̄dē
   We were down at the bottom inside the bottle-gourd. (26.5)
B. kɔ̄ kɛ̄   lower end of a swidden
   cú mā kɛ̄   elbow
   khɛ̄ no kɛ̄   back of heel

khʌ̄ on top of, at the apex of

A. dɤ̀ cho khʌ̄   on the (peak of) mountain
B. lɛ̄ khʌ̄   headwaters
   ʔīthoə khʌ̄   knife edge

210

lē bottom, base of, underneath

A. dɤ́ hi lē   under the house

   dɤ́ dɔ̄ lē   below (downhill from) the village

B. plā lē   armpit

   tēú kē̄ lē   gills

chá next to, near the base of

A. dɤ́ dɔ̄ chá   near and downhill from the village

   dɤ́ Phāʌ chá   next to Pha'a

B. kɛ chá   mouth (of stream); foot (of tree)

Possibly related: (1) nenā chá 'cheek'; (2) chá 'when (future)' (Preposition)

ŋē~béseŋē in front of

A. dɤ́ ŋē   in front

   dɤ́ hi béseŋē   in front of the house (bése 'face')

B. N ŋē   on N's part, N's share

khjā~békhjā in back of, behind

A. dɤ́ hi békhjā   behind the house

   ka dɤ́ khjā   come later

B. khjā sé   back again, in response (VPtc)

   kəkhjā   backwards (Bound Directional)

lo on the non-horizontal surface of

A. dɤ́ là lo   on the cliffside

klē in among, in stg not construed as an aperture

A. dɤ́ dɔ̄ klē   in the village

   dɤ́ mi klē   in the forest

rɔ̄klē beside

A. dɤ́ hi rɔ̄klē   beside the house

   dɤ́ rɔ̄klē cáci   on the left (side)

B. rɔ̄   side

   rɔ̄ khrwí   rib

ple~ple kū in (the narrow space) between

A. dɤ́ dɔ́ ple   inside the wall (e.g. a lizard)

   dɤ́ X né Y ple kū between X and Y (e.g. people standing in

                        a row)

B. ʔaple   a crack

klē mē kū ~ cɔkū in the middle of, between

A. dɤ́ dɔ̄ klē mē kū between the villages

   dɤ́ dɔ̄ cɔkū   id.

   (dɤ́ X né ʏ klē mē kū between X and Y

B. təklē mē   one half

thɯ̄ on the edge of

A. dɤ́ dɔ̄ thɯ̄   on the edge of the village

B. thʌ̄ thɯ̄   river bank

   ʔathɯ̄   edge, seam

təkjā in the direction of
A. dɤ́ phrɛ̀ dɔ̄ təkjā   towards the Shan village
   dɤ́ tē təkjā ɛ̄   in which direction?
B. kjā   Classifier for paired body parts (arms, ears, etc.)

ŋū thé uphill from
ŋū lē downhill from

6.6 PP

Prepositions are bound morphemes that form a PP with a following NP (which may be a nominalized clause). There is one exception to this: chá takes only clauses or zero, plus the SPtc pā 'irrealis' (required with zero, optional otherwise).

The Prepositions fall into three groups:

a) Locative

dɤ́   at, when (past); distal, unmarked for evidentiality; 'at:U' in glosses.

mú   id., known by inference or hearsay, not in sight; 'at:I' in glosses.

bɤ́   id., proximal, in sight; 'at:P' in glosses. Also forms contraction with ʔⱭ̄ 'this': bɤ́ + ʔⱭ̄ 'at this [place]'— > bⱭ̄ 'here'.

b) Extentive

bá   as much as, _ much

tí   as big as, _ big

tɤ́~thɤ́ as long as, _ long

213

c) Miscellaneous

chá   when (future)

phú~hú like, as

cɛ́~cɛə   the __ part, the ones who __

nɛ́   backgrounded participant, quasi-coordination

a) Locative. The difference among these three is that of evidentiality, i.e. the speaker's basis for knowing the truth of the proposition he utters. mú and bɤ́ have positive evidential connotations, as indicated; dɤ́ seems to have less, and may be considered unmarked. It is by far the most common preposition. All three may be used to indicate time, but it must be past time; future time requires chá. dɤ́ at times is better translated 'as for':

(6-16) <u>dɤ́</u> ʔa mē nʌ rʌ . . . <u>dɤ́</u> ʔa phē nʌ . . .
         3 wife NØ rØ   3 father NØ
The wife, for her part, . . . the father, for his part, . . . (53.2)

b) Extentive. These usually precede lexical NP's (not nominalized clauses); for example:

(6-17) ʔa bésɛplɔ ʔo   <u>tí</u> chā   dʌ
       3 eye   exist   chicken egg
He had eyes as big as chicken eggs. (95.5)

They may form interrogative sentences in conjunction with the SPtc tē, as:

(6-18) ʔa thū <u>tɤ́</u> tē   ɔ
       3 long   what Huh
How long is it, huh? (10/18)

A form bá occurs in bá CLF tē 'how many?' (cf. 7.4).
Although similar in meaning to the Extentive Preposition with
this phonological shape, bá in this expression must be considered
a Quantifier, since it takes a Classifier Object, something no
(other) Preposition is known to do. Notice that the other Extentive Prepositions do not have this property, as in (18), where tɤ́
takes the interrogative Noun tē 'what'.

c) Miscellaneous. For an example of the use of cɛ́, cf. the
following:

(6-19) Ɂū dʌ́ phɛ́   cɛ́ Ɂū mi Ɂo nʌ
      3i give simply   3i name exist NØ
      They only give to the ones whose names they have [writ-
      ten down]. (263.2)

Here cɛ́ takes as Object the nominalized clause Ɂū mi Ɂo nʌ
'they have [their] names'. Notice that the PP headed by cɛ́ here
functions as (Indirect) Object.

chá indicates future time. Its commonest uses are (1) chá
pā meaning 'soon'; (2) with short time expressions, most of
which can be analyzed as clauses. For example:

chá mɔ̀ hé pā	this evening (mɔ̀ 'sun', hé 'late, be evening')
chá no pā	later on (for no as a verb cf. 4.2.4)
chá lē the tənʌ̄ pā	on the coming first day of the waxing moon (lē 'moon', the 'ascend', tənʌ̄ 'one day')
chá pā ro pā	tomorrow (pā ro 'tomorrow', analysis uncertain)

215

Finally, note the possible relation of chá to the homophonous Localizer meaning 'place nearby, at the base of'.

For né see 5.5.2.

We next examine the grammatical functions that PP's may have. Besides filling the post-verbal slot that I have referred to as Obl (5.5), PP's are also quite common as Topics. This is especially true of time-when expressions referring to the past, which usually appear in that position—for instance, the standard story-telling opener dɤ́ ŋjā nʌ 'long ago' (ŋjā 'be a long time'). Cf. also:

(6-20) dɤ́ [vē̄ jì   bó nʌ] vē̄ bá   hē̄   chā ‖ ʔa ri   mē̄
      at:U 1s thresh rice NØ   1s divine go:FH chicken 3 good PTC
      When I was threshing, I divined[2] about going [to work];
      [the indication] was auspicious! (183.6)

Future-time expressions are introduced by chá and are normally in the Oblique position.

There are also examples of PP's functioning as Object, including (6-19) above and the following:

(6-21) ʔa|lā   síŋē   rʌ́ phɛ́ | céə [rāmá rʌ́ nʌ] phɛ́
       3 intrusively understand RØ simply those.who write.down RØ NØ simply
       They know only what they write down. (302.3)

(6-22) ʔa |nɔ̄ hē̄ dʌ́ rʌ́ | dɤ́ ʔaro təphre ǂ nʌ
       3   order go:FH give RØ   at:U other one-C:human NØ
       He got another person to go give it. (100.5)

---

[2] bá chā is the practice of divining by inserting splinters of wood into holes in the leg-bones of a chicken.

(6-23) ʔa phjá dɤ́ təcē nʌ

    3   take   at:U sickle NØ

He took his sickle. (472.3)

Of these, the PP's in (21) and (23) are Direct Objects, and those in (19) and (22) are Indirect Objects (or would be if there were co-occurring Direct Objects, cf. the discussion in 5.4.1 above).

    This ability to function as Object is one way in which Kayah Li PP's are not very different from NP's. Note also that most of the meanings associated with the prepositions of English and other languages are not borne by prepositions in Kayah, for example:

        Directional/configurational

into	nō (Verb)
under	lē (Localizer)
from	ʔo X V (V' series)

        Temporal

after	clause sequence, 'having done X, then did Y'

        Case- or semantic-role marking

for	pè (Verb Particle)
of	(concatenation of NP's)
to (Recipient)	Obj-1 (structural postion)

The 'locative' Prepositions especially can be thought of as evidential markers of NP's, which only incidentally tend to be locative in meaning. In this view, it may be the Localizer constituent of a locative expression, as much as the Preposition, that assigns or marks the Oblique grammatical relation.

6.7 The Abstract Noun lè

The Noun lè can be given a core meaning of 'place'. Along with Karen cognates such as Pa-O lâm 'house', it is a reflex of a widespread Tibeto-Burman etymon most often glossed 'road'. The Kayah Li reflex is a Bound Noun, with special grammatical characteristics and a meaning ranging into fairly abstract territory.

Like any noun, it may be modified either by a preposed nominal or a postposed verbal construction. But lè has the following special characteristics. (1) each type of modifier is associated with a different shade of meaning of the head lè. (2) when the two modifier types co-occur, the whole construction has the semantics of the verbal-modifier type. (3) the postposed modifier of lè is at most a VP, whereas postposed verbal modifiers of ordinary Nouns are clauses (8.2).

6.7.1 N lè

With preposed nominal modifier, the meaning is 'because of N, with the undesirable influence of N'. This construction occurs only in Object position; examples:

(6-24) síʔichē vē lè
     fear   1s place.for
     be afraid of me

(6-25) klɛ pɔ̄khī lè
     run tiger   place.for
     run from [i.e. because of] the tiger

(6-26) khjɔ́   ʔa lè

      surrender 3s place.for

      give in to him/her

(6-27) ʔa phʌ̄   nʌ rʌ ʔonē lɛ   nì kʌ̄ pa lū lè   to

      3s grandmother NØ RØ sit   descend get COM DUR OBV place.for NEG

      His Grandmother can't sit down, because of him. (250.2)

6.7.2 lè VP

With postposed verbal modifier, the meaning is 'place for V-ing, thing for X'. Simple examples, with the modifying VP consisting of a single verb, include lè mʌ̄ 'bedroom' (mʌ̄ 'sleep'), lè ʔi 'toilet' (ʔi 'defecate'), and lè ʔe 'food' (ʔe 'eat'). Notice that in the first two examples, which have concrete meanings denoting physical locations, lè may still be glossed as 'place'; whereas the last example has a more abstract denotation—the meaning is not 'eating place' but 'thing for eating'.

The verbal modifier of lè is a VP. An example including both Verb and Object is lè ʔílò thʌ̄ 'bathing place' (ʔílò 'bathe', thʌ̄ 'water'). Further expansion of the modifying VP to include ClfP and PP is exemplified below:

      lè + [V NP ClfP]

(6-28) təcē ma lè   ché thuú pwā cɤ

      trap be.so place.for trap bird   every C:kind

      A tajeh is [a thing] for trapping all kinds of birds. (6.iv) lè + [V PP]

(6-29) thorəsap ma lè   ʔíbe dɤ́ ʔaja

    telephone   be.so place.for   speak   at:U   ITS-far

A telephone is [a thing] for talking to far-away. (26.iv)

Notice that the PP in the last example is not specified by the verb ʔíbe 'speak' and so is a constituent of VP, not of V (5.1).

Finally, both types of modifiers of lè may co-occur. The whole expression retains the 'place-for' semantics, rather than the 'because-of' semantics shown in (1) above, with preposed nominal only. Examples:

(6-30) khruɯ lè   bɔ́   thé

    machine   place.for weave cloth

    loom (machine for weaving cloth)

(6-31) səklʌ̄ lè   dɛ   kəjē̄ nʌ̄chʌ̄

    boat   place.for transport person   two-ten

    a boat for transporting 20 people (26.iv)

(6-32) víjuə lè   ʔíbe

    radio   place.for speak

    radio (cf. Thai wíthájú) (10/8)

(6-33) dī   təkɔ̄ lè   sɛ́ ʔe   rʌ́ hō

    cooked.rice container place.for put.in for.use RØ unhusked.rice

    a rice-container for putting rice in[to the pot] (199.7)

In the above examples the preposed Nouns (khruɯ, səklʌ̄, víjuə̂) have a sort of identity with lè, in that both are interpretable as 'thing-for'. All denote inanimate objects; when the preposed Noun denotes a human, as in the following examples, it does not have this identity with lè, being interpreted as Agent while lè retains the 'thing-for' interpretation:

(6-34) phrekhū   lè   ʔílò   thā̄
      human-male place.for bathe water
      men's bathing place

(6-35) dɤ́ ʔū lè   sī   tā   kúkhu
      at:U 3i place.for wash fall hand
      at the place under where they wash their hands (461.1)

The instrumental meaning of lè+VP is attested by an informant's metalinguistic comments about the sentence kəjē mū pù 'person beats ox': kəjē ma phre mū, pù ma phre chē, lè mū ma ʔímū 'the person is the one who beats, the ox is the one who hurts, the thing for beating is the stick'. Notice especially the contrast in grammatical form: N+AttrC in kəjē mū 'the one who beats' and phre chē 'the one who hurts', versus the lè construction in lè mū 'the thing for beating'.

However, this 'instrumental' meaning ranges far beyond literal instrumentality, as is illustrated further in the following examples:

(6-36) swá mo lè   ŋjā
      friend fun place.for laugh
      a happy friend to laugh with

(6-37) vē lè   nɔ̄cɔ̀ ʔo
      1s place.for order exist
      I have something to order [you to do]. (470.6)

221

(6-38) dujὲ ʔo rʌ́ lὲ   donē   sūrɛ ʔo rʌ́ lὲ   pǝcʌ

      rich   exist RØ place.for tell.legends difficult exist RØ place.for gossip

If [my descendants] are rich they will be a matter of legend, if they are poor they will be a matter for gossip. (51.6) (possibly better: they will exist as a matter of legend . . .)

Although both of the lὲ constructions may include a preposed nominal modifier, they remain distinct syntactically as well as semantically. The N+lὲ 'because-of' construction is the more restricted: not only may it not include any postposed verbal modifier, but it is also limited to Object position in the clause.

lὲ with verbal modifier can be identified as the source of several lexicalized compounds. With literal 'place-for' semantics: lὲ to 'bed', lὲ sɯ 'shed, granary', in which to and sɯ do not occur elsewhere. lὲ may also appear in lὲ klō, a khwe-class Verb particle (4.3.2) meaning 'have ever V'd, experienced'; if klō here is 'language', the meaning could be 'thing for speaking-about', i.e. something I have experienced becomes something I can speak about.

Chapter 7

Sentence Types and Sentence Particles

7.1 Sentence Types

This study has thus far been devoted to the grammar of the simple clause. In this chapter I will look beyond the simple clause, by situating the simple autonomous clause within a more inclusive inventory of sentence and clause types. I will then go on to describe the class of Sentence Particles, the only clause constituent not yet considered. This also seems the best place for a discussion of questions and question words, although only a few of the question words are Sentence Particles.

Let us begin with a set of definitions, some repeated:

A Verb is any morpheme that can stand on its own in construction with lāí, ʎ, pa, or some other member of the rʎ-class Verb Particles.

A Clause is any construction that both (a) contains a verb and (b) can be terminated by the Sentence Particles to 'negative' or pā 'irrealis'.

A Sentence is any construction that can stand on its own as an utterance bearing an illocutionary force; it may consist either of one or more clauses, or of an NP. Let us call the former a verbal sentence and the latter a nominal sentence; both types may end in a Sentence Particle (although only a subset of the SPtc's may terminate a nominal sentence). A verbal sentence may also be classified as an autonomous clause; clauses that cannot stand on their own (do not qualify as sentences) are termed non-autonomous clauses. Examples:

Verbal sentence = autonomous clause

(7-1) nō   nɔ́   hóhé   to   ɛ̄   ɔ
      enter at.all school   NEG QUES HUH
      Aren't you going to school, hey? (130.4)

Nominal sentence

(7-2) thwá ke
      cat   PRH
      (on hearing a noise:) Maybe it was the cat.
      (in conversation)

Non-autonomous clauses

  a) modifying a preceding noun

(7-3) kəjē̄   [ré   to]
      person   good NEG
      a bad person

  b) modifying a following Clf'

(7-4) ʔa ʔe tēú təhe
      3   eat fish one-C:group
      the ones who were eating fish (198.6)

c) as object of a preposition

(7-5) ʔa phā̄   nʌ ʔo dɤ̌ hi   thūū hú pe ʔo ʔā̄ nʌ
    3 grandmother NØ exist at:U house edge as 1p exist this NØ

His grandmother lived at the edge of the village, like we
live here. (204.4)

The non-autonomous clauses in (3) and (4), which modify nouns,
are called Attributive Clauses (AtrC). Their function is similar to
relative clauses, but I do not use that term because the Kayah Li
constructions includes no equivalent of the relative pronoun. The
difference between preposed and postposed AtrC parallels the
contrast between nouns (which typically precede what they modify) and verbs (which typically follow what they modify); for
more on this point see 9.2. The preposed AtrC's often end in nʌ;
since clauses ending with nʌ also resemble nouns in being capable of acting as object of a preposition, I interpret nʌ as a nominalizer (see also 8.3).

We therefore have, in addition to [autonomous], another
possible feature for classifying clauses: [nominalized]. We have
seen examples of [−autonomous +nominalized] (4 above),
[−autonomous −nominalized] (3), and [+autonomous −nominal-
ized] (1). It turns out that the fourth possibility also exists: there
are what appear to be autonomous clauses ending with nʌ, which
might be analyzed as autonomous nominalized clauses. Autonomous nominalized clauses might further be taken to be instances
of nominal sentences. Since they are extremely common, I have
instead generally treated these autonomous nominalized clauses
as verbal sentences with nʌ functioning, like the (other) Sentence
Particles, to mark illocutionary force. See, however, the discus-

sion of nʌ (8.3 below). It may be noted here that autonomous nominalized clauses, or something like them, seem to be a widespread Tibeto-Burman trait.

It will be seen in the following section that only a small number of Sentence Particles can occur in non-autonomous clauses; the large number that cannot include most of the illocutionary-force markers. This is consistent with the definition of autonomous clause/verbal sentence as being able to bear illocutionary force: since an embedded clause generally cannot have any illocutionary force distinct from that of the main clause, we would not expect illocutionary-force markers to occur in it.

7.2 Sentence Particles

The Sentence Particles (SPtc) terminate the clause; as suggested above (6.2), they are adjoined to the clause in a configuration like . . .]S Ptc]S Ptc]S. There are some eighteen SPtc's known; they can be sub-classified on the basis of two formal properties. The first is ability to reduplicate (cf. 2.4 above); the second is occurrence in non-autonomous clauses.

Reduplication. Certain SPtc's can reduplicate, as in the following:

(7-6) dʌ́ cwá vē̄ to ‖ vē̄ cwá to   to
      let go 1s NEG 1s go   NEG RDP
[If you] won't let me go, I won't go, then. (0.5)

(7-7) m̩ síʔichē ké   rò he   he
         afraid   AMB cold LEST RDP
Mm, I'm afraid it'll be cold, too. [e.g. in addition to raining] (2/24)

(7-8)   thɛ́ phra kʌ̄ ke ke

        pig to.sound COM PRH RDP

    It might also be a pig making noise. (2/24)

Others cannot:

(7-9a)   vē cwá kʌ̄ ní ‖ *vē cwá kʌ̄ ní ní

        1s go   COM ATT

    I'm going along! I'm going along too!

Compare:

(7-9b)   vē cwá kʌ̄ ní ‖ vē cwá kʌ̄ kʌ̄ ní

    (same meaning as 9a)

For a similar example:

(7-10a)   ma Pímò te mē ‖ *ma Kāmɛ̀ te mē mē

        be.so (name) 's PTC

    It's Pimo's, and it's also Kameh's!

(7-10b)   ma Pímò te mē ‖ ma Kāmɛ̀ te te mē

    (same meaning)

    Occurrence in non-autonomous clauses. This property is found only in to 'negative' and pā 'irrealis, future'. Examples with to:

(7-11)   dī [vā   lāí to] ʔo pa dɤ́ dīpɔ kū

        rice cooked yet NEG exist DUR at:U pot   inside

    The rice that is not yet cooked is in the pot. (11/24)

(7-12)   ma | kəjē [mò ʔo to phē ʔo to]

        be.so person mother exist NEG father exist NEG

    [they] are people without a mother or father. (267.2)

And with pā:

(7-13) ma | dɤ́ [vɛ̄ | dʌ́ pè kʌ̄ | vɛ̄ pò ǂ pā nʌ] təbe
       be.so at:U 1s give TRN COM 1s YS IRR NØ one-C:flat
       It's the one [a tool] that I'm going to give to my brother.
       (11/24)

(7-14) pənè [cwi ʔithá pā] ʔo tōútē
       buffalo pull plough IRR exist where
       Where's the buffalo that will pull the plow? (11/24)

Since these two formal properties do not coincide completely, they delineate three subclasses of SPtc's:

	subclass		
	A	B	C
reduplicates	+	+	-
occurs in non-autonomous clause	+	-	-

There may be another distinguishing feature: if the zero initial is really an underlying /h/ (2.2), then it deletes in the C-class particles ɛ̄ and ɔ, but not in the B-class particle he. This would probably correlate with a difference in prosodic or metrical position between the two classes of particles.

Some at least of the SPtc's can terminate nominal sentences—which is indeed the evidence compelling us to recognize those constructions as sentences. Thus the class B SPtc ke in (2) above; also the negative in ʔū rò mɤ̄ to '[it was] not other people's country'.

There is a rough correlation of semantic values with the three subclasses. A relates to polarity (positive/negative) and the realis/irrealis status of the proposition; C consists entirely of

228

markers of illocutionary force, while B is a mixture; e.g. the B class SPtc he 'possible undesirable event' combines polarity ('possible') with expression of the speaker's attitude ('undesirable').

The illocutionary force-marking function is typical of morphemes of this type, i.e. sentence-final bound morphemes, often unstressed. This is true at least for Southeast Asian languages, in which they are often known as Sentence Particles or Final Particles (cf. also Okell's Verb-Clause Markers). It is often said that the lexical function of tone in these languages limits the possibilities of exploitation of phrase and sentence intonation for expressing illocutionary force, hence such meanings must be encoded in this class of lexical items. What is certain is that these illocutionary force markers are invariably among those aspects of the language that are the most difficult to capture and explain. Although I have made a start at delineating differences among those SPtc's that share a general meaning (particularly that of urging), there is undoubtedly much remaining to be discovered about the semantics and pragmatics of these morphemes.

Subclass A

to   Negative. The relationship between this particle and the Extent expression has been discussed above (5.5.1). Here it may suffice to recall that, while to seems to derive from a Clf' made up of the numeral tə- 'one' plus some other unknown element, which originally functioned as one half of an emphatic negative 'not even one', it has undergone sufficient evolution that it is no longer a true Clf', although it retains enough ties to the Extent expression Clf' that the two are in near-complementary distribution. to is also related to the phonologically aberrant too 'only' (cf. 2.4), which occurs only after Extent expressions. Consider the following contrastive sets:

(7-15a) rū̄   ʔo ŋēcwè too
money exist 500
I have only 500 [Baht]. (2/27)

(7-15b) rū̄   ŋēcwè ʔo to
money 500   exist
I don't have 500 [Baht]. (2/27)

(7-16a) ʔa khé be   thuú sō dō   too
3 shoot strike bird   three C:animal
He shot only three birds. (2/27)

(7-16b) nʌ sō dō   ʔa khé be   to
that three C:animal 3 shoot strike
He didn't shoot [shot at and missed] those three. (2/27)

Examples of reduplication of the negative have been given above; too 'only' may also reduplicate:

(7-17)   dīpɔ ʔo təmē too ‖ pē ʔo phɛ́ təmē   too too
pot exist one-C:large   bottle exist only one-C:large   RDP
There's only one pot; and only one bottle as well. (2/27)

pā   irrealis, future hypothetical, upcoming. Very frequent in clauses introduced by the Prepostion chá, which indicates near-future time-when expressions. E.g:
chá mɔ̀ hé pā   this [coming] evening (mɔ̀ 'sun' + hé 'evening')

chá lē the tənʌ̄ pā the [coming] first day of the waxing
moon (lē 'moon', the 'ascend', tənʌ 'one day')
cwá chá pā will go pretty soon

> pā contrasts with ke (subclass B), which expresses uncer-
> tainty about events that are (or may have been) com-
> pleted, usually in the past. The Kayah equivalent of
> 'maybe, possibly, might' is not a modal auxiliary but a use
> of pā, as in hē pā ē, to ē literally 'may come, may not',
> corresponding to may come, maybe will come, and very
> often followed by síŋē to 'don't know'.

Subclass A could also be known as the Clause Particles:
since these SPtc's are the only ones that can occur in all sorts of
clause, it has been useful to single them out in discussing intra-
clausal syntax. But from the perspective of the sentence to and pā
are simply a special subtype of a larger class.

Subclass B

ke   past or perfective irrealis. Examples:

(7-18) pe lā   síplɔnō lū   to   nʌ   <u>ke</u>
       1p intrusively understand 3OBV NEG NØ
       We just don't understand them. (45.5)

> (Note the sequence of three SPtc's). Also ʔĩphri ka ke
> '[they] may have bought [it]'.

he   lest, possible undesirable event. Examples:

231

(7-19) sí dɛ khrā, síʔichē ʔa ʔɔ́   <u>he</u>

      want put dry   afraid 3 mildew

I want to put it out to dry; I'm afraid it may mildew. (cf. I want to put it out to dry lest it mildew)

(7-20) sī súplī pè ʔa, ʔa kəsévà lū   <u>he</u>   ní

      2p wash BEN 3 3 itch   3OBV EMPH

You wash him, or he'll get itchy again, now! (lest he get itchy) (249.4)

me   don't, negative imperative. Examples:

(7-21) mɛ́ pəthɛ <u>me</u> ní

      look upwards   EMPH

Don't look up, now!

(7-22) thɛ́ ma kɔ́no <u>me</u> me

      needle be.so play   RDP

Don't play with the needle either. (note reduplication)

lē   and what about . . . ?. Seems to occur only in nominal sentences. Examples:

Phrèʌ cwá nɔ́ to ‖ . . . ʔa mò <u>lē</u> ɔ

A: Phre'a didn't go. B: What about his mother? (146.2)

vē lʌ <u>lē</u>   Where's my grandchild?

The last example is from a narrative, where it is the utterance of a grandmother speaking to people who had gone fishing with her grandchild and were returning without him/her.

Subclass C

The remaining SPtc's will be grouped according to general types of illocutionary force.

Interrogative

ε̄   yes-no question. Example: ʔ大 tən大 ʔo kō ε̲ 'Are you free today?' Also occurs in the idiom dý tē tə-CLF ε̲ 'which one?'

pē   discontinuous component of ʔū . . . pē 'who?'(lē, subclass B)

ɔ   prompt-question. Can follow other interrogative indicators, or may turn a statement into a question, somewhat like English *huh*. E.g. ne cwá ɔ̲ 'you're going, huh?'

As for WH-questions, most terminate with the interrogative Bound Noun tē, which has some of the characteristics of a SPtc; see 7.4 below.

Imperative

kɔ   urging, offering for consideration, 'suggest that you do this/agree with this'.

tɛ~tɛē   urging, 'let's'. This particle urges the hearer to join the speaker in doing something. It often occurs with the rʌ́-class Verb Particle m大 (mild imperative), as in:

(7-23) ba m大 t̲ɛ̲ē̲, ph大 //   to, dɛ se mī ʔa, ʔa hé lū nʌ
     pick sugg   grandmother NEG put fruit ripe 3   3   say 3OBV NØ
Let's pick it, OK Grandma? No, leave it to ripen, she said to them. (161.5)

233

tɛɛ̄ may also appear at the end of a sentence with the force of 'Right? Isn't that so?', as in:

(7-24) khrā   khri nʌ ʔa ʔo kā̄ pa hé nʌ <u>tɛɛ̄</u>
calabash shard NØ 3   exist COM DUR say NØ

They say that pieces of the calabash still exist, right? (159.1)

The connection between urging and this tag-question is probably a matter of the hearer being urged to agree with the speaker in the truth of the preceding assertion.

ū~ú   urging, 'you go ahead and'. This particle urges the hearer to go on and do something. It contrasts with the preceding item, as neatly exemplified in the following:

(7-25) ʔó: chwakhriə təbe,   pʉ̀ ʔa tɛɛ̄ //
oh   crab   one-C:flat catch 3 let's

to, pʉ̀ <u>ú</u>   ʔa hé vɛ̄ nʌ
NEG catch   3 say 1s NØ

'Oh, a crab, let's catch it.' [I said] 'No, you go ahead', he said to me. (174.6)

ú is probably a component of the form dúū~duə, which also has the function of urging or trying to persuade. This can be analyzed as ú following a element that also appears in the forms dɤə~duə~dɛə, which are used by parents in calling their children. This element may be represented as /dV/, possibly with high tone, although given its usual occurence with the suffix /-ə/, with its pre-emptive high-falling tone, it is difficult to be sure of any intrinsic tone for this element.

pó~pō   urging, "why don't you'. Urges with less force than ú and tɛ̄ɛ̄; is not restricted to urging hearer alone. Examples:

(7-26)   ʔa hé kʌ̄   lū   pe ʔíla p̱ō̱ ʔa hé

           3 say COM each.other 1p call   3 say

           They said to each other, 'Let's call them [cattle]', they said. (462.2)

(7-27)   ne thɔ̄ təmē   ʔa dʌ́ jū   vɛ̄ p̱ó̱

           2s drum one-C:large 3 give easy 1s

           Your drum, won't you give it to me? (408.5)

Other morphemes with imperative force include Verb Particle mʌ̄, the negative imperative me (Sentence Particle class B) and ní in 'Assertive' below).

Assertive

təkoʌ   concessive assertion, nevertheless, still. Example:

(7-28)   ʔū bé   bɤ̌ té: || ʔū síjɯ kʌ̄   nʌ ṯə̱ḵo̱ʌ̱

           3   endowed at:V what-SH 3   want   COM NØ

           However rich they are, they still want some. (269.6)

mó   concessive: 'sure, but. . . .' Example (in Conversation 2 in Texts):

(7-29)   ʔa lɔ̄   m̱ó̱ nachi

           3 use.up   oil

           Sure it does [use up gasoline] . . . (164.1)

tədɤ́   concessive: although, nevertheless.

(7-30)   vɛ̄ lɛkhuí ṯə̱ḏɤ̱́ ma sī hɛ̄ lɔ́plú tè vɛ̄ me níˀ

           1s fall.over   be.so 2p go:FH across don't 1s don't EMPH

           Even though I fall, don't step over me. (382.4)

235

lé   counter-assertion.

(7-31)   pe já   pé lɤ̆ sɛ́   Ɂū lé

          1p go.and dumb more in.reaction 3i

[We should have been smarter,] but we're dumber than them! (109.3)

mē   mild counter-assertion, also used in answers to questions.

(7-32)   Ɂa me sɅ̄ Ʌ́ lū   mē

          3 do   die NS mutually

They would have killed each other [if I hadn't stopped them]. (241.2)

ní   strong assertion or imperative, 'be sure and pay attention to what I say'.

lā~lá   exclamation.

(7-33)   Ɂíbe cɛ̀ pɤ́ lā

          speak able INT

[They] can speak very well! (300.5)

vā ~   medium-strong assertion, sure it's true that X. Sen-
təpa vā tences with this Particle tend not to have overt NP Objects, but they can have afterthought-like expressions:

(7-34)   Ɂa kléə síŋē   pwā cɤ   vā, Ɂū Ɂíbe

          3 should understand every C:kind   3i speak

She should understand everything [by now], of their language! (221.6)

This is probably the reason for the acceptability of the following constructed sentences, with vā occurring on either side of an Object NP:

(7-35) ʔa ʔe ʎ tə̄pa vā dī   ~   ʔa ʔe ʎ tə̄pa dī vā
   3 eat NS   cooked.rice [id.]
   S/he has eaten! (12/5)

The rʎ-class Verb Particle phέ (4.3.5) may also be repeated in the Sentence Particle position, as in ʔe phέ təklέ phέ 'eat only half'.

The particle nʌ also has a very frequent use for neutral assertion, but it has complexities that are best discussed separately. For discussion and examples of this item, see the following section (7.3).

Multiple Sentence Particles. Below is a rough indication of the co-occurrence possibilities of the SPtc's:

to	nʌ	me ke he tədɤ́	mē ɛ̄	tɛɛ̄ ɔ ní
	pā			
				*

Among the SPtc's that can appear in the position marked with the asterisk (*) are lē, pó, dūú, kɔ, mó, lé and possibly others. This chart treats nʌ as just another SPtc; for its special characteristics see below.

7.3 Unique and Problematic Particles

7.3.1 ke 'if' and da 'if, whenever'

These morphemes appear between Subject and VC, with the meaning 'if':

> mò ke ʔo to ma . . . if they have no mother . . . (11.3)
>
> pe ke bwí ré rʌ . . . if our luck is good . . . (30.6)

(7-36) ʔū dā dʌ́ tə́ra ɔ ʔū dʌ́ sálá lɔ̄

> 3i if give anyway HUH 3i give used.up exhaust
>
> Anyway, if they gave [to the rich] they'd run out of them. (270.4)

This ke is probably related to the Subclass B SPtc ke 'perfective irrealis' described above: conditionality and irrealis are semantically similar. The pre-VC ke and dā are not khwe-class Verb Particles (4.2): they freely occur before the khwe-class VPtc's whereas the true members of that class occur with each other only in circumscribed conditions. I therefore recognize a separate category consisting of ke and dā.

7.3.2 nʌ: Assertion Marker, Nominalizer/Complementizer

The syllable nʌ is variegated and elusive in its function, both syntactically and semantically, perhaps in large part because it is nearly always optional rather than required. Assuming the distal demonstrative nʌ 'that' to be unrelated, two particles nʌ can be distinguished, both of them extremely common: a topic-marker and what I have been calling the nominalizing Sentence Particle.

Topic marker. The topic marker follows NP's:

(7-37) Mĩʌ nʌ ma vē phē mē
        (name)   be.so 1s father EXCL
        Mi'a is my father! (266.1)

(7-38) phrèjwi nʌ kwi ʔe kè
        Thai   request for.use country
        The Thais asked for some land. (202.6)

(7-39) ʔa phú lʌ nʌ nɔ̄ ka lɔ́ lū dɤ̀ sínō nʌ
        3 child gchld command go:TH inter 3OBV at:U West NØ
        His descendants were told to go bury him in the West.
        (201.5)

Nominalizer. The nominalizing SPtc occurs with both autonomous and non-autonomous clauses.

With autonomous clauses:

(7-40) ʔa ka ʔe lɔ̄ lū nʌ
        3 go:TH eat use.up 3OBV
        They came and ate them all up. (206.2)

(7-41) thɛ me ʔichē tò ʔa mĩú ʔa mwĩ
        ascend do fear arrive 3 (name) 3 namesake

        dɤ̀ hi dɔ́ kū nʌ
        at:U house wall inside NØ
        [He] went up and frightened Mi'u's namesake in the
        house. (242.6)

With non-autonomous clauses:

(7-42) dʌ́ pè k̄ʌ ʔa təkhʌ̄ ja nʌ təphre
        give TRN COM 3 muntjac meat one-C:hum
        the person that you gave muntjac meat to

(7-43) dɤ́ vē jì   bó nʌ
       at:U 1s thresh rice NØ
       when I was threshing (183.6)

(7-44) bɤ́ ʔa phʌ̄   ʔo rʌ́ nʌ
       at:V 3 grandmother exist RØ NØ
       where the grandmother lived (209.2)

And in locative expressions consisting of Preposition+Directional Verb+nʌ, such as dɤ́ thɛ nʌ 'up there' (the 'ascend'), dɤ́ nō nʌ 'in there' (nō 'enter'). The verbs here are one-word clauses, nominalized by nʌ and functioning as object of the preposition (see also 8.1.2).

    This nominalizing function of nʌ is not very salient. While non-autonomous clauses with nʌ do indeed have the noun characteristics of modifying following Clf' and of acting as objects of Prepositions, nʌ is optional in both cases. There are some examples that show what looks like nominalization in the classical sense of 'that which S', but they are better interpreted as Topics marked by nʌ:

(7-45) [chá lū   nʌ] ma ʔūpē
       fight each.other be.so who
       Who was it who was fighting? (227.4)

(7-46) ʔa chʌ́ nʌ thwā rū ʔa kōdó nʌ thwā thē
       3 clear become silver 3 muddy become gold
       The clear one [container of water] turned to silver, the muddy one turned to gold. (40.5)

(7-47) [pɔə   thɛ ʔiswá títí nʌ]ma ʔʌ̄ təphre kɔ
       dght.in.law go.up teach constantly be.so this one-C:hum PRMPT
       This is the one you go teach all the time, huh? (220.1)

240

And we would expect to find nominalized clauses in other functions as well, such as object (of verbs like *know, believe, see*) or subject (e.g. *That he arrived late annoys me; For John to arrive late would be surprising*). Clausal subjects seem not to occur in Kayah Li, and while clauses do occur as Direct Objects (see 8.3), they also do not require nʌ:

(7-48) nìhō ʔa ʔé mò   ʔé phē to
      hear 3 call mother call father NEG
[We] don't hear him call his mother and father. (249.6)

Setting aside for the moment the question of the nominalizing function of nʌ, let us examine some of its sentence-final uses. It is especially common in narratives, in which the following uses can be distinguished:

1. After reported speech or thought, in ʔa hé nʌ 's/he said', ʔa ne nʌ 's/he thought', where any pronoun may substitute for ʔa (see also 8.3.3). Legendary narratives are sprinkled with ʔū hé nʌ 'they say', with the indefinite/backgrounded third-person pronoun; it is often reduced to hé nʌ. Similarly in all sorts of narrative, sentences may be followed by (ʔa) me nʌ 'they did it', perhaps better rendered as 'that's what they did', or 'that's what happened'.

2. Asserting occurrence of an anticipated event. For example:

(7-49) ʔa nɔ̄ phjá dʌ́ ʔamē súba //
      3 order take give 3-wife hemp
    ʔamē rʌ phjá súba dʌ́ ʔavē nʌ
      3-wife RØ take hemp give 3-husb
He told his wife to take hemp and give it to him; his wife took some hemp and gave it to him. (480.2)

In another example, a king offers to employ the hero to guard his pumpkin garden, because, he says:

(7-50) jò ka   ʔa təmō phɛ́
        rat go:TH eat often   simply
        A rat is always coming and eating them. (467.1)

After several clauses in which the bargain is struck and the hero goes every day to guard the pumpkin garden, the rat appears:

(7-51) jò nʌ rʌ: ka   ʔe pè lū   léhēse nʌ
        rat NØ rØ: go:TH eat BEN 3:OBV pumpkin
        The rat came and ate their pumpkins. (486.2)

The first appearance of nʌ here is the Topic-marker, following jò.

    3. Restating or reformulating an event already described. E.g:

(7-52) décho lɔ̄   ʔa swá ʔa khō rʌ:sé: rē dī   sērē thʌ̄
        tell   use.up 3 friend 3 comp. RØ: prepare c.rice prepare water

        ʌ́ me aː ʔé nìː lɔ̄   rʌ́ ʔa swá ʔa khō nʌ
        NS do PTC call get use.up RØ 3 friend 3 comp.

        He told all his friends and companions; and they pre-
        pared food and drink. He called together all his friends
        and companions. (477.4)

Here the first and third sentences describe the same event, although in slightly different terms.

    What all of the above have in common is that the content of the nʌ-terminated sentence comes as no surprise: either it has already been asserted once, or it is the anticipated outcome of a preceding event. Even with the type ʔū hé nʌ, ʔa me nʌ, it is usually fairly obvious that something or other has just been said or done, and ʔū hé nʌ simply confirms that fact. Therefore the function of nʌ in these sentences is to mark the entire propositional content as having a particular information status, one that can probably be identified as a type of Given (Chafe 1970).

If autonomous clauses with nʌ are truly nominalized, as indicated previously, we could place them in the category of nominal sentence, needed independently for those sentences made up of NP's headed by lexical Nouns. The semantic connection between nominalization and assertion has been described by Matisoff in relation to the Lahu particle ve, which resembles nʌ in many respects:

> From this point of view, every verb occurring in the environment __ + ve + {,/#/Pu} would be considered 'objectified' or 'reified'. Its verbality is set up as a neutral fact, endowed with a reality like that inhering in physical objects. (Matisoff 1973, 362)

7.4 Excursus: Interrogative and Indefinite Morphemes

The interrogative morphemes include a Sentence Particle, a bound noun, and one discontinuous constituent of a compound.

Yes-no questions are signaled by the SPtc ε̄

ʔʌ̄ tənʌ̄ ʔo kō ε̄   Are you free today?

Question-word questions (WH-questions) are formed with the following question words, all but one involving the interrogative Bound Noun tē 'what'. ʔitē 'what, anything' is its Free equivalent (here again a prefix serves to allow a bound morpheme to occur on its own).

ʔitē	what?
me tē	why?
tō ú tē	where?
bɔ́ kē tē	when?
bá CLF tē	how many?
bɤ̄ tē	where? (nearby)
hú tē	how?
dɤ̄ tē tə-CLF . . . ɛ̄	which one?
ʔū . . . pē	who?

ʔū is the pronoun 'they, other people, someone', while pē, whose only function is to trigger the interrogative meaning of ʔū, must be considered a SPtc: e.g. it may follow the negative, as in ʔū mɛ́ to pē 'who doesn't look?'. Most of the other question words are analyzable:

me tē	Verb+Object 'do what = why?'
bá CLF tē	Quantifier+Classifier 'as-much-as-what clf's = how many?'
bɤ̄ tē	Preposition+Object 'at what = where?'
hú tē	Preposition+Object 'like what = how?'
dɤ̄ tē tə-CLF . . . ɛ̄	Preposition+Object+SPtc

in the last, the object of dɤ̄ is an NP consisting of N tē and Clf': 'what one-clf — which one?' (dɤ̄ here is not locative).

bɔ́ kē tē 'when?' is not analyzable. tō ú tē 'where?' is probably grammaticalized from an expression including a Resultative V-V whose second verb is tō 'strike, correct, exactly' (4.5.1), as if 'to V exactly at what?'. Cf. méthʌ ʔa tō bɤ̄ tē ~ méthʌ tō ʔa bɤ̄ tē, both 'where did [you] see him?' ú must then be a Preposition, perhaps a reduced form of mú 'at, not in sight'.

244

In terms of grammatical relations, the expressions other than ʔitē 'what' and ʔū pē 'who' can be considered to have Oblique relations of various sorts (5.5). This is natural for those interrogative expressions that are syntactically PP's, such as bɤ́ tē 'where (nearby)'; others, such as bɔ́kētē and tōútē, join some time expressions in a small category of Adverbs (5.5.3).

All of these interrogative expressions show a strong attraction to sentence-final position, which may partly be explained by that being the place in which all illocutionary force is marked. In addition, sentence-final position is also universally a position of 'focus', i.e. not the background or reference-point established by the Topic, but its complement, the portion of information to which the hearer's attention is directed. Obviously the question-word in a question is quintessentially a focus, since it is, in effect, a blank that the hearer is being asked to fill in.

WH-questions must also indicate the grammatical position of the questioned item in the clause; when that position is not one that is normally at or near the end of the clause, various measures are taken to ensure that both functions of the interrogative expression are fulfilled. Sometimes, of course, there is no conflict: interrogatives like hú tē 'how?' would, as PP's, normally be clause-final, or could at most be followed by a Clf'. me tē 'how?' is invariably sentence-final regardless of any other considerations.

ʔū . . . pē 'who' shows a neat division of labor: ʔū shows the proper grammatical position of the queried element, and pē marks the illocutionary force in the appropriate position. In a similar fashion, 'which' would probably be adequately conveyed by dɤ́ tē tə-CLF, literally 'at what one-CLF'. The addition of the question particle ɛ̄ might seem semantically redundant, but it ensures that there is an interrogative element in final position, even when the queried item is in sentence-initial Subject position:

(7-53)   dɤ́ tē   təcɤ   ʔa vī   lɤ́   ɛ̄
           at:U what one-C:kind 3 delicious more QUES
           Which kind tastes better? (29.iv)

Sometimes there is repetition of the element tē, as in:

(7-54)   ʔa síʔichē ʔitē lè   tē
           3 fear   what place.for PTC
           What is he afraid of? (29.iv)

Here the Object of síʔiche 'to fear' must be an NP headed by the abstract noun lè (6.7). Since ʔitē 'what?' is a noun, it must precede the modified head, which would leave the head lè terminating the sentence. Repetition of tē avoids this. In another example, the queried element is followed by a locative PP, again necessitating a repetition of tē:

(7-55)   ne phjá ʔitē dɤ́ klébe tē
           2s take what at:U market PTC
           What did you get at the market? (29.iv)

Finally, clauses that would have the queried element in non-final position are often recast as clause sequences, often linked by ma 'be so' (8.4). E.g. (53) above could also be phrased as:

(7-56)   ʔa vī   lɤ́ ma dɤ́ tē təcɤ   ɛ̄
           3 delicious more be.so at:U what one-C:kind QUES
           Which kind tastes better? (29.iv)

And the preferred version of (55) is:

(7-57) ne cwá dɤ́ klébe já   phjá ʔitē
       2s go   at:U market go.and take   what
       What did you get at the market? (29.iv)

This is probably the most common strategy in actual speech.

All question words may have indefinite meaning; in fact it is better to think of interrogative and indefinite as conditioned variants of a single 'meaning'. The indefinite meaning is usually triggered by the conjunction/verb ma (8.4), e.g.:

cwá bɔ́ kē tē ma rɛ́   to go whenever is good: it's good any time

(7-58) báté: ma síʔichē to ʔa be phri
      how.much be.so fear   NEG 3 must buy
      However much it is, don't be afraid, he must buy it.
      (174.2)

247

Chapter 8

Interclausal Syntax

This chapter will first sketch some of the ways in which clauses may be embedded in each other, including clauses modifying a nominal (8.1.2, 8.2) and clauses embedded as constituents of other clauses (8.1.1, 8.3); finally we will consider sequences of linked clauses, with no embedding (8.4).

8.1 Non-autonomous Nominalized Clauses

A nominalized clause is any clause followed by nʌ, or by a Clf' before which nʌ can be inserted. If the nominalized clause is autonomous (in which case there is no following Clf'), the nʌ functions as an illocutionary force-marking SPtc, as discussed above (7.3). If the clause is non-autonomous and has the following Clf', it is a preposed attributive clause; if there is no following Clf' I will simply term it an embedded clause.

8.1.1 Embedded Clauses

Embedded clauses are typically the objects of prepositions:

(8-1) bɤ̃ [Jepu hē   nʌ] ma tēú ʔo pa   mē
      at   Japan go:FH NØ be.so fish exist DUR PTC
      When the Japanese came, there were still [many] fish.
      (205.3)

(8-2) tē   təduɯ bɤ̃ [ʔa sō   né ʔa li   nʌ]
      measure go.on at:V 3 green Né 3 red NØ
      Measure up to where it's green and red. (287.4)

(8-3) ʔa dʌ láteá li   phá hú [phē ʔíro] hé nʌ
      3 give instead book skin like father sing say NØ
      He gave a hide book instead, as Father sang, it's said.
      (100.4)

PP's containing embedded clauses may occur in all the typical PP
functions: Topic as in (1), Oblique/Locative(Goal) as in (2),
Oblique/Adjunct as in (3). Note that the embedded clause in (3)
lacks nʌ; my analysis of it as nominalized rests largely on the
definition of Prepositions as taking NP objects.

8.1.2 Preposed Attributive Clauses

The idealized maximal form containing a preposed
attributive clause (AtrC) is:

P S nʌ Clf'

However, many preposed AtrC lack nʌ:

(8-4) ʔa bé rʌ̀   təba
      3 mold beforehand one-C:sheet
      the first one he made (337.5)

Since nʌ acturally occurs in only a portion of preposed AtrC, it may be better to analyze nʌ and S as alternative fillers of a Determiner position, as shown below:

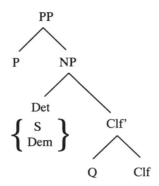

The Preposition may be omitted as well, as in the following:

(8-5) ʔa ʔe tēú təhe
      3   eat fish   one-C:group
      the ones who were eating fish (198.6)

The impression that presence or absence of nʌ is not of especially great moment is reinforced by examples like the following two, the first repeated from (4) above, the second from a later portion of the same narrative:

(8-6) ʔa bé   rʌ̀   təba   (= 8-4)
      3   mold beforehand one-C:sheet
      the first one he made (337.5)

(8-7) ʔa bé   rʌ̀   nʌ nʌ̄ ba
      3   mold beforehand NØ two C:sheet
      the first two he made (340.3)

250

The semantic relation between the AtrC and the head Clf' can usually be thought of in terms of a semantic role or syntactic position that the (referent of the) Clf' plays in the AtrC. In (5) above, the head has the Subject/Actor role; in (6) it has the Object/Undergoer role. With V_d both Direct and Indirect Object are possible:

Indirect Object

(8-8) kəjē dɤ́ ʔíphē dʌ́ lū   rūū   nʌ cwá thō ʌ́
       person at:U Father give 3OBV money NØ go   finish NS
       The person who Father gave money to has gone.

Direct Object

(8-9) ma | dɤ́ [vɛ̄ | dʌ́ pè   kʌ̄ | vɛ̄ pò ǂ pā nʌ] təbe
       be.so at:U 1s give TRN COM 1s YS   IRR NØ one-C:flat
       It's the one that I'm going to give to my brother. (11/24)

And relations occur that are even 'more oblique':

(8-10) kwā nʌ ma dɤ́ ʔa mūū lípəna kuklɔ́ nʌ təbe
       axe NØ be.so at:U 3 hit nail   head   NØ one-C:flat
       The axe is the one in whose head he pounded a nail.
       (252.1) ('the one that he pounded a nail into its head')

Here the axe's role in the AtrC might be characterized as 'possessive' or 'genitive'.

Notice that in all of the above examples the AtrC includes a Subject NP. The presence of a Subject seems quite consistent, with the notable exception of those AtrC that occur as part of a Locative expression (8.1.3 below).

As the preceding examples show, there may or may not be an element (usually a pronoun) present in the AtrC, marking the position that relates to the head, as for example ʔū 'they' in ʔū ré to təhe 'the group that's not good' (271.2). If the head relates to Subject, as in this example, there is generally a pronoun in that position in the AtrC, cf. also (5) above. If the head relates to an Object, there usually is no pronoun in that position, as in (6, 7, 9).

8.1.3 Embedded Clauses as Locatives

A distinct subtype of nominalized clause that should be mentioned occurs in Locative expressions. Most simply, and quite commonly, these are of the form $[_{PP}$ dɤ́ V $(n\Lambda)]$, where V is any of the Type B Directionals (4.2.1.2), with the probable exception of tò and təka. Usually '__ there' is a good translation:

dɤ́ thɛ nʌ   up there

dɤ́ nō nʌ   in there

dɤ́ thō nʌ   over there

These can be viewed as an abbreviation of $[$dɤ́ $[[S$ nʌ$]_{NP}$ $[$təkjā $]_{Clf'}]_{NP}]_{PP}$ where the nominalized clause S nʌ modifies a Clf' headed by kjā 'side, direction'. An extremely literal translation reflecting this analysis might be 'at the direction in which one ascends'. These embedded clauses are not, however, completely identifiable with preposed Attributive Clauses. It is true that in a few cases the Clf' is more explicit:

(8-11) dɤ́   thō   təphre

     at   go-over one-C:hum

     the person [who lives] over there (265.5)

And, since these expressions are clauses, they may contain constituents in addition to the verb:

dɤ́ lɛ Thóká hi nʌ   down there at Thoka's house
dɤ́ thɛ dɔ̄ du   up there at the big village
ʔo phɛ́ dɤ́ thɛ vī kū   it's up there in the city (369.v)

But these Locative embedded clauses differ from the usual AtrC in that they never include Subject NP's. Note also that the post-verbal NP's in the above examples are Locative in meaning but Direct Objects rather than PP's in function. In an autonomous clause the Locative expression would be a PP; e.g. 'go down to Thoka's house' would be lɛ dɤ́ Thóká hi. If that autonomous clause were embedded as object of a preposition we would have *dɤ́ lɛ dɤ́ Thóká hi; there may be some constraint against sequences of Prepositions requiring that the second dɤ́ be omitted.

Nominalized clauses that do not contain a directional verb may nevertheless have Locative meaning, as in the following, repeated from (2) above:

(8-12) tē   təduɯ bɤ́ [ʔa sō   né ʔa li   nʌ]   (= 8-2)
     measure go.on at:V 3   green Né 3 red NØ
Measure up to where it's green and red. (287.4)

But this example is better analyzed as an AtrC, since it contains Subject NP's, the two pronouns ʔa.

8.2 Postposed Attributive Clause

Kayah Li postposed attributive clauses (PsAtrC) resemble English adjectival and participial constructions more then they do English relative clauses. kəjē̄ li 'red person', dī chwí 'chilled rice', thwá kúmì thū 'long-tailed cat', thwi ʔe dī 'rice-eating dog', súplʌ cɔ̄ dɯ 'self-tying rope'. In contrast to the preposed attributive clause, the postposed type is less than a full clause, in a sense that is hard to specify (but see below). Certainly they tend to be smaller than the Preposed AtrC, very commonly consisting only of a single verb:

pɔ̄cī du	big pagoda
bē̄ʔū bū	thin cloth
dī chwí	cold cooked rice
kəjē̄ vī	driver (driving person)
lè dɛ	place to put [stg]

The postposed clause may contain other constituents:

VPtc:

(8-13) ʔīswí hɛ́ chílū

curry   hot excessive

curry that's too hot

(8-14) súplʌ cɔ̄ dɯ

rope   tie own.accord

self-tying rope [a magical object]

Obj-x:

(8-15) pənè cwī ʔīthá

buffalo pull plow

a buffalo to pull the plow

(8-16) kəjḗ chōdō mò   chōdō phē

person lack   mother lack   father

a person with no father or mother (6.vii)

Subject:

(8-17) thwá kúmì thū

cat   tail   long

cat whose tail is long, long-tailed cat

(8-18) kəjḗ bése khi

person face   dark

blind person (461.1)

V-V:

(8-19) mɔ̀   kɔ̀   rɛ́

doctor inspect good

doctor who examines well

SPtc:

(8-20) kəjḗ pā tha   pā

person cut sesame IRR

people who will harvest sesame

(8-21) kəjḗ mò   ʔo to   phē ʔo to

person mother exist NEG father exist NEG

people without mother or father

PsAtrC's tend to be distinctly shorter than their preposed nominalized counterparts, the vast majority containing at most five morphemes. The restriction is not simply on morpheme count, but (also) on structure: there are no known cases of a PsAtrC including both Subject and Object NP's, and the only cases including two NP's of any type are elicited examples in which one NP is a Clf' (NP's underlined, AtrC bracketed):

(8-22) vē mɛ́ thʌ thwá [kúmì ʔo nʌ̄ bō] təphó to
1s look see cat   tail   exist two C:long one-time NEG
I've never seen a two-tailed cat. (6.vii)

If a Subject is present in a PsAtrC, the verb is always a one-argument verb naming a state or a process; in examples above, thū 'long' and khi 'dark', cf. also kəjē rū̄ ʔo to 'a person with no money', with Subject rū̄ 'money' and state verb ʔo 'exist' (literally, 'a person whose money does not exist'). Note that although the expression bése khi 'face+dark: blind' is a lex-icalized Subject-Predicate compound, the other examples show that lexicalization is not a requirement for a Subject-Predicate expression to occur in a PsAtrC.

The abstract noun lè 'place/thing for V-ing' (6.7) takes postposed verbal modifiers that resemble PsAtrC, but are clearly VP since they cannot include a Subject.

That PsAtrC's must be treated as clauses is shown by their ability to include both Subjects and SPtc's. It is not fully clear how to account for the restrictions on their size and structure, but it is likely that the explanation involves semantic/pragmatic as well as structural factors.

Any postposed AtrC has an equivalent preposed AtrC, although the modified head must differ: noun for the former, Clf' for the latter. E.g. to refer to people driving cars we may have either kəjē vī mɔ̀rəká (postposed), ʔa vī mɔ̀rəká (nʌ) təphre (preposed), with vī 'drive' and mɔ̀rəká 'car'. The question arises of the semantic or rhetorical difference between the two. Definiteness is a factor: in this case, the preposed construction would most likely be translated with the definite article, 'the person who drives (the) car(s)'. The postposed version could have the same translation but could also be indefinite: 'a person who drives, a driver'. The postposed construction is likely to connotate purpose, as in 'a person to drive', cf. also 'buffalo to pull the plow' in (14) above, which could also be rendered 'a buffalo for pulling the plow'. A third point is that only postposed AC's are found in lexicalized compounds:

tétabō thʌ ʔo	pencil+water+exist —> pen
kəjɛ̄ li	person+red —> Kayah Li
bó ʔ ĩ	rice.plant+sticky —> glutinous rice
tē bū	fish+white —> a species of fish (not just any fish that happens to be white)
mi dā	fire+to.forge —> lighter, flint-and-steel

Lahu has a similar distinction between preposed and postposed modifying clauses; Matisoff suggests that the postposed variety ('RRC', right relative clause) 'ascribes some more or less permanent quality' (490; italics in original). However permanence is not essential in the Kayah equivalent; e.g. phre nɔ̄ 'the person ordering' can simply pick out the speaker of a command, whether or not that person is characteristically or habitually a commander. What is more important is the different types of nominals that the two types of AC modify; in particular the difference in discourse-pragmatic status between common nouns and classifiers. A unique feature of classifiers (except for time classifiers) is that

257

they cannot be used unless some antecedent (in a non-technical sense) is available, whether in the linguistic context or the real-world setting. E.g. I can use the expression ʔĀ təmē 'this one' only if some house (or some other of the types of object lexically associated with mē) is in view or has been mentioned. Classifiers, then, are 'given' or 'evoked', but in a special sense: while the common noun may have definite reference, it may also merely name a category, of which the Clf' picks out a specific instance(s) or member(s). The consequence is that preposed AC's are part of an NP that is by definition 'given', in the sense described. On the other hand an NP including a postposed AC has no particular inherent pragmatic status: it may be 'given' or not.

It is even possible to construct pairs of AC's that contrast in referential opacity:

Preposed AtrC, transparent—

(8-23) ʔa cwá mé dɛ́ cɛ̀   təchē nʌ təphre

     3s go look ride know.how elephant that one-C:human

He goes to look for that person who can ride elephants. (3.vi)

Postposed AtrC, opaque—

(8-24) ʔa cwá mɛ́ phre dɛ́ cɛ̀   təchē

     3s go look human ride know.how elephant

He goes to look for somebody who can ride elephants. (3.vi)

8.3 Clause as Argument of Verb

Some verbs may be followed by a clause functioning as Object. These verbs include méthʌ 'see'; nìhō 'hear, smell'; síʔichē 'fear'; təré 'susupect', and ŋjá 'encounter some bad event'[1]. All these verbs can take either NP or clausal Object:

(8-25) ne ʔírɛ to   chápā ma ne ŋjá   ʔíkwa ní

      2   work NEG soon   be.so 2 encounter stick   ATT

[If] you don't work you're going to encounter a stick, now! (11/9) i.e. you're going to get a beating

(8-26) ne sí   ŋjá   [lokhrɯ̄   pɔ̀] mē

      2   want encounter motorcycle bump EXCL

You're going to have a collision! (11/9)

(8-27) ʔa méthʌ [ʔū kū   ʔū sɛ́]   ʔa síjɯ kʌ̄   hú nʌ

      3 see   3i wear.lower 3i wear.upper 3 want COM like that

They see others wearing clothes and they want some like those. (274.1)

The clausal Object may or may not be preceded by the preposition dɤ́; cf. the following examples with nìhō 'hear':

(8-28) ʔa cwá nìhō kʌ̄   dɤ́ [kəjē̄ ké   təhʌ̄]   nʌ

      3 go   hear COM at:U person harvest thatch.tree NØ

They went and heard people harvesting thatch-tree [leaves]. (461.6)

(8-29) nìhō [ʔa ʔé mò   ʔé phē] to

      hear   3   call mother call father NEG

[We] don't hear him call his mother and father. (249.6)

---

[1] This recent Shan loan is considered by some to be 'not real Kayah'; however its syntactic behavior does not seem to differ from that of the other verbs listed.

The SPtc to in (29) belongs both syntactically and semantically to the matrix clause. Semantically the structure is more like 'It is not the case that we heard him call' than like 'We heard it to not be the case that he called'. The same is true for the following:

(8-30) méthʌ [Doʌ   phē ka]   to   nʌ

    see   (name) father go:TH NEG NØ

(I) haven't seen Do'a's father come back. (316.4)

(8-31) ne méthʌ mo   [Phēluídu me hú   ʔʌ̄] to

    2 see   happy (name)   do like this NEG

You are unhappy seeing P. act like that; seeing P. act like that makes you unhappy. (11/21)

Example (31) does not mean 'You are happy not seeing P. act like that', since the context makes it clear that it is a case of P. acting in some way and the addressee being unhappy about it.

However, it is also possible for these SPtc's to apply semantically to the embedded clause rather than the matrix. For example, the following is ambiguous:

(8-32) vē síʔichē [ké   cɯ] to

    1s fear   AMB   rain NEG

I'm not afraid that it will rain. (matrix clause negated)
or I'm afraid that it won't rain. (embedded clause negated)

The following shows that the same is true of Verb Particles:

(8-33) vē nìhō [pɔ̄cí ʔíbe chɯ   nɔ́ pè lū]   təphóː to

    1s hear pagoda speak confronting at.all BEN 3OBV one-C: NEG

I've never once heard the pagoda speak to him. (12.v)

Here the VPtc nɔ́ occurs in the embedded clause even though the meaning is clearly vē nìhō nɔ́ təphɔ́ to 'I've never once heard it'. (32) and (33) differ in that in (32) the matrix-clause morpheme applies semantically to the embedded clause (in the second reading) while in (33) the embedded-clause morpheme applies semantically to the matrix clause. The general point is that there is a kind of semantic permeability of the boundary between the two clauses.

This also relates to the matter of occurrence of nʌ as a nominalizer of the embedded clause. nʌ is absent from most of the examples cited; where it is present, as in (28) and (30), it could be taken either as nominalizer of the embedded clause or as illocutionary force marker of the matrix clause. Since the two syntactic positions are adjacent—

$$[\text{NP V }[\text{NP V NP SPtc}]_S \text{ SPtc}]_S$$

—there may be a sort of haplology at work, allowing only one occurrence of a given SPtc.

To disambiguate (32), the two following structures can be used:

(8-34) vē síʔichē ké   cɯ lè   to
      1s fear   AMB rain place.for NEG
      I'm not afraid of it raining.

(8-35) vē síʔichē ké   cɯ to   he
      1s fear   AMB rain NEG lest
      I'm afraid that it won't rain.

261

Example (34) also shows this semantic permeability: *to* again negates the embedded clause although it syntactically belongs to the matrix clause. Also he is a constituent of the matrix clause (recall that as a class-B SPtc, he cannot occur in a non-autonomous clause, 7.2 above), but its semantics, 'possible undesirable event', apply to the embedded clause.

Clauses do not function as Subject in Kayah Li, with the possible exception of the first of two clauses joined by the verb/conjunction ma (8.4). Constructions that might seem to have that analysis are actually clause sequences, with the first clause relating to the second in a Topic-like fashion. E.g. (clauses bracketed):

(8-36) [ʔa sítərē] seʔo kā ʔū təcɤ̀ː   to
    3   ashamed useful COM 3i one-C:kind NEG
Being ashamed isn't any use to him! (265.1)

(8-37) [bɔ́ kʌ   bɤ̀ ʔa khu nʌ né ʔa kē nʌ] twà kā né ke
    weave striped at:V 3   top NØ Né 3 base NØ pretty COM Né PRH
Weaving it striped at both ends might be pretty. (277.3)

(8-38) [ʔa ka   nɔ́ to] ʔo ʌ́ nā lē   ʌ́
    3   go:TH at.all NEG exist NS two month NS
He hasn't been back for two months. (2/20)

In the last example, one might claim that the first clause functions as Subject of the verb ʔo 'exist', i.e. 'his not coming back has existed for two months. But the anaysis is rather as a sequence 'he hasn't come back; it's been two months'. This pattern of clause sequence is discussed further in 8.4 below.

8.4 Quotatives

The pattern for reported speech (or, less commonly, reported thought) is:

$$S \; N_1 \; hé \; (rʌ́) \; N_2 \; nʌ$$

where S is a clause representing the quote, the reported speech; N_1 denotes the the speaker of the quote, the person who uttered S; hé is the verb 'say'; and N_2 denotes either the addressee of the quote or sometimes the entity that the quote is about. Examples:

(8-39) [ne chá mʌ̄ phrè tē   Sɛthɯ̄phē] ʔa hé nʌ
      2 fight sugg Shan let's (name)   3 say NØ
'Attack the Shans, Sɛthɯphe!' she said. (353.1)

(8-40) [dɔ phrē phrē tərú   ʔó chwa chwa]
      beat fast fast go.ahead blow strong strong

hé rʌ́ ʔa pòvè du lɤ̀   nʌ   təhe
say RØ 3 sibling big more that one-C:group
'Beat [the drums] fast, go ahead and blow [the flutes] loudly,' he said to his older siblings. (54.6)

(8-41) [ma sí ʔɛ ma ʔo kʌ̄ dɯ   pa təmjō
      be.so want lucky be.so exist COM own.accord DUR one-C:sort

sí   thwā ʔo kʌ̄ dɯ   pa təcɤ]
want lucky exist COM own.accord DUR one-C:kind

ʔa hé rʌ́ ʔa lʌ   nʌ
3 say RØ 3   grandchild NØ
'[You] will be lucky of your own accord; [you] will be fortunate on your own account,' he said to his grandchildren. (88.6)

263

(8-42) [chápā ʔū jɯ̀ʔe vɛ̄ to he vɛ̄ ʔo kɛ̄   dɯə   ʌ]
     soon   3i   believe 1   NEG lest 1s exist NEW.LOC own.accord PTC

ʔa ré   ne   kɑ̄   nʌ
3   should think COM NØ

He should think, 'Soon nobody will trust me and I'll be an
outcast,' (but he probably won't). (313.2)

The following has N₂ as the entity the quote is about:

(8-43) [thwākhwí] ʔa hé   kɑ̄   rʎ   ʔanè
    king   3   say   COM RØ 3-body

They called themselves kings ('king,' they said of themselves). (466.5)

To distinguish between the addressee and the entity about-which,
the following clause sequence must be used (overheard in conversation):

(8-44) hé rʎ ʔa phú hé kɑ̄   pjà ʔa phɛ̄
    say RØ 3 child say COM BEN 3 father

say something about the child to the father.

As to the syntactic analysis of this pattern, it is best seen
as a special case of clause sequence. The hé nʌ clause has some
of the feel of an 'afterthought', particularly in legendary narratives, in which virtually every sentence ends with a muttered hé
nʌ or ʔū hé nʌ. It may well be on its way to grammaticalization
as a quotative marker. Looking back to its historical source, we
may speculate that the quotative pattern is a vestige of verb-final
syntax: the quoted S would then have originally been a clausal
Object of the verb hé.

8.5 Clause Sequences and ma

ma is a verb meaning 'be so, be true'. It occurs in the criterial verb environments: ma ʌ́ 'it's so, yes', ma to 'not so, no'. There is also a more expanded pattern [X ma Y], where X and Y may be NP, PP, or S.

When both X and Y are NP's, ma has the flavor of a copula:

(8-45) ʔʌ̄ hō <u>ma</u> ʔilū   This is an Ilu. (47.1)

(8-46) bōlò   <u>ma</u> dīklwí mɔ̀ nʌ ʔa lò ʔo dɤ̌ ʔa kū   nʌ
banana.heart   banana plant NØ 3 pith have at:U 3 inside NØ
'Bo-lo' is a banana plant; the 'lo' is inside it. (298.1)

(8-47) pe <u>ma</u> kəjē̄ li   phú cé
1s   Kayah red child real
We are genuine Kayah. (lp.3)

(8-48) ne təphre   <u>ma</u> təklí ŋara phé   nʌ
2 one-C:hum   turtle sin   simply NØ
You[rs] is a sin involving turtles. (173.2)

As (48) shows, the relation between X and Y is not one of simple equation, but has a value that can only be called Topic-Comment: 'as for you, it's a turtle sin'. It is important to note that the order of X and Y cannot be reversed: X is the thing in evidence, the word to be defined, and Y is the information supplied that is relevant to X.

ma is a one-argument verb, taking Subject only. Where both X and Y are NP's, as in (45–48) above, Y is not the Direct Object of ma, but must be considered a separate nominal sentence. The clearest evidence of this is the ungrammaticality of *X ma Y to. The way to negate statements like (45–48) is Y ma to, as in the following exchange:

(8-49) A: ʔʌ ma ʔilū   B: ʔilū ma to   (*ʔʌ ma ʔilū to)

    A: This is an Ilu   B: It's not an Ilu

Therefore the proper analysis of X ma Y is [[X ma] Y].

The frequent cases in which the X element is a clause are the exception to the rule (8.3) that Kayah Li clauses cannot function as Subject: ma is the only verb that can take such clausal Subjects. Before investigating this point further, let us first consider the range of relations between X and Y when either or both are S or PP. Several subtypes can be recognized, all related in meaning:

Topic-Comment—

(8-50) thʌ̄ʔɔ nʌ <u>ma</u> kəjē ʔíjē tā phrɔ bōʌ thwā thʌ̄ʔɔ nʌ

    pond   NØ   person jump fall cave.in then become pond   NØ

The pond, now, a person jumped so that [the earth] caved in, and it became a pond. (164.5)

(8-51) Sō   ʔa phē te dɤ̆ Lɛ̄   mɔ̀khí <u>ma</u> ʔa plɛ̄ ʔà   tò

    (name) 3 father's   at:U creek dark   3 ear bite arrive

So's father's, at Dark Creek, [they] ate [everything,] even the ears [of grain]. (182.4)

Setting—

(8-52) dɤ̆ ŋjá   nʌ <u>ma</u> ʔū chá lū   nʌ

    at:U long.time NØ   3i fight each.other NØ

Long ago, they had a war. (230.2)

(8-53) dɤ̀ ʔa lē   nʌ <u>ma</u> ʔakū ʔo   rʌ́

      at:U 3 underneath NØ   hole exist RØ

Under it there was a hole. (212.2)

Antecedent-Consequent—

(8-54) vē ke pù̀ nì jòkhró tədō <u>ma</u> vē có lúlɤ̀ khɛ təkjā

      1s if catch get rat one-C:animal   1s tie dangle leg   one-C:side

If I can catch one rat, I'll tie it up hanging by one leg. (182.10)

(8-55) bó rɛ́   to <u>ma</u> ʔū   do

      rice good NEG   1s:humilific abstain

Because the crops aren't good, I'm fasting. (175.1)

Interrogative—>Indefinite—

(8-56) nɔ̄ʔe rʌ́ ʔitē <u>ma</u> rɛ́

      use RØ what   good

Whatever you use is good. (91.4)

(8-57) bá tɛ́ʼ   <u>ma</u> síʔichē to ʔa be   phri

      how.much   fear   NEG 3 must buy

However much it is, don't be afraid, he must buy it. (174.2)

The basic meaning of [[X ma] Y]] can be put as 'given X, Y is pertinent'. In all the above types the X is taken for granted, recoverable, presupposed, etc., while Y is the relevant information, the consequence. [[X ma] Y] is effectively a grammatical-ized Topic-Comment structure. In (56) and (57) question words are given an indefinite reading by their appearence in the X con-stituent of the ma- construction, which is also consistent with this basic meaning. The question word in an interrogative sentence is a non-Topic, a 'focus' virtually by definition, as mentioned in 8.3 above. Appearence in the X constituent, which is by definition 'topical', can be said to cause the question-word to have its non-interrogative meaning.

The overlap among Topic-Comment, if-then, and time-event can be seen in the English translations of the following:

(8-58) <u>ma</u> ke hé kəjē ŋē <u>ma</u> tō   síjɔ chálè phέ

       if say person part   should care.for honor simply

<u>ma</u> bó ŋē <u>ma</u> hé cὲ pa to ʌ

     rice part   say able DUR NEG PTC

If you're talking of people, they must care about honor; as for rice-plants, you can't really say [anything]. (175.5)

       or As for people . . . (Topic-Comment)

       or When it comes to people . . . (time)

The preceding example is quite typical in the multiple use of ma. Kayah Li discourse of all genres is generally peppered with this morpheme, which is one of the most common in the language, and often seems to function as little more than a pause-filler. At the same time it is quite common to encounter sequences of clauses that are simply juxtaposed, without ma or any other linking morpheme, but with the same relation as that just described for elements linked by ma. The following is an if-then sequence with simple juxtaposition (clauses bracketed):

(8-59) [jὺʔe to] [pāro   ne hē   kʌ̄   dūú]

     believe NEG tomorrow 2s go:FH COM URGE

If you don't believe [me], come with me tomorrow. (474.5)

The indefinite reading of interrogative morphemes can also be triggered without ma:

(8-60) [ʔa ʔé ʔojwā lū   bѓ tē] [ʔojwā kʌ̄   lū   to]
    3 call wait 3OBV at:V what wait COM 3OBV NEG
Wherever he called to them to wait, they didn't wait for him. (157.1; also in example 5-14))

Insofar as ma is a verb, it is the only Kayah Li verb that can take a clausal Subject, examples being the initial clauses in (54–56). However ma in such contexts has much of the quality of a conjunction, specifically one joining clause with clause or else Topic with clause. If it is a conjunction, its immediate constituency is still with the element that precedes it, i.e.:

[[S Cnj] [S]]

Classing ma in its conjunction-like use as something other than a verb allows it to join several other connective morphemes, some of which indeed are compounds that include ma, in a class of Nonfinal Particles. Among them are:

rʌ	unmarked pause (usually rʌ:, no final glottal stop)
bō ʌ~bō rʌ	and then
manɛ́	but
toíma	otherwise; if not for X, then Y
nʌíma	consequently, if . . . then
loíma	consequently, if . . . then, whenever . . . then
nɛ́kū	(similar to preceding)
nʌhō	(similar to preceding)

269

Example:

(8-61) ʔū ke phjá phe   nʌ íma kəjḗ phú nʌ ma

    3i if   take   supplanting consequently Kayah DIS   NØ be.so

    thʌ̄ kè   lɔ̄   plīchá: ʔū hé nʌ

    water country use.up completely-SH 3i say NØ

    If they took it, then the Kayah, absolutely all the countries
    [would be theirs]. (332.4)

These can be opposed to the Class B and C SPtc's, with which
they are mutually exclusive, for the most part. They are Nonfinal
in that part of their function is to signal that the clause they terminate is a nonfinal member of a sequence.

Chapter 9

Elaborate Expressions and Parallelism

9.1 Introduction

Like other languages of the mainland Southeast Asia-China area, Kayah Li makes widespread use of the four-syllable structures known as Elaborate Expressions. This term, first used by Haas (e.g. 1964) for Thai, refers to a four-part expression ABCD, in which various pairs of the component elements are linked by either phonetic or semantic parallelism or both.

Some examples of phonetic parallelism are təplotəpjā 'hurried', təvītəva~təvītəvɔ 'winding back and forth'. In the second, for example, the prefix tə- repeats to form the first and third elements, and the initial v- repeats in the second and fourth.

The parallelism is purely semantic in mi khu sɔ klē 'forest on tree among' —> 'in the forest among the trees' (274.3).

More common is the co-occurrence of both phonetic and semantic parallelism, as in hʌ le ca le 'pants+warm+shirt+warm: warm clothes', where the phonetic parallelism is the full repetition of le 'warm'. Another example is thā sú kè sá 'water + com- + land+ -plicated: country is complicated' (thākè 'water+country: country, land'; súsá 'complicated'). Here the phonetic parallelism is the repeated initial s- in the second and fourth syllables, while the semantic parallelism is the combination of 'water' and 'land' to mean 'country' (thākè also occurs as a two-syllable compound with that meaning).

In this chapter we will see that these types of parallelism are in fact operative in all sizes of structure, from disyllabic expressions to multi-clause stretches of discourse. For an exploration of parallelism as a discourse phenomenon, see Solnit 1995; in this chapter I will concentrate on outlining a typology of parallelistic structures and on suggesting the place of parallelism in the grammar.

Before proceeding, though, I will add a few words about Kayah Li discourse. Much remains to be done in studying this topic; what I set down here are impressions formed while listening to, transcribing and doing grammatical analysis of many hours of tape-recorded material. The Texts section includes examples of everyday conversation and of ordinary narrative.

There are two special genres of oral literature that should be mentioned: Donē, which recounts legendary history, and Írō, which is chanted. The first three texts in Part II of this book are examples of ordinary narrative. Text 3, the Magic Drum story does indeed deal with legendary history, but its style is not Donē. Both Donē and Írō texts are partially or wholly memorized, display extensive parallelism, are quite lengthy, and use many words that are obscure or unknown to many speakers. Tellers

vary in their knowledge of Donē narratives; some seem entirely
familiar with the plot but narrate in a more everyday style, while
others remember chunks of elaborate parallelistic clauses and
phrases but do not know the story all the way through.

A few notes on the Írō style. The singing is at the upper
end of the vocal range, in a thin, pinched-sounding voice, but not
falsetto. There are only three pitches: a middle pitch that serves
(to my ears, at least), as a tonic; an upper pitch that begins about
a major second or major third above the tonic and slides
upwards; and a lower pitch that starts about a minor third below
the tonic and slides down about a major second. I can say very
little about the content. Most speakers of my acquaintance could
understand and explain individual words and short phrases of Írō
texts, but did not manage to make me understand the overall
meaning. This genre is a topic for much further research.

9.2 Types of Parallelism in Kayah Li

Let us begin with some definitions.

Parallelism may be defined as the repetition of linguistic
features to produce binary structure. As exemplified in the Elaborate Expressions above, such features may be phonological or
semantic. I use 'semantic feature' loosely, to cover the notions of
synonymy, antonymy and the like, with no commitment to any
particular feature-based theory of semantics. Any two items that
share such repeated features are said to be linked by parallelism,
and may be called members of a couplet or couplet-partners.

From this definition it follows that reduplication is a subtype of parallelism, namely the repetition of all features of an

item. The opposite classification is also possible: some authors treat alliteration and rhyme as types of 'partial reduplication', while here I consider them to be rather subtypes of phonetic parallelism.

It is also common to simply keep (full) reduplication separate from repetition of less than the full complement of features. In particular, Elaborate Expressions are treated as distinct from reduplication by both Haas (1964, xvii) for Thai and Matisoff (1973/1982, 81–82 and footnote 47) for Lahu.

More could perhaps be said about the unity versus distinctness of these phenomena; I put them together in this chapter because they form a common theme in Kayah Li, which might otherwise be unapparent if left distributed piecemeal through the grammatical description.

9.2.1 Full Reduplication

Kayah Li makes use of reduplication as a morphological device in the sentence-final morpheme of reduplication (3.4.3). Here we may also mention two further instances, involving Classifiers:

A Clf including the Quantifier pwā may reduplicate, with the meaning 'every', as in pwā nā̄ pwā nā̄ (often with expressive high pitch on the first Clf: pwā nʌ́: pwā nā̄) 'every day, day in day out'.

Slightly different are examples like (repeated from example 5-53): ʔithɔ́ təphre təpɯ təphre təpɯ 'cover with one [blanket] per person' (272.5). This exemplifies the 'distributive' Extent expression pattern (5.5.1). But the single Clf' may repeat as well, as shown by the an interlocutor's response to the pre-

274

ceding: ʔa tɤɔ́ cɛ̀, ʔithɔ́ phɛ́ təpɯ təpɯ ʔa tɤɔ́ cɛ̀ 'that's effective, covering just one by one is effective' (272.6).

9.2.2 Other Types, Including Elaborate Expressions

We now turn to parallelism that repeats less than the full complement of features. Two types can be recognized, of which the second includes Elaborate Expressions.

9.2.2.1 Type A: Derived, with No Syntactic Structure

This type has the following four characteristics:

1. It is always in four parts.

2. It has no internal syntactic structure.

3. The pattern is consistently ABAC; i.e. the first and fourth parts are identical.

4. The phonological patterning suggests that many of these expressions can be analyzed as derivationally related to the part C morpheme.

In the following examples, the four-part expression is followed by those of its component parts that are identifiable from other contexts, or that seem otherwise relevant:

(9-1) kɛ́kīkɛ́kwa 'V stg long so part remains'; cf. kwa (Clf) 'half', kɛ́kwa (V) 'be in half crosswise, on short axis'.

(9-2) təvītəvaa~təvītəvɔ 'winding back and forth'; cf. vī 'wind up, twist', va 'stir', təva 'around, encircling', vɔ 'around, circumventing'.

(9-3) təplotəpjā 'hurried'. No occurrence of smaller pieces (pjā 'bag', təpjā 'shoot a bow', plo se k. of fruit).

(9-4)   təlwātəpè 'run, hurry, rush around' (180.2). Cf. perhaps lwā 'to shuttle in weaving'.

(9-5)   tatītatè~tatūtatè 'unclear, halting (speech)'; cf. tè 'V the wrong one' (Movable Dscr Pv), sətè 'suppose wrongly', tātè 'unskillfully'.

(9-6)   kənīkōnò 'to play', cf. kōnò 'play'.

(9-7)   təkī təka~təkū təka 'winding, curving', ka 'go towards home', təka 'curved, hooked'.

(9-8)   təvátədā 'misfortune from wrong actions', cf. təpatəva 'do what one knows one shouldn't', me tədā súí 'do stg wrong'.

(9-9)   Possibly the ethnic designations kúlí kulā, pəkū pəkhrō, khómú khómé. The meanings of these Elaborate Expressions are unclear, but kulā means 'Westerner, European' and pəkū is 'Sgaw Karen' (cf. the Karen group known as Paku or Pakü).

Note that the four parts are either four full syllables, as tatītatè, or two prefix+syllable pairs, as təkī təka.

The lack of syntactic structure in type A contrasts with type B, to be described momentarily. To see this, consider, from the preceding list, kənīkōnò 'to play': there are no grammatical relations (modification, predication) holding between any of the parts. Contrast an example of the type B, hʌ le ca le 'warm clothes'. Here hʌ 'pants' and le 'warm' form an NP with hʌ as head and le as modifier. This grammatical relation between the first two items is then repeated in the second pair ca le 'warm shirt'. No such grammatical relations hold between any of the parts of such type A examples as təplotəpjā 'hurried', kənīkōnò 'to play'. In this type the whole expression is either a Verb or a Verb Particle (Descriptive?). In the pattern ABAC, the last part C or last unit AC is in many cases also an independent morpheme of related meaning.

As to the phonological parallelism, not only is the pattern ABAC, there is also a strong tendency for the initials of B and C to be similar or identical, and for the vowel of B to be high, mostly /i/ with a few /u/ (but no /ɯ/). This phonological patterning suggests that many of these can be analyzed as derivationally related to the part C morpheme. For those with high vowels in the B syllable we can posit a derivational rule which may either produce a 'new' morphemic component or sanction occurrence of an independently existing morph like vī in təvītəva. One way of handling this would be as a preposed derivational morpheme of the shape $/C_1VC_2i/$, where C_1 and C_2 copy the corresponding elements of a following C_1VC_2V. This is only a sketch of a possible analysis, and leaves much unexplored, such as the assignment of tones to the CVCi morpheme.

I will nevertheless use 'derived' as a label for this type of parallel structure.

9.2.2.2 Type B: Underived, with Syntactic Structure

These are of all sizes, from disyllabic to paired clauses. The structure is in all cases binary, the number of syllables being 2n where n≥1.

In the following examples, items that occur only in parallel expressions are glossed X.CP, for 'Bound couplet-partner of X' (e.g. ʔehí occurs only in parallel expressions with ʔeho 'steal', so is glossed 'steal.CP' in expressions like ʔeho ʔehí 'steal+steal.CP: steal and pilfer'):

Disyllabic word. hʌ 'pants' + ca 'shirt' = hʌca 'clothes'; súsá 'complicated' (not analyzable)

Two prefixed syllables. ʔamò ʔaphē 'pfx+mother+pfx+father: parents'

Two disyllabic compounds. ʔeho ʔehí 'steal+steal.CP'; ʔokhrɛ́ ʔotɛ̀ 'orphaned+orphaned.CP'

Four full syllables. hʌ le ca le 'pants+warm+shirt+warm: warm clothes'; bo phú mō mē 'nourish+child+feed+wife: support a family'; thʌ̄ sú kè sá 'water+com-+land+-plicated: country is complicated' (thʌ̄kè 'water+country: country, land'; súsá 'complicated')

Repetition of [pfxd syll + single syll]. ʔiswá li ʔiswá la 'study+book+study+book.CP: study'

Repetition of [disyllabic compound + single syllable]. síplɔ du sothʌ̄ thū 'heart+big+gall+long: angry'

Three pairs of full syllables. khé sʌ̄ pā sʌ̄ pɔ̀ sʌ̄ 'shot to death, cut to death, collided to death' (256.4)

Four pairs of full syllables. kəjē [ʔokhrɛ́ ʔotɛ̀ ʔolɤ́ ʔoklɔ̄] 'orphans, solitaries, without families or relatives' (267.2)

Two units of three full syllables each. vē hʌ jē vē kē mɯ '1s+pants+ragged, 1s+blanket+ragged.CP: my pants are ragged, my blanket is tattered' (478.4)

Longer structures. pe [pò ʔo rò vè ʔo ʔé] 'our younger.sib-
lings exist plurally, older.siblings exist many'; mɔ̀ lɛ hé ʔa
domé lū ʔiplí sɔsō, mɔ̀ lɛ tā domɛ lū ʔimū sɔplɔ 'at
evening they showed him a greenwood whip, at sundown
they showed him a seedwood switch' (450.4)

Phonetic parallelism is common in type B, though not
required, as shown by bo phú mō mē 'support a family'. Phonetic parallelism can be illustrated by ʔeho ʔehí 'steal+steal.CP',
which has full repetition in the first and third syllables, and alliteration in the second and fourth.

As mentioned previously, expressions of this type with
four syllables or more (n≥2) have grammatical structure. For four
syllables ABCD, the first two items AB bear a grammatical relation to each other, such as Verb-Object or Modifier/Head, which
is repeated between the third and fourth items CD. Examples:

Expression	gloss	Repeated grammatical relation
hʌ le ca le	pants warm shirt warm	Sbj-Pred
bo phú mō mē	feed child nourish wife	V-Obj
pe swá pe khō	our companions our friends	Modifier-Head
te súi te plú	things wrong things bad	Head-Modifier
klɛ sʌ̄ klɛ ʔo	run die run live	V-V (Resultative?)

There are some distinctions between two-syllable expressions and all other sizes of this type. At the 2-syllable level, some
pairs of parallelistically linked morphemes may occur, as hʌca
'clothes', but others may not, such as those in bo phú mō mē
'feed child support wife', which has no corresponding *phúmē

279

or *bomō. Disyllabic occurrence does seem to be ruled out for pairs including CP members; e.g. we have ʔiswá li ʔiswá la 'study', but not *lila. Another difference is that pairs occurring as disyllables seem not to exhibit any phonological parallelism, but phonological parallelism is common in expressions occurring at the 4-part level and up.

Patterns. For four-part expressions, the basic pattern is $A_IB_JC_ID_J$, where subscribed indices identify items linked by parallelism. Variants are achieved by having one or the other of the linked pairs be a case of full repetition, either A=C or B=D. Some examples:

$A_IB_JC_ID_J$, all four distinct

(9-10) síplɔ du sothʌ̄ thū   'heart+big+gall+thick —> angry'

(9-11) mi khu sɔ klē   'forest+on+tree+among —> in the forest among the trees' (note the usual expression is mi klē 'in the forest')

$A_IB_JC_ID_J$ where A=C

(9-12) ʔiswá li ʔiswá lā   'learn+book+learn+book(cp) —> study, teach' cf. liʔú 'book'

sí the sí hā   'heart+ascend+heart+bad(?) —> envious, resentful'

(9-13) dɤ̃ là dɤ̃ cho   'at+cliff+at+mountain —> in the mountains'

$$A_I B_J C_I D_J \text{ where } B=D$$

hʌ le ca le   'pants+warm+shirt+warm —>
warm clothes'

For larger expressions, one can still distinguish those made up entirely of parallelistic pairs from those involving some repetition; for the latter it seems of little use to specify exactly which constituents are repeated, but one may count the number of non-repeated, parallelistic pairs (members of pair underlined):

(9-14) One:

ʔo dɤ̌ <u>sɔ</u> kū tā the nɔ́ to   ʔo   <u>ve</u> kū tā the nɔ́ to
'doesn't fall out of a tree   doesn't fall out of bamboo'

(9-15) Two:

dɤ̌ <u>klúi</u> du sō <u>mē</u>   dɤ̌ <u>kəlō</u>   sō <u>khri</u>
'on three big knolls   on three hills'

(9-16) Three:

<u>cho</u> sō cho pe sí <u>ʔílū</u> cho <u>cūi</u>
'three hills we want to combine as one

<u>dɔ̄</u> sō dɔ̄ sí <u>cūi</u> lū dɔ̄ <u>tùi</u>
three villages we want to join as one'

(9-17) All:

hē̄ ʔe tɯ   ka ʔō plɔ
'go eat in groups'   'come drink in herds'

Notice that the syntactic parallelism simply concatenates, producing strings of identical constructions such as [N V]$_{NP}$ [N V]$_{NP}$ . . . etc. On the other hand the lexical parallelistic linkage alternates: in $A_IB_JC_ID_J$, A goes with C and B goes with D as lexical (semantic) parallels. This produces interlocking relations: $[A_I \ B_J][C_I \ D_J]$. The two aspects of parallelism can be displayed as 2-dimensional matrix:

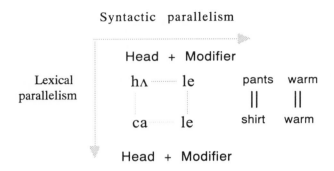

This is what is at work in longer expressions, up to and including the multi-clause parallelism of Donē style. E.g. repeating (14) above:

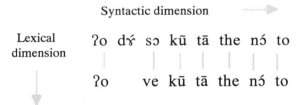

9.3 Place of These Expressions in the Grammar

9.3.1 General

Unstructured-derived 4-part EE's are lexical items, to many of which can be added an account of derivation from a base morpheme, as indicated above. There is no obstacle to listing them as lexical entries, with cross-reference to the listings of component items when identifiable. The underived type, with its many possible sizes and patterns, requires a more complex analysis. I do not advocate taking one size of these expressions as basic and deriving the others from it by expansion or reduction. They are not derived in the usual sense, but arise from the interaction between the principles of parallelism on one hand and the usual components of the grammar on the other.

9.3.2 Underived Are Not Expansions/Contractions of Each Other

For an analysis of structured parallelistic expressions as derived from some basic form, the contenders for that base-form would seem to be disyllabic words like hʌca and four-part expressions like ʔiswá li ʔiswá la.

Disyllabic words might seem to be a natural place to list any special semantics not derivable from simple juxtaposition of meanings, as in perhaps thʌ̄kè 'country', dī̃ʔiswí 'cooked.rice+ curry: food'. Larger structures could then be derived by expansion, inserting additional material either preceding or following the two base items. But a great many parallelistically linked items do not occur as disyllabic words; one would then have to posit 'underlying' words that exist in the lexicon but are never realized as such. For example:

> *phúmē 'child+wife' realized in bo phú mō mē 'feed child support wife'
> *lila 'book+book.CP' realized in ʔiswá li ʔiswá la 'study'

Deriving two-part from four-part expressions has the opposite problem: many, perhaps all couplets are not confined to occurrence with any particular other pair. E.g. thʌkè 'water+ country: land' would be analyzed as an abbreviation of which of the following? pe thʌ pe kè 'our land', ne thʌ ne kè 'your land', Ɂa thʌ Ɂa kè 'his/her/their land', thʌ sú kè sá 'land is complicated', and so on. The only possibility would be to posit an abstract form like (W)thʌ(X)(Y)kè(Z), which would have to be accompanied by stipulations about the realization of W . . . Y and X . . . Z, to ensure that one or the other is realized but not both, and that the fillers of the slots have the required parallelism.

9.3.3 Parallelism as Lexical and Syntactic Attribute

All grammatically structured parallelistic expressions can be accounted for by two mechanisms:

a. parallelism as a relation between lexical items.

b. parallelism as an attribute of syntactic structures.

9.3.3.1 The Lexical Aspect

Items that occur with linkage by parallelism such as hʌ and ca, thʌ and kè, are best listed in the lexicon with that information as part of the lexical entry. CP items like la of (Ɂiswá)li (Ɂiswá)la 'study' or hí of Ɂeho Ɂehí 'steal' would have no further information in their entries. If the paired items occur with no additional material, as a two-syllable word, that word would have its own listing, which would be the place for any special semantics. Finally, the lexical entries must specify the order of paired items, since it is always the same. There is a partial regularity if one is Free and one is Bound, namely the Free item usually comes first:

jò . . . thu 'rats . . . birds'

súí . . . plá 'wrong . . . wrong.CP'

But there are exceptions:

mi . . . sɔ 'forest . . . woods' (mi normally only in te mi 'thing+forest: wild animals' and a few other expressions, such as dɤ́ mi klē 'in the forest')

In this view, the relation between lexical items that are linked by parallelism is similar to the relation between nouns and their associated classifiers, a matter of cross-referencing.

9.3.3.2 The Syntactic Aspect

I conceive of parallelism as a possible attribute of syntactic structures, which might be notated as a feature, perhaps marked on the head consituent. Below I will sketch a few of the ways in which syntactic structures with this attribute differ from those without. I will refer to the latter—structures without parallelism—with the term 'ordinarily'.

One special characteristic of parallelistic syntactic structures is that they allow the Free occurrence of ordinarily Bound morphemes. Examples:

(1) The word for 'bird' in general is normally thuú. But it occurs as thu in:

(9-18) jò bá   dō   thu bá   be tē   ma
     rat how.many C:animal bird how.many C:flat what be.so
     However many rats, however many birds . . . (178.6)

Similarly in ma sí ʔɛ jò ɛ́ ma sí ʔɛ thu 'have the luck of mice and birds' (79.3). Ordinarily the names of birds are thu+X, as thu tò 'drongo', thu thwaə 'bulbul', thu tōú 'bee-eater', while 'bird' in general is thuú with the diminuitive/instantiating suffix phú~hú~ú.

(2) thʌ̄ sú kè sá 'the land is complicated, the country is troubled'. Ordinarily súsá is an unanalyzable compound.

(3) The word for blanket is usually ʔikē, but it occurs without the prefix in vē hʌ jē vē <u>kē</u> mɯ 'my pants are ragged, my blanket is tattered' (478.4).

(4) The following is from a Kèkhu Donē̄:

(9-19) təkō   lū   hú chāmò bē,   təke lū   hú chāmò hó
    grudge 3OBV like hen   yellow grudge 3OBV like hen   brood
[His parents] begrudged him like a yellow hen, begrudged him like a brooding hen. (450.3)

təko is ordinarily Bound, occurring only in parallel with təke, but here it is head Verb of its own clause. For təke as main V, cf. ʔa mòphē təke (rʌ́) ʔa phú dī 'his parents begrudged their child rice' (17.iv).

(5) khɛ dá plā kè 'leg+broken.off+arm+snapped: with uneven limbs' (94.6). Both the first and the fourth item would normally not appear on their own. Normally the first expression would be khēdo dá (found in the Elaborate Expression khēdo dá bése khí 'lame and blind'); khɛ~khē is usually Bound, as in khēdo 'lower leg', khēkʌ 'thigh' and khɛmā 'knee' (see 3.4.2). For the second expression, the verb (4th item) would normally be lɛkè, i.e. plā lɛkè 'broken arm'; the Verb ke is normally Bound, occurring in lɛkè 'be broken-off' or with more specific first verbs

like jó 'bend stg' (jóke 'bend stg so it breaks') or khéjìlɛkè 'step-trample-break off'.

A second characteristic is that parallelism allows the intrusion of Nouns into the Verb Complex. An ordinary VC cannot contain a Noun, with exceptions only for the four 'incorporating' morphemes (4.4.3) Contrast [ʔiswá li ʔiswá lā nó]$_{VC}$ to 'not study at all': this VC, terminated by the VPtc nó, includes no incorporating morphemes but contains two Nouns: li 'written matter' and lā, the CP of li.

Chapter 10

Dialects, Position in Karen, and Orthographies

10.1 Introduction

The aim of this chapter[1] is to summarize all currently available linguistic data on the dialects of Kayah Li. Since nothing remotely like a survey of the Kayah area has been done, and will not be—pending substantial political change in Burma—the coverage is extremely spotty, and much of what I say must be regarded as provisional. All of the data on Kayah Li of Burma cited in this chapter has been recorded with the assistance of refugees along the Thai-Burmese border.

This chapter deals largely with phonology. I state inter-dialect correspondences in terms of proto-Karen as outlined by Haudricourt (1946, 1953, 1975; see also Mazaudon 1985). The reconstructed system of initial consonants and tones, and their

---

[1] A slightly different version of this chapter, entitled 'Kayah Li Dialects', was presented at the 24th International Conference on Sino-Tibetan Languages & Linguistics, October 1991, Bangkok.

288

subsequent interaction are very much like those of Tai, relevant exceptions being: (1) the proto-Karen tone system has a two-way contrast in unchecked syllables (Tai has three); (2) the split according to initial consonant type may in Karen produce or add phonation contrasts as well as tones.

In displaying the tonal reflexes of modern dialects, I use an arrangement like that first used by Haudricourt, similar to the above chart, and found in many studies of Tai tonology. I label the original tones A and B,[2] with D standing for the originally atonal checked syllables that acquired a tonal contrast along with the tone split of checked syllables. I also use A1 A2 etc. for the modern categories conditioned by voiceless/glottalized (added numeral 1) and voiced (added numeral 2) initials. As an example, the tone system of Lower Eastern Kayah Li, the language described in this grammar, is as follows:

	A	B	D
ph, p, ɓ>b, m̥>m	33/ā/	22/a/	55/á/
b>p, m	22/a/	21ˀ /à/	33/a/

Modern reflexes are arranged horizontally according to proto-tone category, indicated by A B D across the top, with vertical arrangement according to the proto-initial laryngeal types that conditioned splits and mergers. These laryngeal types are labeled down the left edge of the chart, with labials standing for all points of articulation. Simply giving the proto-initial laryngeal category

---

[2] Haudricourt's (1975) third proto-tone (Mazaudon's B') has in Kayah reflexes that are identical with those of tone D1 (the reflex conditioned by non-voiced initials).

means that particular category remains unchanged in the modern language (thus ph means that proto-voiceless unaspirated stops remain voiceless unaspirates). b>p and the like give the proto-form on the left and its modern reflex on the right. Both the phonetic value and the notation used herein are given for each prosody. Pitch is written using the Chao five-level pitch scale (1 lowest, 5 highest) and breathy phonation is indicated by a subscribed pair of dots, e.g. /ạ/. The notation used when citing words is given in slanting brackets and attached to the arbitrary vowel symbol /a/.

The following table, adapted from Mazaudon 1985, shows the equivalent tone and initial categories in the correspondence sets of Luce (1959) in roman numerals, followed by comma and the reconstruction of Jones 1961:

proto-initials	proto-tones			
	*A	*B	B'	*D
voiceless aspirate	III, `h (asp)	VI, ´q (asp)	Va	VIII, ´?
voiceless unaspirate and glottalized	II, `'	VIa, ´q	V, `h	VIII, `h
voiced	I, `' (asp)	IV, ´' (asp)		VII, `?

10.2 General Picture, Situation of Kayah in Karen

Clear enough boundaries, both linguistic and cultural, could in principle be drawn for Kayah on the east, north and south. On the west, according to Lehman, there is no discernible linguistic frontier:

> ... The present Kayah or Red Karen dialects form a continuous chain of mutually intelligible neighbors stretching from ... Thailand westward to Kyèbogyi, and the latter dialect is virtually identical with that of the Manumanaw ... Indeed, there are villages in these low foothills that are indifferently identified by both sides as either Manumanaw or Kayah, and traditional Kayah costume is a variant of Manumanaw, or vice versa. (Lehman 1979, 223–4)

Manumanaw is the Burmese name for people who call themselves /manə/ (Lehman's transcription, tones not given), meaning 'west' or 'westerner', cf. Eastern Kayah (Huai Dya) /lɛ̄ bɛ́ nō/ 'the western region'. Lehman goes on to say that Manumanaw 'is mutually intelligible with' so-called Southern Brè, which is definitely not Kayah. Note, however, that Lehman reports of the Southern Brè that

> Several villages in the eastern foothills, next to Kayah, speak a dialect very like Brè, but dress like Kayah and call themselves Kayah. (Lehman 1967b, 67)

The foregoing is intended to convey just a sample of the complexity of the ethnolinguistic situation in Western Kayah state. Given such complexity, the following two phonological criteria can only hope to set off Kayah from other *known* Karen languages:

291

1. Kayah preserves certain *velar+liquid initial clusters which in most other Karen are represented by fricatives/ affricates. Examples:

	Western Kayah	Pa-O	Pho	Sgaw
bone	krwí	chút	xwî	xí
dry	krā	sèŋ	xên	xê

2. Kayah has undergone a general raising of vowels, including (Eastern Kayah reflexes) *a > e, *e > i, *o > u. Examples:

	Eastern Kayah	Pa-O	Pho	Sgaw
bitter	khe	khá	khâ	khâ
fire	mi	mé	mê	mê ʔú
child	phú	pò	phô Tâ	phó Tâ

Proto-Karen high vowels have also shifted in Kayah; reflexes will be discussed below.

Kayah in other respects resembles most other Karen languages. All final consonants have dropped; even the final glottal stop occurring as a tonal feature in Kayah has no relation to older final oral stops, unlike the case in e.g. Pho and Sgaw, where final glottal stop is the reflex of all proto-Karen final oral stops. Older initial laryngeal features have given rise to laryngeal prosodies, including both tone split and contrastive phonation type (cf. Solnit 1989).[3] I will now turn to the dialects themselves.

---

[3] These general Karen characteristics of course have exceptions: final nasal consonants are preserved to differing extents in Pa-O, Padaung and Pho (the latter taking the form of vowel nasalization); and the proto-Karen laryngeal contrasts are preserved for initial stops in Blimaw Bwe (Henderson 1961 and 1979 'Western Bwe').

10.3 The East-West Divide

The primary division among Kayah dialects is between East and West, with the boundary following the line of either the Pun or the Salween river. This is noted by Lehman ('variation is from west to east' [1967, 110]), and is the view of the Kayah themselves, who divide their country and their language into /lɛ̄ bɛ́ the/ 'the East' and /lɛ̄ bɛ́ nō/ 'the West' (citations are Eastern Kayah Li as described in this book, unless otherwise noted). In the following sections I will describe the speech Ma Khraw Shie, Kayah State, Burma, as representative of Western; then compare it with the Eastern variety that is the subject of this book. I choose these two dialects because I have the best data on them; in addition, Ma Khraw Shie is linguistically and geographically very close to Kyèbogyi, mentioned in the citation from Lehman above and of some socio-historical importance.

10.3.1 Western: mā khrɔ̄ shié

/mā khrɔ̄ shié/, called Maphrowshi in Lehman 1967b (i.e. /má phrɔ shié/; informants also cite /má pǝshié/), is 15 minutes travel west of Kyèbogyi, Kayah State, Burma. The language is virtually identical to that of Kyèbogyi, according to the principal informant. Kyèbogyi is a large village which is the center of one of the Kayah Li statelets (Karenni States, in older terminology). Lehman 1967b contains much ethnographic data recorded in Kyèbogyi. The segmental inventory is as follows:

293

p	t	c	k	ʔ	pl	pr	i	ɯ	u
ph	th	sh	kh		kl	kr	ie	ɯə	uo
b	d						e	ə	o
m	n		ŋ				ɛ	a	ɔ
	θ			h					
w	l						iu	ui	ia
	r	ᵶ							

Below is the pitch/phonation system, arranged in terms of its proto-Karen antecedents:

	A	B	D
ph, p, ɓ>b, m̥>m	33 /ā/	11 /a/	55 /á/
b>p, m	11 /a̠/	45 /á̠/	33 /ā̠/

The symbols generally have standard (IPA) values, with the following points to be noted:

1. /c sh/ are alveo-palatal [tɕ ɕʰ] before high vowels and alveolar [ts sʰ] before non-high. /sh/ has less aspiration in the former case.

2. /θ/ sometimes and for some speakers verges on /s/.

3. /ŋ/ has the allophone [ŋʲ ~ ɲ] (fronted velar or palatal nasal) before front vowels and glide /j/. Otherwise it is velar [ŋ].

4. /ie ɯə uo/ are falling diphthongs, the second element being quite weak, except in /ɯə/ after the apical (af)fricates /c sh/, in which case the offglide is more prominent. In /iu ui ia/

the two components are about equal in duration and intensity.[4] The second component of /iu/ is midway between IPA /u/ and /o/.

5. Note that the tone system (or better, laryngeal prosody system) can be treated as the intersection of a three-way pitch contrast and a 2-way phonation contrast. The pitches of the high level (modal) 55 and the high rising (breathy) 4̱5̱ tones may then be seen as conditioned variants of a single high tone.

6. Phonation is contrastive only after sonorants and voiceless unaspirated stops.

7. All syllable types may end in glottal stop in isolation.

8. The foregoing applies to full syllables; these may be preceded by prefixes, written directly before the main syllable with vowel /ə/ as in Eastern.

10.3.2 West and East Compared

Initials. The phonological systems are virtually identical, but there are two salient phonetic differences.

1. Stop+liquid clusters in Western are uniformly unaspirated /pl pr kl kr/, while Eastern has aspiration conditioned by the medial /pl phr kl khr/. Aspiration in clusters thus remains noncontrastive in both.

2. Eastern /c ch/ lack the allophonic variation exhibited by their Western counterparts /c sh/.

---

[4] This corrects an error in Solnit 1989, which omitted /iu/, and stated that all diphthongs had equal components. I have also changed /w j/ to /u i/ in diphthongs since they are more vowel-like than glide-like.

Vowels. Viewed synchronically, Western is notable for the diphthongs /ie ɯə uo/, a symmetrical set of three high vowels each followed by a very slight glide one step downwards in the vowel space. In Eastern we may remark on the three back unrounded vowels /ɯ ɤ ʌ/. While it is quite common for languages in mainland Southeast Asia to include the two /ɯ ɤ/, the presence of a third such vowel is somewhat unusual. Etymologically the following correspondences are evident, with Western given to the left, Eastern to the right:

W=E	W=E	W=E
ie=ʌ	ɯə=o	uo=wa
i=i	ɯ=ɯ	u=u
e=e	ə=ɤ,ɯ	o=o
ɛ=e		
ia=ɛ	a=a	ɔ=ɔ
ia=ja	wi=wi	

The pairs /ie=ʌ/ and /ɯə=o/ correspond to simple high vowels in other Karen (I limit consideration to proto-Karen open syllables):

	W.Kayah	E. Kayah	Pa-O	Pho	Sgaw
water	thiē	thʌ̄	thì	thì	thí
two	niē	nʌ̄	nì	nì	khí
rat	ʑɯə̰́	jò	jû	jú	jỳ
thread	lɯə	lo	lú	lû	lỳ

296

This seems to be the top end of the Kayah vowel raising: original high vowels had nowhere to raise to, so instead broke to diphthongs in Western, then monophthongized at the mid level in Eastern.

Tones. The correspondences are straightforward. Eastern has no trace of the phonation contrast, merging those categories that are distinguished only by phonation in Western, namely A1 with D2, and A2 with B1. The difference between the two B2 tones is striking: Western high rising breathy and Eastern low falling creaky are opposite in every respect.

Prefixes. Western does not have tonal dissimilation of the prefix ʔi-, which is always low-level tone. Eastern ʔíchē 'sell' and (sí)ʔichē 'afraid', distinguished only by prefix tone, are in Western are distinguished by main vowel rather than prefix: /ʔiɕʰɛ̄/ 'sell', /(θɛ)ʔiɕʰē/ 'afraid'. The Cə- type of prefix does not exhibit vowel harmony in Western.

10.4 Other Dialects

10.4.1 Upper Eastern

The Kayah in Thailand recognize a difference in speech between /kè khu/ 'upper' and /kè kɛ̄/ 'lower'[5], the boundary corresponding approximately to an east-west line drawn through Mae Hong Son town. I have no idea how this division corresponds to the situation on the Burmese side of the border. Huai Dya, described in this book, is Lower. My Upper material is from

---

[5] /kè/ 'country', /khu/ '(on the) upper surface', /kɛ̄/ '(down on the) lower inner surface'.

the village of Huai Pong, Thai /hûaj pòoŋ/, Kayah /mē lē̄/, not far from the town of Mok Cham Pae /mɔ̀ɔk cam pɛɛ/.

Two differences between Upper and Lower are noteworthy. One is that the Upper counterpart of the Lower high-falling tone (52) is a suffix /u^{52}/; that is, Upper preserves segmental features of the suffix that Lower is realized as tone only (high falling). Cf. the following, including reflexes from Western, which lacks this suffix:

	Lower East	Upper East	West
OTTER	cɔ́ kəre^{52}	cɔ kɛrɛu^{52}	cɔ́ kərī̠
BAT	təple^{52}	təpleu^{52}	plɛ́
SHRIMP	chi ko^{52}	—	si kɔ̠́

Western attests the etymological tone that has been pre-empted in both Eastern dialects: D2 for OTTER, D1 for BAT, B2 for SHRIMP.

The second noteworthy difference is that Upper shows no split of proto-tones A and B:

	A	B	D
ph, p, ɓ>b, m̥>m	33	11	55
b>p, m	33	11	33

But the D 'tone' has split; or rather, since the syllables labeled D were originally atonal syllables with final stop, they have lost final consonants, acquired contrastive tone, and split that newly acquired tone under the influence of the initials, not necessarily in that order. The fact that the D tone has split (to put it in shorthand) suggests that, contrary to appearances, A and B have indeed split, then re-merged. This is an unlikely scenario, but it seems equally improbable that checked (D) syllables have split and unchecked have not. I know of no such case among the hundreds of languages showing tone splits (cf. the dozens of Thai dialects in Brown 1985).

10.4.2 Three Htopu Dialects

In this section I will sketch out some features of three dialects, all located on a plain that centers on a lake known as Htopu on available maps, located between Kyèbogyi and the Pun river, and about 3–5 kilometers northeast of Bawlakè. By singling out this small area, which I arbitrarily name after the lake, I do not mean to claim that it is more important than any other Kayah-speaking area, linguistically or otherwise, but the data is worth presenting as a sample of the linguistic diversity within Kayah, and it includes some phonologically interesting syllabic fricatives. Data on two of the three dialects is from Bennett 1991, which contains more extensive description and examples. Bennett reports that these three village dialects 'are generally recognized by other Kayah speakers as the most difficult to understand'.

The dialects are those of three villages:

village	abbreviation	data source
dɔ ŋe khu	DNK	my notes
dɔ təma	DTM	Bennett 1991
dɔ sɔ pja	DSP	Bennett 1991

I have recorded these names in Eastern Kayah pronunciation as /dɔ ŋē khu/[6], /dɔ təmá/ and /dɔ sɔ pjá/, but I am uncertain of the relation of the tones to those of the pronunciation in the dialects in question. It is at least clear that dɔ in all three is 'village'.

Vowels. The three high vowels /i ɯ u/ found in other Kayah dialects have in DNK and DTM raised even farther, becoming syllabic consonants, or perhaps fricated vowels.[7] In DSP only /u/ has undergone this raising. I now quote Bennett's descriptions of the three DTM syllabic fricatives:

r   retroflexed apical alveolar fricative

ʁ̣   phonetically similar to ɣ, but weakly constricted towards ɣ or ʁ near the end

ʋ   labiovelar syllabic fricative

My own less precise impressions of the DNK equivalents are largely identical. I would add that DNK ʐ̣ , which corresponds to DTM r, may resemble ʁ̣ in sounding more vocalic at its beginning and consonantal towards the end, the vocalic stretch having an ɨ -like quality.

In the following examples, DNK forms are listed in narrow transcription (tones excepted) followed by Eastern cognates. Note that the raising of the three high vowels applies to simple (monophthong) rhymes only, e.g. 'dog' is /thwí/, segmentally the same as in all other Karen.

---

6 Literally 'village'+'ahead, front'+'upper surface'. /ŋē/ here is said to mean 'flat ground', thus 'village on the flats'.

7 Palaychi (Jones 1961) is another Karen language with syllabic consonants.

<u>i</u> reflexes   <u>ɯ</u> reflexes   <u>u</u> reflexes

tɕȵ̩ = ci 'left (side)'   tɕʁ̩ = cɯ 'to rain'   tɕɣ̍ = cu 'scar'

sʰȵ̩ = chi 'chop up'   sʰʁ̩ = chɯ 'body hair'   sʰɣ̍ = chu 'plug' (N,V)

kʰɹ̥ȵ̩ = khrì 'packbasket'   kʰɹ̥ʁ̩ = khrɯ   kʰɹ̥ɣ̍ = khru 'firewood'
                            'mushroom'

mȵ̩ = mi 'fire'   ʔìdʁ̩ = ʔídɯ 'knife'   plɣ̀ = plú 'to punch'

plȵ̩ = plí 'whip'

Note that, as in Eastern, the medial /r/ in 'packbasket', 'mushroom' and 'firewood' is devoiced by the preceding aspiration.

     Other vowel reflexes are as in the chart below, repeated from above with DNK, DTM and DSP added (DTM and DSP reflexes from Bennett op.cit.). 'Western' is /mā khrɔ̄ shié/, 'Eastern' is Huai Dya.

Western	Eastern	DNK	DTM	DSP
ie	ʌ	a	ʌ	ʌa
ɯə	o	o	ʌ	o
uo	wa	wa	wa	wa
i	i	ȵ̩	ɹ̩	ɣ
ɯ	ɯ	ʁ̩	ʁ̩	ɣ
u	u	ɣ̩	ɣ̩	ɣᵛ
e	e	i	i	i
ə	ɣ,ɯ	(?)	ə	ə
o	o	u	u	o

ε	e	e	e	e
a	a	a	a	a
ɔ	ɔ	ɔ	ɔ	ɔ
ia	ε	e	ε	ε
ui	wi	ui	ui	ui

It is apparent that the three Htopu dialects have taken the Kayah vowel raising further to various degrees. Besides the frication of the three high vowels, the mid vowels /e o/ have been raised to /i u/ with the exception of /o/ in DSP, and the set Western ia = Eastern ε has risen to /e/ in DNK. In the set Western ie = Eastern ʌ we see rather a further degree of lowering in DNK /a / and partially in DSP /ʌa/. Below are listed examples of some of these correspondences in DNK, Eastern, Western, plus Pa-O to attest a state that better preserves the proto-Karen vowel height:

	DNK	Eastern	Western	Pa-O
bear	thī	thē	thē	thàm
country	kì	kè	kẹ́	khâm
watercourse	klū	klō	klō	khrɔ̀ŋ
gong	mū	mo	mọ	môŋ
elephant	təçʰē	təchē	təshiā	chàŋ
five	ŋʲé	ŋē	ŋiạ̈	ŋát
water	thā	thʌ̄	thiē	thì
ten	sʰà	chʌ́	shié	chì

Consonants. The three Htopu dialects have allophonic cluster aspiration as in Eastern (r with aspirates, l with unaspirates):

kʰr̥ẕ̌ 'packbasket'   tʰá klú 'watercourse'

kʰr̥ý 'firewood'   plā 'arm'

pʰr̥ì 'Shan'   plẕ̌ 'whip'

kʰr̥á sé 'calabash'   təklà 'flea'

Tones. DTM and DSP, but not DNK, have breathy phonation as the reflex of former voiced stops and sonorants.

Daw Nye Khu	A	B	D
ph, p, ɓ>b, m̥>m	33 /ā/	55/á/	31/à/
b>p, m	33 /ā/	31/à/	55/á/

Daw Tamah	A	B	D
ph, p, ɓ>b, m̥>m	33	11	55
b>p, m	5̤5̤	3̤1̤	3̤3̤

Daw Shopya	A	B	D
ph, p, ɓ>b, m̥>m	55	11	31
b>p, m	3̤3̤	2̤1̤	1̤1̤

Remarks: the DNK tone A, like that of Upper Eastern, is either unsplit or re-merged. DNK tones B and D exhibit an unusual 'crisscross' merger of B1 with D2, D1 with B2. DSP may provide a hint about the stage leading up to the D1-B2 merger, with both D1 and B2 as falling tones but still distinguished by onset pitch as well as by phonation. Notice that phonation is fully distinctive at only one pitch level in DSP, namely low level (11); otherwise high (55) and mid-falling (31) are only modal, and mid (33) is only breathy.

Although the three Htopu dialects are west of the Pun, and although I have been contrasting them with Lower Eastern, they in fact resemble Eastern in this aspiration of stop+r clusters (all), as well as in the non-high vowel in the rhyme corresponding to Western ie and other Karen /i/ (DNK and DSP). DNK's lack of a phonation contrast is also more like Eastern. The indication is that, unsurprisingly, the boundary between Eastern and Western is neither straight nor a one-dimensional line.

10.4.3 Orthographies

Kayah Li has no established written form, although orthographies for Kayah languages have been devised. A Roman-letter orthography has been developed by Catholic missionaries for a language of the western portion of the Kayah area, and several prayer books exist in this orthography. The language is either a type of Western Kayah or one of the transitional dialects between Kayah and Kayaw (Lehman 1967 mentions a Catholic script used for Manaw; this is probably a reference to the same orthography).

There also exists a script of recent invention used principally by members of the indigenous self-determination organization, the Karenni National Progressive Party.

The following chart displays the characters in alphabetical order:

Consonants

ꤊ	k	ꤒ	t	ꤚ	r
ꤋ	kh	ꤓ	th	ꤛ	j
ꤌ	g	ꤔ	n	ꤜ	l
ꤍ	ŋ	ꤕ	p	ꤝ	w
ꤎ	s	ꤖ	ph	ꤞ	θ
ꤏ	sh	ꤗ	m	ꤟ	h
ꤐ	ʑ	ꤘ	d	ꤠ	v
ꤑ	ɲ	ꤙ	b	ꤡ	c

Vowels		Tones		Digraphs	
ꤢ	a	◌꤫	(high*)	ꤛꤢꤩ	ie
ꤣ	ə	◌꤬	low	ꤝꤥ	uo
ꤤ	i	◌꤭	mid	ꤛꤣ	ɯə
ꤥ	o			X+ꤟ	breathy phonation
ꤢꤦ	ɯ				
ꤢꤧ	ɛ				
ꤢꤨ	u				
ꤢꤩ	e				
ꤢꤪ	ɔ				

This script is in the Indic style, consisting of main graphs for initial consonants and certain vowels, plus secondary graphs, superscripts and subscripts for tones and the remaining vowels. The alphabetical order also follows the Indic tradition, starting with velar obstruents and moving forward in place of articulation (palatal, dental, labial), after which come nonnasal sonorants and fricatives. Within each obstruent series the order is by manner of articulation: voiceless unaspirate, voiceless aspirate, voiced, nasal. The nonnasal sonorants and fricatives are not ordered by manner in this way.

The following rearrangement may make this Indic ordering clearer (the alphabetical order is retained, but the arrangement is left to right first, then down):

	plain	asp	vcd	nas	(vcd)	
velar	Ꮇ	ᗺ	ᖋ	ᕐ		
palatal	ᖴ	ᖋ	β	ᖴ		
dental	ᖴ	ᑌ		ᖯ	(ᘔ	ᖇ)
labial	ᕮ	ᖋ		ᖇ		
son	ᖇ	ᨕ	ᖇ	ᖳ		
fric	ᖇ	ᖻ	ᖶ	ᖴ		

The regular 'voiced' column does include the voiced obstruents [g] and [z̧], but only [z̧] is a Kayah Li phoneme; contrariwise the voiced stops [d] and [b] are not in their expected locations, which would be directly following [th] and [ph] respectively. This is most likely due to the Burmese milieu in which the script was created. As a good Indic-style script, the Burmese writing system includes letters for both voiced and 'voiced aspirated' stops, which occur largely in loanwords. They are pronounced as voiced, but voicing in Burmese phonology is largely a matter of close juncture, with the result that any orthographic voiceless obstruent may be pronounced voiced in the proper environment. This may be why the Kayah Li letters <b d> are separated out: the script's creator felt (correctly) that voicing of obstruents has a different status in Kayah Li than it does in Burmese.

Some of the spelling conventions of Kayah Li are:

1. The character ej, besides standing for initial [h], also is written following the initial consonant to indicate breathy voice.

2. The diphthong /ɯə/ has three different spellings:

a) /ɯə/ (non-breathy) is ej꜕u <hkɯ> after non-coronal initials.

b) /ṳə/ (breathy) is ejʌu <hgɯ> after non-coronal initials.

c) /ɯə/ both breathy and non-breathy are spelled ɯu <jɯ> after coronal initials.

3. The high tone is normally indicated by the absence of any tone mark; thus ŋɛ̄ /lɛ́/ 'chase', ŋɛ̰̄ /lɛ̄/ 'moon', ŋɛ̰̄ /lɛ/ 'leaf' (the Eastern cognates are lé 'keep up with', lē 'moon', le 'leaf'). The first tone mark listed above, a subscribed dot, represents a high glottalized tone according to Bennett. The status of this tone mark is uncertain. Bennett states that it occurs rarely, and I have been unable to hear any difference between it and the ordinary high tone when speakers claimed to be producing minimal pairs. It may have originated for writing loanwords, possi-

bly Burmese checked syllables or those in the Burmese creaky tone although I have no concrete examples. It may be that this mark is used in a few instances to differentiate homophonous morphemes, such as Western ဧ̄ /ʔɛ́/ 'many' and /ɛ̄/ ʔɛ́ 'call' (both ʔɛ́ in Eastern), although my consultants say that this is a minimal pair.

Part II

Texts

1. Blind Men Steal a Gong

Kèkhu Dialect

Told by Nāʌ at Mē Lȝē̄, 22 April 1988. (457.1–460.7)

kúnè ma   dɤ̄ vē pòvè
now   be.so   at:U   1s   YSib-OSib
Now, as for my brother

dɤ̄ kulā   ʔa sí   nìhō kʌ̄ dɤ̄ pe kəjē̄ ʔíbe
at:U European   3   want   hear   COM   at:U   1p   Kayah   speak
as for the European, he wants to hear some of our Kayah speech.

ʔa donē̄   dɤ̄ a lʌ dɤ̄ ŋjáo
3   tell.legends   at:U   3   old   at:U   long.time-SFX
They tell of times long ago;

ʔū mòphre lʌ   bése khí
3i   old(hum)   old(nonhum)   face   dark
some old people . . .   [they were] blind . . .

cwá mɛ́ ʔeho kʌ̄ ʔū síjɯ   kʌ̄ ʔū mo
go   look   steal   COM   3i   want.to.get   COM   3i   gong
They went looking to steal somebody's—they wanted somebody's gong;

311

cwá mɛ́ ʔeho ʔehí   kā   ʔa hé
go   look steal steal.CP COM 3 say
they went seeking to steal and thieve, it's said.

ʔa cwá cwá cwá ʔe   thɛ   bé kā   ʔū hi
3 go go go exploit ascend able COM 3i house
They went and went and went and managed to get up into somebody's house

thɛ   bé kā ʔū hi   rʌ cwá mɛ́ ʔeho kā   nʌ
ascend able COM 3i house rØ go look steal COM NØ
They were able to get up into the house, they went looking
to steal;

thɛ   phjá nì bé kā   ʔū mo du
ascend take get able COM 3i gong big
they managed to get up and take their big gong,

lɛ   jɛ́   chɯ   kā lū ʔa:
descend carry.on.shldr confronting COM OBV INT
and came back down carrying it between them [i.e. suspended
from a stick with a person shouldering each end].

cwá kā nʌ cwá cwá cwá cwá ja kā lā ʌ́ ʔa hé nʌ
go COM NØ go go go go far COM very NS 3 say NØ
Going together; they went and went a long way, it's said.

lē   təva   phɛ́   ʔū hi   ʔa:
move.around curving   simply   3i   house   INT
[But] they just moved in a circle around the house.

ʔa cwá cwá cwá khē nō   tò
3   go   go   go   step   enter   arrive
They went and went until they stepped

dɤ̀   pəʔá klē   dɤ̀   ʔū lè   sī   tā   kúkhu nʌ
at:U   mud   amidst   at:U   3i   place.for   wash   fall   hand   NØ
into the mud, the place [under the house] where the water falls
when people wash their hands.

ʔa:ɯ̄ɯ ʔʌ̄ təphó ma   pe cwá ja nɛne ʌ́ cwá tò   ʌ́   mú
INT   this one-time be.so 1p   go   far really NS go   arrive NS   at:I
'Ah! this time we've gone a long way; we've gone all the
way into

nó   khu ʔa hé kʌ̄   lū   nʌ
swamp on   3   say   COM   each.other   NØ
a swampy place,' they said to each other.

ʔa: pe dɔ mɛ́ mɛ́ ma phra   ɛ̄   phra   to   ɛ̄   ʔa hé lū
INT 1p beat look look be.so to.sound QS to.sound NEG QS 3   say each.other
Ah, 'Let's beat it to see if it makes sound,' they said to each other

ʔa dɔ mɛ́ kā rʌ́ təphó hi bɛce nìhō sɛ́   phɛ́ a:
3 beat look COM RØ one-time house owner hear in.reaction simply
they beat it once to try it out, and the owner of the house heard

hi bɛce lɯ tā lɛ   phjá phe   sɛ́   phɛ́ lū rʌ
house owner chase fall descend take supplanting in.reaction simply OBV rØ
the owner of the house came down after them and took it away
from them

ʔa lɛ   dʌ́ lū ʔíkwa təphre təphō   rʌ
3 descend give 3OBV stick   one-C:hum one-C:bloom rØ
he came down and gave each of them a stick

ʔa lɛ   mɯ̄ chē lū rʌ hŋ təphó rʌ
3 descend hit   hurt 3OBV rØ INT one-time rØ
he went down and struck them once

ʔa chɛtɛ̀   rʌ́ ʔū mɯ̄ ʔa
3 suppose.wrongly RØ 3i hit 3
they thought somebody was beating them

jesī rʌ ʔa phjá kā ʔíkwa təphre   mɯ̄ lʌ̄   mɯ̄
3p rØ 3 take COM stick   one-C:hum hit each.other hit
they all took a stick and beat

ke   dɯ   lū   rʌ
each.other.CP   own.accord   each.other   rØ
each other [each thinking he was defending himself]

ʔa mū mū pɤ̀   thō   ʎ   rʌ
3   hit   hit   finish   finish   NS   rØ
and when they had finished beating

ʔá: pɔ   ʎ mū pa lū   me ʔa chē phé   ʔa hé   lū
INT enough NS hit   DUR each.other don't   3   hurt   simply 3   say   each.other
'Ah! Enough! don't hit [us] any more, it really hurts!' they said
to each other

təphré   ʔa plwā sé   lū   rʌ:
one-C:hum-SH   3   release   in.reaction   OBV   rØ
every one of them put it [stick] down

təphré: ʔa ka   rò   sé   phé lū   hú   nʌ
one-C:hum-SH 3   go.TH   many   in.reaction   simply   each.other   like   NØ
each of them just went home again

ʔa tədɯ   ʎ   ʔaklé   thū   to
3   go.until   NS   ITS-road   long   NEG
that's as far as it [this story] goes, it isn't long

2. The Magic Drum

Told 29 Feb. 1984 at Thāmɛdɣlɛkhā. (325.1–333.5)

boʌ: ʔa phú nʌ hō rʌ, ʔa nōo   kē   kā   rā ʔa
and.then 3   child   NØ   as.for   RØ   3   command-exist   NEW.LOC   COM   RØ   3

phú lʌ   mú   mɔ̀ seklē, ʔa hé nʌ
child   grandchild   at:INV   sun   daytime   3   say   NØ

and then, as for the children, they told their children to stay
(home) during the day, it's said

ʔa mɔ̀   phē nʌ rʌ, ʔa hē   ʔó   ʔúklē   nʌ
3   mother father NØ RØ   3   go:FH   away   swidden   NØ

the parents, they went away to the fields

ʔa hē   kúklē pwa nʌ́   pwa nā
3   go:FH   swidden   every   day-SH   every   day

they went to the field every day

[gap on tape]

ʔa hē   ʔó   kúklē pā sɔ pā ve   hē   ʔó   nʌ rʌ
3   go:FH   away   swidden   cut tree   cut bamboo   go:FH   away   NØ   RØ

they went to the fields to cut wood and bamboo, they went away

mɔ̀   phē nʌ si   ke sí   ʔe   dī   ʔa:
mother   father NØ [hesitation] if   want eat   c.rice   INT

the parents—if they were hungry, ahh—

kɤ́ dī   ka   bɤ́ ʔʌ̄ ʔa hé pʉ́: ʔa plὲ dī   nʌ ka
_   c.rice go:TH at:V this 3 say _   3 slap c.rice NØ go:TH
Kö! '[I] call rice to come here,' they said; puh! they hit [the drum], and rice came

ʔa sí ʔe chā   ja ma ʔa dɔ ma   ʔa ka ka me nʌ̄ʔ ʔa hé nʌ
3 want eat chicken flesh be.so 3 beat be.so 3 go:TH RDP do that 3 say NØ
if they wanted to eat chicken, they beat it and it came too; it happened like that, it's said

bōrʌ ʔa phú lʌ   nʌ ʔo kē   nʌ
then 3 child grandchild NØ exist NEW.LOC NØ
and so their children stayed home

ʔa dɛ thɛ   dɤ́: plò   kū   dɤ́ phrὲ khu nʌ
3 put ascend at:U storage.box inside at:U shelf on   NØ
they [the parents] put it up in a box, on a shelf

cwá mé lēkhē tɛ   me ní   ʔa hé rʌ́ phú lʌ   nʌ,
go   look PL.AC don't don't EMPH 3 say RØ child grandchild NØ
cwá kōnò me ní   ʔa hé nʌ
go   play don't EMPH 3 say NØ
'don't you go look at it now!' they said to the children, 'don't you go and play with it!'

phú lʌ   nʌ ʔa kléŋē nʌ rʌ, ʔa thɛ   phjá tā nʌ
child grandchild NØ 3 laugh NØ RØ 3 ascend take fall NØ
the children laughed, they went up and took it down

317

phōa: kɤ́ dī ka bʌ̄ ʔa hé nʌ ʔa plὲ ʔa dī nʌ ka kʌ̄ kʌ̄
and.then _c.rice go:TH here 3 say NØ 3 slap 3 c.rice NØ go:TH COM RDP
So, 'Kö! Rice come here,' they said, they hit it, and the rice came

phōa: ʔa ʔe ʔa ʔe lɔ̄ pè jʌ́ pa to nʌ̄
and.then 3 eat 3 eat use.up able NS DUR NEG NØ
then they couldn't eat it all

phōʌ: dɔ ka thwi ʔa hé nʌ dɔ ka thwi rʌ
and.then beat go:TH dog 3 say NØ beat go:TH dog RØ
so they said, 'Drum and get dogs . . . drum and get dogs'

pɤ́ɤ́ ʔa plὲ nʌ ʔa kɤ́ thwi ka bʌ̄ ʔa hé nʌ,
_ 3 slap NØ 3 _ dog go:TH here 3 say NØ
puh! they hit it, and kuh! 'Dogs come here!' they said

pɤ́ɤ́ plὲ bōʌ thwi nʌ ka rɔ́: lo nʌ
_ slap and.then dog NØ go:TH many very NØ
Puh! they hit it; then a huge number of dogs appeared

thwi nʌ ka ʔe ʌ́ dī nʌ
dog NØ go:TH eat NS c.rice NØ
the dogs came and ate the rice

ʔe ʔe ʔe lɔ̄   pè pa to, ʔa ʔe nʌ ʔi təpɯ lɔ̄   bɤ̌
eat eat eat use.up able DUR NEG 3 eat NØ shit heedless use.up at:V

hi   dɔ́ kū   nʌ, ʔa mé nʌ
house wall inside NØ 3 do NØ

they ate and ate; they couldn't eat it all; and they shat all over the
place in the house; that's what they did

ʔé: ʔi təpɯ lɔ̄   ʌ́ hi dɔ́ kū   nʌ rʌ phōa: ʔa súplī,
_   shit heedless use.up NS house wall inside NØ RØ and.then 3 wash

ʔa súplī tā rʌ́ thwi ʔi nʌ̄ʌ ʔa súplī ʔɛ   pa to
3 wash fall RØ dog shit NØ 3 wash (not)much DUR NEG

Eh! shat all over in the house; so then they [tried to] wash the
dogshit down [out of the house, but] they [couldn't] clean it very
much

phōa: dɔ thɛ   ʔíkwa ʔa hé lū   nʌ
and.then beat ascend stick 3 say each.other NØ

then they said to each other, 'Drum up some sticks'

dɔ thɛ   ʔíkwa bjaphɛ́ hú ʔʌ̄ nʌ hé   nʌ
beat ascend stick ordinary like this NØ simply NØ

they drummed up ordinary sticks, like this

kɤ̌ ʔíkwa ka   bʌ̄ ʔa hé púɨú ʔa plè
_ stick   go:TH here 3 say _ 3 slap

Kö! 'Sticks come here!' they said; Puh! they beat

319

phō?a: ?íkwa nʌ thɛ   ?é   təlwá   nʌ
and.then stick   NØ ascend many excessively NØ
then too many sticks came up

?a súplī lɔ̄   pè pé   rʌ́ pa ?íkwa to   ?a təsɔ́   lɔ̄
3 wash use.up able turn.out RØ DUR stick   NEG 3 disordered use.up

hi   dɔ́ kū   nʌ
house wall inside NØ
they couldn't clean up all of the sticks; they were every which
way all over the house

?ōó chá   mò hé   pa ma, vē mò   ka   toó ma
 _   when:FUT sun evening DUR be.so 1s mother go:TH arrive be.so

ka   mūū ʌ́   vē ?ā ?a hé nʌ
go:TH hit   NS 1s _ 3 say NØ
'Oh-h, this evening, when my mother comes home, she'll beat
me,' [they] said

phōʌ me hú tē   sī hé nʌ dɔ   thɛ   thʌ̄ ?a hé nʌ
and.then do like what 3p say NØ beat ascend water 3   say NØ
then they said, 'What will we do?' 'Drum up water,' they said

dɔ thɛ   thʌ̄ kúcù hú ?ʌ̄ təklɔ́   lè   ?ō nʌ
beat ascend water plain like this one-C:group place.for drink NØ
they drummed up plain water—like this, the kind for drinking

320

ʔū dɔ thɛ   thā̄ kúcù nʌ rʌ, ʔa dɔ sídō ma   ré   rʌ
3i beat ascend water plain   NØ RØ 3   beat gently be.so good RØ
they drummed up plain water; it would have been better if they
had drummed gently

kɤ̃ thā̄   ka   bʌ́ ʔā̄ hé nʌ
_   water go:TH at:V this say NØ
Kö! Water come here!' they said

púɯ́ dɔ̄   rʌ phōa: hŋ thā̄ nʌ thé: lɔ̄   lū dɔ̄   nʌ
_   beat RØ and.then _   water NØ ascend-SH use.up OBV village NØ
Puh! They drummed, then; hmm, water rose all over their village

thɛ   lɔ̄   ʌ́ bō̄ʔa: ʔa nɛbɛce thɛ   ʔo   vā
ascend use.up NS and.then 3 owner   ascend exist cross

dɤ̃ tɔcɔ   khu hú ʔʌ nʌ, thɛ ʔo dɤ̃ nʌ
at:U crossbeam on like this NØ ascend exist at:U that
it rose up all over; then the owner [the children] rose [floated] up
onto the horizontal roof-beam, like this [gesturing], rose up there

dé ʔa jɔ́ kè   thɔ̄ khri   təkí   klá ʔa vī   tā
_ 3 bend broken.off drum fragment one-C:bit _ 3 throw fall
Ding! they broke off a small piece of the drum; Klah! they threw
it down

thā̰ nʌ dé ʔa kəlɛ
water NØ _ 3 descend
Ding! the water went down

dé ʔa phjá təki   plɔ́ ʔa vī   tā   dé ʔa kəlɛ   nʌ
_ 3 take one-C:bit _ 3 throw fall _ 3 descend NØ
Ding! they took a little, Plaw! they threw it down, Ding! it [water] went down

ʔúú ʔa pəjè phɛ́ ʔa hé nʌ bōa: túú ʔa tā tā
_ 3 slow simply 3 say NØ and.then _ 3 fall fall
chī mē lɔ̄ nʌ
entire C:large use.up NØ
'Ooh, it's really slow,' they said, then 'Doo! they dropped the whole thing

tā tā bɤ̀ thā̰ ʔɔ kū   nʌ bōʌ   thā̰ hɛɛ́:
fall fall at:V water pond inside NØ and.then water go:FH-SH
rʌ́ mú   thā̰ du təva   nʌ
RØ at:INV water big curving NØ
down into the (pool of) water; then the water went off to the (big encircling water:) ocean

ka   ʔo mú kulā   kè   nʌ hé nʌ
go:TH exist at:INV European country NØ say NØ
it [the drum] went back to the Europeans' country, it's said

kəjē li phú nʌ ke cwá phɯ dɤ́ nʌ íma
Kayah red DIS NØ if go near at:U that consequently
If the Kayah Li went near to there

thɔ̄likheú nʌ ma the chɯ ʔa hé nʌ
[name] NØ be.so go.out confronting 3 say NØ
Tawlikheyu would come out to meet them

thɔlikheú ma ʔo dɤ̄ꞏ thā du klēm- thã̄ du təva klēmē nʌ
[name] be.so exist at:U water big between water big curving between NØ
Tawlikheyu is out in the big w— out in the ocean

kəjē li phú ke hē pè lū nʌ íma
Kayah red DIS if go:FH BEN OBV NØ consequently

ʔa theē tō nʌ hé nʌ
3 go.out-SH correct NØ say NØ
if the Kayah Li came for it, it would come out right to them, it's
said

mənɤ́ ʔū dʌ́ hē phɯ to hé wá kəjē li phú ɔ dɤ́ nʌ
but 3i give go:FH near NEG say sure! Kayah red DIS huh? at:U that
but they don't let us go near, that's what they say—us Kayah Li,
right?—near there

kəjē ke hē tò dɤ́ nʌ ma phjá nì rʌ́ sɛ́ ʔa hé nʌ
Kayah if go:FH arrive at:U that be.so take get RØ in.reaction 3 say NØ
if the Kayah went there, they'd get it back

phjá nì sé   tholikheú hú ʔā̰ nʌ

take get in.reaction [name]   like this NØ

they'd get Tawlikheyu back, like this

ʔū dʌ́ hḛ̄   pā to   kəjḛ̄ phú nʌ

3i give go:FH IRR NEG Kayah DIS NØ

[a listener says:] they won't let them go, the Kayah

m̰ ʔū dʌ́ cwá to

_ 3i give go   NEG

[narrator replies:] Mm, they won't let us

ʔū dʌ́ cwá pa to

3i give go   DUR NEG

[the listener continues:] they won't let us go

síʔichḛ̄ ʔū hḛ̄   phjá phe   sé   tholikheú rʌ

fear   3i go:FH take supplanting in.reaction [name]   RØ

they're afraid they [the Kayah] would get it back from them, the Tawlikheyu

ʔū ke phjá phe   nʌ íma   kəjḛ̄ phú nʌ ma

3i if take supplanting NØ consequently Kayah DIS NØ be.so

thā̰ kè   lɔ̄   plīchá: ʔū hé nʌ

water country use.up completely-SH 3i say NØ

[the narrator resumes:] if they took it, then the Kayah, absolutely all the countries

324

kulā   kè   ma kəjē li phú thΛ̄ kè   kè
European country be.so Kayah red DIS water country RDP
the Europeans' country would be the Kayah's too

mɛ   kè   ma, kəjē li phú me pè   Λ́   hΛ́   ʔa hé nΛΛ̄?
Burmese country be.so Kayah red DIS do   win NS RDP 3 say NØ-_
Burma, the Kayah Li would conquer it too

ke phjá nì nΛΛ̄ jΛ: dɔɔ̄ sΛ̄ lɔ̄   lɔ̄   Λ́   ʔū
if   take get NØ- _   beat die use.up RDP NS 3i
if they got it, they'd drum them all to death [laughs]

ʔíkhu ma kəjē li phú te   lɔ̄   Λ́
earth be.so Kayah red DIS 's.thing use.up NS
[DBS says:] the earth would belong to the Kayah Li

ke phjá nì Λ́
if take get NS
[narrator:] if they got it

thwā kəjē li phú te   lɔ̄   plīchaə nΛ
be   Kayah red DIS 's thing use.up completely   NØ
[another listener:] it would be the Kayah Li's, every bit of it

bɤ́ téé: bɤ́ téé   ma mɔrəká hosɔphɔ́ sī
at:V what-SH at:V what-SH be.so car   airplane   and.them

325

ʔitéé   ʔitē ma kəjē li hú te   lɔɔ́   nʌ

what -SH   what be.so Kayah red DIS 's.thing use.up-NS   NØ

[narrator:] anything at all; automobiles, aircraft and that sort of thing, whatever it is it would all be the Kayah Li's

hʌ   ca   sī   rūu thē sī   nʌ hé nʌ   ma

lower.garment upper.garment and.them silver gold and.them NØ say NØ be.so

clothing and so on, gold and silver and that sort of thing, it's said

kəjē   li   phú te   lɔ̄   ʌ́ ne ke phjá nì nʌ́ nʌʌ̄ jʌ

Kayah red DIS 's.thing use.up NS 2s if   take   get ?   ?   ?

would belong to the Kayah Li completely, if you could get it

ne phjá cè rʌ́ pa to   nʌ ka   ʔo   múː thʌ̄ du təva nʌ

2s take   able RØ DUR NEG NØ go.TH exist at:l   water big curving NØ

you can't get it, it's gone off and stays in the ocean

ka   bé   bé   rʌ́ pa   to

go:TH cross able RØ DUR NEG

it isn't able to come back

326

3. Conversation 1

30.vi.83, Baan Huai Dya, home of Phrēmὲ and Doʌ

Interlocutors:

X, name unknown

Kāmὲ, operates a taxi service along with her husband

X: cwá tò   ʌ́ ʔa jū   ʌ́ ʔū hé ʌ né ʔʌ̄ rʌ:
    go   arrive NS 3 easy NS 3i say _ OBL this RØ
    [I] have arrived; it's easy, I say

    thε   sɤ́ dɯ   rū dɤ́ lú   nʌ ʔō ʔa hé nʌ
    ascend insert own.accord silver at:U district NØ _ 3 say NØ
    [I'm going to] go up to town and pay at the District Office

Ka: thε   sɤ́ dɤ́ mɔ ē thε   sɤ́ dɤ́ lú   ɔ
    ascend insert at:U doctor QS ascend insert at:U district huh?
    you're going to pay at the hospital? going to pay at the District, huh?

<u>X</u>: ŋ   <u>Ka</u>: sí   thε   dɤ́ vī kū ɔ   páro   pā
    _   want ascend at:U city inside huh? tomorrow IRR
    Mm.   You want to go to town, huh? tomorrow?

X: thε ʔíkɔ̄   Ka: dέ vē mɔrəká pā níː
    ascend sure   ride 1s car   IRR EMPH
    Yes, sure   Go in my car, hey.

X: dʌ́ pā ʔaŋu to   Ka: dʌ́ to hú tē
    give DUR ITS-price NEG   give NEG like what
    I can't/won't pay the fare.   Why won't you pay?

X: já   kwī títíː   ʔū rūɯ ma

go.and beg   constantly-SH 3i silver PTC

You're always asking me for money!

Ka: kwī to ʔa me tē   ā   ʔa lɔ̄ː   nachi nā̄

beg NEG 3 do   what _   3 use.up-SH gasoline NØ

Why shouldn't I ask for money? it uses gas.

X: ʔa lɔ̄   mó   nā̄ ɛ̄   beé thɛ   dɤ̄ nʌ pā mē

3   use.up yes.but NØ QS   must ascend at:U that IRR EXCL

Well, sure it does, but, ah   well, I do have to go there!

Ka: thɛ   bá   mūɯ tē   ɔ   X: ɔ̄ɔ́

ascend how.many C:strokes what huh?   _

What time are you going?   Huh?

Ka: thɛ   bá   mūɯ tē   X: jʌ̀

ascend how.many C:strokes what   _

What time are you going?   Hmph!

ʔū thɛ   bá   mūɯ   tēé síŋē lāí to   hé rʌ dɯ

3i   ascend how.many C:strokes what know yet NEG say RØ own.accord

What time am I going? don't know yet, I say.

4. Conversation 2

Baan Huai Dya 1.xii.83
ref (254.1–258.2)

Interlocutors:

Phrèmè,   older woman (abbreviated Phrè)

DS,   David Solnit

Kāmè,   Phrèmè's daughter-in-law

Lēmè,   a neighbor, Kāmè's age

Phrè: təmjō təmjō ʔū hé phé nʌ   DS: təmjō
one-C:sort one-C:sort 3i say simply NØ   one-C:sort
They just say, 'one kind, one kind'   one kind

Phrè: m̥   Kāmè: lōné təmjō
    _   ghost one-C:sort
Hm   one ghost

Phrè: m̥ lōné ʔʌ̄ təmjō ʔa me
  _ ghost this one-sort 3s do
this (kind of) ghost did it

Lēmè: ma hé kʌ̄ lōné me be nʌ kɔ̄
be.so say COM ghost do strike NØ SUGGEST

ʔa hé: lōné témô nʌ ɛ̄ hé
3s say ghost whatsit NØ QS say
when speaking of ghosts, they say, 'it must have done it,
was it a whatsit ghost,' they say

329

Kāmè: ʔa hé lōné lō təphrɛ sī   nʌ ma (ʔité)

3s say ghost ghost (die)badly and.them NØ be.so what

they say, ghosts and bad-death ghosts and all that are . . .
what? (whispered)

ʔa sʌ̄ ré to ma təphre hé nʌ ɛ̄

3s die good NEG be.so one-C:human say NØ QS

if somebody dies badly, do you say 'one (person)'?

Phrè: n̩ sʌ̄ ré to ma təphre hé phé ʌ́ nʌ

_ die good NEG be.so one-C:human say simply NS NØ

Mm, for dying badly you just say 'one of them [human]'

já hé ʔarò ma hé cɛ̀ pa ú tē

go.and say ITS-other be.so say able DUR like what

how could you say it any other way?

sʌ̄ ré to ma ʔʌ̄ təphre təphre ʔū hé phé ʌ́ nʌ

die good NEG be.so this one-C:hum one-C:human 3i say simply NS NØ

for dying badly, they just say 'this one [human], one of
them'

DS: sʌ̄ ré to ma ɛ̄

die good NEG be.so QS

dying badly, right?

Phrè: sʌ̄ ré to ma hú ʔū tā sʌ̄ thʌ̄ sī

die good NEG be.so like 3i fall die water and.them

dying badly is like those who drown

ʔū... kwā sʌ̄ ʔū nè né sɔ sī

3i chop die 3i self OBL tree and.them

those . . . who get killed chopping down trees [chop down
tree which falls on and kills them, a common logging
accident]

330

Lēmè: mɔká pɔ̀   sʌ̄ sī   Phrɛ̀: m̩, mɔká pɔ̀   sʌ̄

car   collide die and.them   _ car   collide die

those who are run over by cars   Mm, get run over

DS: ʔūrò   me sʌ̄ ma ɛ̄

3i -other   do die be.so QS

if somebody else kills them, right?

Phrɛ̀: m̩, sʌ̄ təphre   təphre,   ʔū hé phé nʌ   .

_ die one-C:human one-C:human 3i say simply NØ

Mm, they just say 'one [human] died'

Lēmè: khé sʌ̄ lū   Phrɛ̀: khé sʌ̄ pā sʌ̄

shoot die OBV   shoot die cut die

[somebody] shoots them   shot or cut (to death)

Kāmè: ʔū hé rʌ́ sʌ̄ təphrɛ

3i   say RØ die (die) badly

they call it 'dying badly'

Lēmè: ʔū sʌ̄ rɛ́ ʔū hé ma ʔū chwí sʌ̄ dɯ   ʔū cɛ̄́:

3i die good 3i say be.so 3i chilled die own.accord 3i those.who

when they say, 'dying well', it's when they die of fever, those who . . .

ʔū da khé sʌ̄ pā sʌ̄ pɔ̀   sʌ̄ nʌ ɛ́ʌ̄ sʌ̄   təphrɛ

3i if   shoot die cut die collide   die NØ _ die (die) badly

if they shot or cut or runover, then its dying badly

ʔū phú ʔo ʔū sʌ̄ nʌ sī   ʔū hé rʌ́ sʌ̄ múmè hé nʌ

3i child exist 3i die NØ them 3i say RØ die ugly   say NØ

if they have a child and they die, they call it 'an ugly death'

phú ʔo sā̄ nʌ ma sā̄ təphrɛphrɛ ʎ́
child exist die NØ be.so die (die)badly-RDP NS
to die in childbirth, that's also dying badly

Phrɛ̀: ŋ, sā̄ təphrɛ, sā̄ múmɛ̀
_   die (die)badly die ugly
Mm, a bad death, an ugly death

[pause] kúu phá pɔ̀ tū lɔ̄ phɛ́ ké rò me tē a:
mouth skin crack sever use.up simply AMB cold do what _
my lips are all cracked, it's cold (so what can y'do?)

Kāmɛ̀:mɔ̀ khí ké rò cɛ̀jʎ́pato:
sun dark AMB cold really
at night it's REALLY cold

Phrɛ̀: [pause] teē sē ʔitēa:,
one-some night what

ké rò chwa thō ʔomā̄ kā̄ ne mò dɤ̀ Rùsɔ̄lɛ̄ a:
AMB cold strong go.over lie.down COM 2s mother at:U [place] _
some nights, it's so cold, I go over to sleep with your
mother at Rùsɔlɛ̄

ké rò cɛ̀jʎ́pato mané vē ʔomā̄ kā̄ Mòphrɛ̀ né [pause]
AMB cold really but 1s lie.down COM [name] OBL _
Pímò sī klēmé:kū a né kənɛə klēmé:kū ʔa leē
[name] and.them between-SH _ OBL youngest between-SH 3 warm
it was really cold, but I slept right between Mòphrɛ̀ and
Pímò, ah, and Kənɛ̂, and I was warm

ʔomā̄ tɯ́ə ké rò cɛ̀jʎ́pato
lie.down alone AMB cold really
sleeping alone is REALLY cold

Kāmὲ:ké rò lɤ̀:   pwā na ʔʌ̄ tǝna
AMB cold more-SH every year this one-year
this year is colder than any other!

Part III

Glossary and Index

Kayah Li-English Glossary

This glossary includes all Kayah Li forms cited in the Grammar and occurring in the Texts, plus selected core vocabulary items. Interjections are omitted.

Clearly-related items with distinct meanings or grammatical categories are combined in a single entry; for example, khri 'be shattered' (V), 'a fragment' (N), 'C:shards' (Clf).

Little attempt has been made to indicate the analysis of polymorphemic items. For example, síʔichē 'afraid' probably consists of sí 'heart' and chē 'hurt'; but the former component is suggested only by the word's alphabetical listing next to other items beginning with sí, while the latter is not indicated at all, although chē may be found in its alphabetically determined place.

The glossary is arranged in ordinary alphabetical order, subject to the following additional conventions:

1. Entries are ordered by the phonological initial of the first full syllable. Ordering by phonological initial rather than by first letter means that aspirates and complex initials are separated out from each other; e.g. p ph phr pl. Prefixed forms (those beginning ʔí ʔi kə tə pə) are listed under the initial of the full syllable; e.g. kəjē follows jē and precedes jō.

2. Zero initial comes first. Glottal stop is between ŋ and p.

3. Order of rhymes is a e ɛ i ja jo ʌ o ɔ u wa we wi ɯ

ɤ ə. Note that the semivowels j w are considered part of the rhyme, not the initial, and are ordered accordingly.

4. Order of tones is mid, low-level (no mark), low-falling, high. E.g. bā ba bà bá.

The form of entries is Kayah Li morpheme, grammatical category, short gloss as used in interlinear glosses, fuller gloss and other comments. For some items, such as cwá 'go', the short gloss is considered sufficient and no fuller gloss is added. The abbreviations for grammatical categories are:

Adv	Adverb
BRE	Bound Result Expression
INT	Interjection
D	Demonstrative
Ins	Intensifier
N	Noun
Nc	Classifier
Nl	Localizer Noun
Np	Pronoun
P	Preposition
Pfx	Prefix
Pnf	Non-final Particle
Ps	Sentence Particle, followed by A/B/C denoting subclasses
Ptc	Particle, indeterminate
Pv	Verb Particle
Q	Quantifier
Sfx	Suffix
V	Verb

ɛ̄ *PsC* QS polarity (yes-no) question marker)

íma *Pnf* consequently consequently, if . . . then, whenever . . . then; also loíma; cf. toíma 'otherwise'

ʌ́ *Pv* NS new situation, change of state; rʌ́-class Postverbal Particle

ɔ *PsC* huh? prompt-question

ú *P* at possible variant of mú 'at:I' in tōútē 'where?'

ú *PsC* go.on also ū; urges hearer to go on and do stg

ə̄ *Sfx* some some, underlying component of təə-ə̄-Clf (təə̄ rising tone)

ə́: *Sfx* SH special high tone (expressive)

ə̂ *Sfx* SFX also written ə

bā *V* full (of containers etc.)

ba *Nc* C:sheet Clf for e.g. mats, hats, the earth, mosquito nets, umbrellas

ba *V* pick

bá *N* fat

bá *Q* how.many also *P* X.much

bá *V* divine to divine using the thigh-bone of a chicken

bēlɔ̀ *N,Nc* bowl bowl, cup, drinking glass

bē?ū *N* cloth

be *Nc* C:flat Classifier for faceted or winglike things

be *V* manifest become manifest, come into being; strike strike, affect adversely, impinge; must modal V

?íbe *V* speak

bé *BRE* across cross, skip, miss

bé *V* able able, have the wherewithal or resources to V

békhjā *Nl* behind behind, in back of

bése *N* face

bése thʌ̄ *N* tears tears

bésenē *Nl* in.front

béseplɔ *N* eye

bē *Nc* C:pole+thatch Classifier: a pole with thatch attached, a unit of roofing

bē *V* yellow

bɛce *N* owner

?íbɛ *N* bmb.shoot bamboo shoot

bɛ́ *V* mold

bébū *Pv* show.way show the way to V, General Descriptive Postverbal Particle, adds IO argument.

béswá *V* be.companion

bí *V* closed

bja *BRE* affect V with drastic, often destructive effect; variant of be

bja *Pv* ordinary General Descriptive Postverbal Particle

bjaphé *Pv* ordinary just V, usually V, V in an ordinary way; General Descriptive Postverbal Particle; can modify N

bʌ̄ here contraction of bɤ́ ?ʌ̄ 'at:V + this'

bō *N* banana k. of banana

bō *Nc* C:long Clf for long objects e.g. ropes, snakes, intestines, trees, lizards bōʌ *Pnf* and.then also bōrʌ

bó *N* rice.plant

bɔ̄klé *V* blink blink the eyes

bɔ́ *V* weave

bɔ́ *V* reach

bɔ́kētē *Adv* when

bɔ́khri *V* close.eyes

bū *V* white

bulɛ *V* exchange

bwí *N* merit merit (Buddhist), blessing

buɯ *Pv* dare Movable Descriptive Postverbal Particle

buɯ *V* fat fat (not thin)

bɤ́ *P* at:V at: visible; proximal, in sight

təcā *V* tight

ca *N* upper.garment upper garment, shirt

cà *V* fall.as.hail

càphrʌ̄ *V* endure Modal V: keep on V-ing (in spite of stg)

təcē *N* sickle

ce *V* dye

cè *V* soft soft, tender

cé *V* real real, genuine

təcē *N* trap

cè *Pv* maybe.not maybe not, tentative negative; rʌ-class Postverbal Particle

cè *Pv* able able, know how to V, be good at V-ing; Movable Descriptive Postverbal Particle

cèjʌ́pato ? really

cé *P* those.who the ones who _, the _ part

ci *V* shear; squeeze squeeze, pinch off

ʔíci *N* scissors

təci *N* binturong Arctictis binturong, a large member of the civet family

cʌ *N* wick

pəcʌ *V* gossip gossip, talk about other people

təcʌ́ *V* cool cool, as water

cōpəriə *V* pointed

co *V* wet

təcoə *Pv* only

cɔ̄ *V* lift

cɔ̄ *V* tie

cɔ *V* wrap; *Nc* C:packages

cɔkū *Nl* middle.of in the middle of, between

təcɔ *N* crossbeam horizontal crossbeam of house

cɔ́ *Pv* insistently insist on V-ing, stubbornly V; Movable Descriptive Postverbal Particle

cɔ́kəreə *N* otter

cū *V* accord agree, V in accordance with, obey

cu *V* melt

təcù *V* bland bland, tasteless

cúkē *N* wrist

cúmākē *N* elbow

cwà *Pv* help help to V; adds an Indirect Object argument. General Descriptive Postverbal Particle.

cwá *V* go

cwè *Q* hundred hundred baht: hundred, of money only; cf. je

340

cwi *V* pull

cɯ *Nc* C:handful

cɯ *V* rain

cɤ *Nc* C:kind

chā *N* chicken

chāmò *N* hen

chāphē *N* cock

cha *N* vinegar

cha *V* sour

cha *V* late.afternoon

ʔícha *V* jump

chá *P* when:FUT when (future, upcoming); *Nl* nearby; chápā *Adv* soon

chá *V* pound

ʔichá *V* pound.in.mortar

chá *V* shine

chálè *N* honor

chē *V* hurt

ʔichē *V* fear also síʔichē

ʔíchē *V* sell

bəche *V* bored

che *N* star

che *N* food usually animal feed

ché *V* sew

ʔiché *V* tell

təchē *N* elephant

chetè *V* suppose.wrongly cf. sətè 'id'; Descriptive Particle tè 'wrongly, V the wrong one'

ché *V* trap usually followed by ʔe 'exploit, for use'

ʔaché *N* thorn

chī *Q* entire whole, the entire

chijá *V* untie

chikoə *N* shrimp

ʔíchi *V* split

chílūū *Pv* extremely rʌ-class Postverbal Particle

chʌ̄ *Q* ten ten, -ty (in numerals 20 through 99)

ʔíchʌ *V* urinate

chʌ́ *Q* ten ten, basic form

chʌ́ *V* clear clear (of water, sky)

chōdō *V* lack lack, not have, be without

chōtəpa *V* forget

cho *N* mountain

ʔícho *V* wash

ʔíchɔ̄ *V* curse

təchɔə *N* slow.loris

chwa *V* strong strong, loud

chwá *V* sibilant rubbing, sibilant sound, as hand on wood, paper on paper

chwí *V* chilled chilled; have a fever

chūū *V* stab

chūū *V* sweet

chɯ *N* b.hair body hair

chɯ *Pv* confronting

chú *V* kindle

dā *N* crotch space between, as crotch of tree, ravine between mountains

dā *Pu* if

dā *V* forge strike stg on stg, strike a light

kədā *N* door

dá *N* wing

dé *V* spread

dɛ *Nc* 8.khwe measure for rice, 8 khwe baskets-full

dɛ *V* transport

de *V* put

dɛke *V* hire Directive V

dɛsíplɔ *V* decide

déplu *N* sprout

dɛ́ *V* ride

dɛ́ *V* dip.up dip up, ladle out

décho *V* tell

dɛ́hʌ̄ *V* ask

désíplɔ *V* decide

détəklwà *V* speechless

dī *N* cooked.rice

dībɛə *N* paper.wasp

dībō *N* navel

dīcò *N* spoon

dīklwí *N* banana

dīpɔ *N* pot rice-pot

dītùì *Pv* keep.on keep on V-ing, undesirable event/action contin-ues; rʌ́-class Postverbal Particle

di *N* frog

dʌ̄ *N* melon melon, cucumber

dʌ *N* egg

dʌ́ *V* give

dō *Nc* C:animal Clf for animals, i.e. non-human mammals

dō *V* thick

tədō *N* leech.l land leech

do *V* chop.up e.g. chop firewood into lengths, chop up burnt brush in a swidden

do *V* abstain

dodē̄ *V* hold.out hold stg out, offer

donē̄ *V* tell.legends

doʌ *N* (name)

domé *V* show

kədó *V* muddy muddy, dirty (of water)

dɔ̄ *N* village also Classifier for villages

dɔ *V* beat

dɔ́ *N* wall

kədɔ́ *N* lid

dū *V* sweep

ʔidū *N* broom

dūú *PsC* go.on

du *V* big

dujè *V* rich

dúlo *V* older.of.sibs

dV *?* hey.kid used by parents in calling children.

dwá *BRE* away away, available for future reference; General Bound Result Expression

duɪ *Pv* own.accord to V on one's own, of one's own accord, to V oneself; rʌ́-class Postverbal Particle

ʔídɪɪ *N* knife

dúí *V* cut slice

tədɪɪ *V* go.until onward, [extend] up to

dɤ́ *P* at:U

tədɤ́ *PsC* although although, nevertheless

hā *V* bad

hā *V* often

hē *N* Chinese

he *N* earth

he *Nc* C:group

he *PsB* lest possible undesirable event

heso *N* dust

hé *Nc* evening

hé *V* say

hē̄ *V* go:FH move away from home, go

pəhē̄ *BRE* ahead ahead, forward; Orientational Directional BRE

hé *V* spicy hot (as chilis)

hi *N* house

hikhu *N* roof

ʔihí *V* spin.thread

təhā̄ *N* thatch.tree

hʌ *N* lower.garment lower garment: pants, skirt, sarong

hʌca *N* clothes lower garment + upper garment

hō̄ *N* husked.rice husked rice, ready to cook

hō̄ *Pnf* as.for in ʔʌ̄hō̄, nʌhō̄; one (NOT numeral), [this/that] one, [this/that] for its part

hōsɔphɔ̄ *N* airplane

ho *Pv* secretly to V secretly, sneakily; General Descriptive Postverbal Particle

hóhé *N* school

pəhó *N* onion

hoə *N* hidden be hidden, missing, out of sight

hɔ́ *N* stomach stomach (organ) hɔ́kū the organ, belly, abdomen (external area) hɔ́ phú

hú *P* like

ja *N* flesh

ʔíja *N* flesh flesh, meat

ja *V* far

jasú *N* gunpowder

jà *V* lick

já *Pv* go.and go and V; does not denote literal motion; Preverbal Particle, called 'Sequential'.

jē̄ *N* (name)

jē̄ *V* old old (things), torn, tattered

je *Np* 3 third person pronoun (Upper)

je *Q* hundred

jechuə *N* Jesus

jepu *N* Japanese

jesī̄ *Np* 3p

ʔíje *N* howdah

pəjè *V* slow slow, slow in accomplishing; contrast jɔ̄ slow in motion

jē̄ *V* deep

kəjē̄ *N* person person, Kayah; also kəjē̄liú Kayah

ʔíjē̄ *V* jiggle

jɛ *N* leech.w water leech, larger

jè *V* difficult often as V₂ in Descriptive V-V

jèjo *V* shadow, image

jé *V* carry.on.shoulder

jì *V* trample step on; _ bó thresh rice

jʌ́ *Pv* EMPH emphatic, exclamatory; rʌ́-class Postverbal Particle

kəjō̄ *V* move

jo *N* shadow

jo *V* fly

jò *N* rat rodent

jòlɛmɔ̄ *N* squirrel

jò *N* basis

jòkhró *N* rat

jòklē *N* chopping.block

jòthúí *N* wart

jɔ̄ *N* monkey esp. gibbon

jɔ̄ *V* slow slow to cover distance (cf. pəjè 'slow to accomplish')

jɔbέbλ *N* mantis

jɔ́ *V* bend bend stg (Vt)

jū *V* easy

jū *V* point point with finger; (as Directive V) order by pointing

jùʔe *V* believe

ka *V* go:TH move towards home, go, come, (sometimes) return

təka *V* curved curved, bent, hooked

kē *V* feed

kēleko *N* ear

kēleko kəʔɔ̄ *V* deaf

kēsé *V* itch

ʔikē *N* blanket

ke *PsB* perhaps

ke *Pu* if

ke *Pv* each.other.CP V each other, V reciprocally; cp. of lλ̄

kè *N* country also AMB, Subject of weather verbs, which dissimilates to ké before low tones

kè *V* broken.off broken-off, of stg long such as string, stick; usually as V₂

kèkjá *V* fold

ké *N* AMB dissimilated form of kè, Subject of weather verbs

ké *V* harvest harvest, peel with knife

təké *V* dwarfed

kē̄ *BRE* NEW.LOC V so that something ends up in some (new) location; general Bound Result Expression

kē̄ *Nl* bottom bottom inner surface, at the bottom of a container

ké *V* burn burn (Vi)

kékwa *V* in.half

ké *N* eggplant

kīlō *Nc* kilogram

təkī *N* grasshopper grasshopper

tə-ki *Pv* a.little a little, a bit; Q+Clf functioning as Verb Particle

kjā *Nc* side

təkjā *Nl* direction in the direction of, towards

kλ̄ *Pv* COM Comitative; rλ́-class Postverbal Particle

kʌ *V* striped striped, patterned, not plain

kō *V* leisure in ʔokō; be free, at leisure

kōnò *V* play

təkō *V* chop.up cut up fine, as meat

ko *Nc* C:gen the general Classifier

ko *V* unwilling Modal V

təkoʌ *PsC* still nevertheless, still, concessive assertion

kò *V* chop.hole chop hole in log with axe

kò *V* inspect inspect, examine

ʔíkò *V* poke jab at quickly with stg curved, as sickle

kó *Pv* temporarily temporarily, V instead for a bit; rλ́-class Postverbal Particle

kóʌ *Pv* temporarily temporarily,
V instead for a bit; rʌ́-class
Postverbal Particle

kó *V* full satiated, full from eating

kólo *N* h.hair hair of the head

kɔ̄ *N* shell shell, container

təkɔ̄ *N* container container,
small box

kɔ *PsC* SUGGEST urging, offering
for consideration, suggest that you
do or agree with this

kɔdɔ́ *N* lid

kū *N* hole

kū *Nl* inside

klēmēkū *Nl* between in between,
in the middle

kūcɛ *N* earring long silver
Kayah-style

kū̄ʔu *N* mouth

ku *V* hot

kuchɔ́ *N* hairpiece hair coiled
and attached to back of head

kukhʌ̄ *N* tooth

kuklɔ́ *N* head

kuklɔ́nɔ̄ *N* brain

kulā *N* European European,
Caucasian

kuphō *N* nose

kusā *N* sweat

kusē *N* earring gold Shan-style

kúbī *N* bean

kúbīsúse *N* peanut

kúcù *V* plain in thʌ̄ kúcù 'plain
water, drinking water'

kúdi *N* handle

kúdū *N* crown.of.head

kújā *N* palm

kúlā *N* necklace

kúkhu *N* hand

kúklē̄ *N* swidden

kúklɔ *V* hold.in.hand

kúmʌ *N* fingernail

kúmì *N* tail

kúnè *Adv* now

kúpè *N* butterfly

kúvē *V* dig

kwā *N* axe; also *V* chop chop,
chop down, cut with axe

kwa *V* half be in half, of stg long;
also in təkwa (Q) half

ʔíkwa *N* stick

kwī *V* beg beg, ask for

kū *V* wear wear on lower body
(pants, sarong)

kūchɯ *N* mortar

kūchɯʔiphō *N* tilt.hammer

pəkū *N* Sgaw Sgaw Karen

təkhā *V* yawn

kha *V* promise Modal V

təkhwa *V* speechless

təkhwá *N* lizard

khē *V* step also C:steps,
Classifier for steps

khe *V* bitter

khé *V* shoot

khē̄ *N* leg form in compounds
before low tone; cf khɛ before
mid tone

khē *V* paddle

khē~lēkhē *Pv* PL.AC plural action,
multiple participants involved;
rʌ́-class Postverbal Particle

345

khēbō *N* neck

khēdo *N* lower.leg

khēkhi *N* shin

khēkʌ *N* thigh

khɛ *N* leg form in compounds
before mid tone; cf khē before
low tone

khɛ kē lē *N* hollow.of.knee

khɛbó *N* leggings

khɛle *N* foot

khɛmā *N* knee

khɛphá *N* shoe

khɛrē *N* paw

təkhémɔ̀ *N* mango.tree

khɛ́ *V* overgrow overgrown
(with weeds), choked, cluttered

khī *N* in.law in-law of opposite
sex, sibling's spouse

khí *V* dark

khjā *Nl* back in back of, behind

kəkhjā **BRE** backwards Orientational Bound Directional

khjɔ́ *V* surrender

khʌ̄ *N* gunny.sack

khʌ̄ *Nl* apex apex, peak; on top of

təkhʌ̄ *N* muntjac muntjac,
barking-deer

təkhʌ *N* tick tick (insect)

khō *N* companion

kho *N* smoke

kho *Pv* as.cover to V as cover
for doing stg else; movable
Descriptive Post-verbal Particle

khonokhá *N* king

khó *Pv* separately

khɔ *N* dam also Classifier for
dams

khɔ *Pv* separately

khɔ́mū *N* bread bread, cake

khū *?* male

khu *Nl* on on the upper surface of

ʔíkhu *N* earth earth, the world

ʔíkhu *V* wind.on.spool to wind,
as thread on a spool; also C:spool,
Classifier for spools of thread,
guns

khwē *Nc* ricebasket measure
for rice, the size of a packbasket
(khrì)

khwe *Pv* midst.of in the midst
of V-ing, continuous action;
khwe-class Preverbal Particle

khwi *N* parrot in thu khwi

təkhuí *V* cough

khrā *N* calabash calabash,
bottle-gourd

khrā *V* dry

khrè *N* bug bedbug; also in other
insect names

ʔikhré *V* winnow

khrē *V* skinny thin (not fat)

təkhrē *V* similar

khré *Pv* what.all plural questioned
entity; rʌ́-class Postverbal Particle

khré *V* orphaned in ʔokhré

khri *V* shattered be shattered,
broken in many pieces; also
N 'fragment'; also Nc Classifier
for shards

khrì *Nc* packbasket conical shape,
carried (ví) by tumpline

pəkhrɔ̄pɔcʌ *V* gossip

təkhrɔ̄ *V* stupid

khru *N* firewood

khrwā *V* follow

khrwí *N* bone

khrwíbá *N* marrow (bone + fat)

təkhrūse *N* hail

khrɯ *N* machine

khrɯ *N* mushroom

khrɯ *Pv* equally as _ as;
Descriptive Post-verbal Particle

klē *Nl* amidst in among, in stg
not construed as an aperture

təklē *V* lazy

Kle *N* (name)

klé *Pv* should epistemic, should be
the case; Modal Pre-verbal Particle

klébe *N* market

Klémè *N* (name)

klḕ *V* chop.contact chop stg by
putting in contact with blade and
bringing them down together

klēmē *Nl* between; also *V*
half be in half, be a half of stg;
also in təklēmē (Q) 'half'

klɛ *V* run

klɛ̀ *V* cut cut weeds in swidden:
klɛ̀ phré; normally using a təpū
hoe

klɛ́ *N* road

kléŋē *V* laugh

təkli *V* gnaw

təklí *N* turtle

klā̄ *N* army

klʌ *N* crossbow

klʌphé *N* bow long bow (not
crossbow); phé perh. 'hug'

klō *N* ditch in thā̄ klō;
also *Nc* C:ditch

klō *N* language; also *Nc* C:language

kló *N* trough

kló *V* cover

klɔ̄ *Nl* outside

klɔ̄ *V* spill

kló *Nc* C:group bunch, bundle,
group, faction (in a conflict),
wad (of cooked rice)

təklwà *V* not.speaking speechless,
quiet

klwī *N* seed

təklù̀ *V* stunted

lā *Ins* very Intensifier for hā 'bad'
and mɯ 'drunk'

lā *Pv* intrusively to V intrusively,
rashly (Quasi-modal Preverbal
Particle)

lāí *Pv* yet must co-occur with
Sentence Particle to 'negative';
rʌ́-class Postverbal Particle

kəlwa *V* slanted

láte *Pv* instead

ʔíla *V* call call an animal by clucking sounds or finger snapping

là *V* clear be clear of (e.g. weeds);
sparse

láte *Pv* on.the.other.hand

láteá *Pv* instead rʌ́-class
Postverbal Particle

təlwá *Pv* past

ledē *N* mat

le *N* moon; also *Nc* month

le *Nl* base bottom, base of;
underneath

le *V* move.around

le *N* leaf

le *V* warm

lehʌ *N* teak

lè *N* place.for place for V-ing, thing for X; because of, from

lèsɯ *N* granary granary, shed

lè *Pv* hurry

lèklō *Pv* have.ever have ever V'd, experiential; khwe-class Preverbal Particle

lé *PsC* CtrA counter-assertion, it might have been X but it's really Y

lé *Pv* overtaking keep up with, catch up with, to V overtaking somebody; General Descriptive Postverbal Particle

léhē *N* pumpkin

léhēse *N* pumpkin

lē̄ *N* ravine ravine, mountain stream; also Classifier for id.

lɛ *V* descend

kəlɛ *V* descend descend, go down (Subject participant moves)

lɛkhɯ́ *V* fall fall over from standing position

lɛsé *V* wind.blows

lè *N* field wet rice field

lī *V* light

līpəna *N* nail

li *N* writing written language

li *V* red

limē̄ *V* smart

liʔú *N* book

lì *N* vagina

liə *Ins* very Intensifier with phrē̄ 'fast'

lʌ *N* grandchild

lʌ *V* old old, usually of nonhumans

lʌ~lʌ̄ *Pv* each.other rʌ-class Postverbal Particle

təlʌbɔ́vī *N* whirlwind

lō *Ins* very intensifier with ŋjā 'long time', ʔé 'many'

lō *N* ghost ghost, corpse

lōné *N* ghost ghost, spirit

lō *Pv* manifest become manifest, apparent, known; General Descriptive Postverbal Particle

kəlō *N* hill

lo *N* thread

lo *Nl* vertical.surface

loíma *Pnf* consequently if . . . then, whenever . . . then

loəkhɯ̄ *N* motorcycle

lò *N* vehicle

lòtɔthé *N* bicycle

lò *N* core in bōlò, the edible heart of a banana stem

lò *Pv* ought ought (by duty); Modal Preverbal Particle

ʔílò *V* bathe bathe, always with Object thʌ̄ 'water'

ʔílò *V* plant to plant (seeds)

lɔ́ *V* inter inter, bury a corpse

təloə *V* medium.sized

lɔ̄ *V* use.up exhaust, expend, use up, (exhaustively=) completely

lɔ *V* black

lɔ̀ *N* rock

lɔ́ *V* pregnant in hɔ́ lɔ́ 'pregnant'

lū *Np* 3OBV obviative third person pronoun; requires preceding clause-mate noncoreferential NP

348

lū **Pv** each.other reciprocally; rʌ-class Postverbal Particle

ʔilū **N** llu the New Year's ritual post and its elaborate bamboo and wood finial

ʔílū **V** combine

təlū **V** roll.up

lù **V** make.merit make merit (as Buddhist practice)

lú **N** district administrative unit below the province, Thai amphəə

lúlɤ́ **V** dangle

təlwá **Pv** excessively excessively, too; Descriptive Postverbal Particle

lwī **Q** four

lwīswá **Q** eight literally 'four doubled'

lwīswátə **Q** nine literally 'four doubled and one'

pəlwī **V** cool cool (ambient), of weather

thulwi **N** pigeon

lɯ **Pv** a.bit rʌ-class Postverbal Particle, often following kóʌ 'temporarily'

lɯ **V** chase

lɯ̀ **N** gourd melon, Momordica

lɤ́ **Pv** more more, comparative degree, very, than; Movable Descriptive Postverbal Particle

mā **N** joint

ma **V** fixed

ma **V** be.so

mané **Pnf** but

mē **N** wife

mē **Nc** C:large clf for large semi-regular shapes, e.g. houses, drums, heads, stomachs, larger fruits

mē **PsC** EXCL mild counter-assertion

me **PsB** don't negative imperative

me **V** do

me **V** try try to do stg undesirable or prohibited; Modal Verb

metē **Adv** why me 'do' + tē 'what'

mēkluí **N** rhythm.pipe rhythm-pipe, a bamboo percussion instrument

mēleké **N** pineapple

mɛ **N** Burmese

mɛ̀ **N** OSib older sibling

mɛ̀ **V** dream

mɛ́ **V** look

mɛ́thʌ **V** see

təmɛ́ **N** pig.tusk

mī **V** ripe

Mīʌ **N** (name)

mīú **N** (name)

mi **N** name

midu **V** famous

mi **N** fire

mipja **N** ash

miplɔ **N** lightbulb

mjō **Nc** C:sort type, way, custom

mā **Pv** sugg. suggestion, mild imperative; rʌ-class Postverbal Particle

mā **V** lie.down in ʔomā 'lie down, sleep'

mʌ **Ps** IMP imperative

mō **V** open

təmō **V** constantly

mo *N* gong

mo *V* happy feel good, healthy, have fun; (as V$_2$ in V-V) enjoyably, enjoy V-ing

Motaəphē *N* (name)

mò *N* mother; also *N* female; also ʔímò *N* Mother one's own mother

mòphrè *V* old(human); also *N* old.person; also a name

mó *PsC* yes.but sure, but . . . ; concessive

mɔ *N* doctor

mɔ̀ *N* sun sun, in compounds

mɔ̀hé *N* evening

mɔ̀khí *N* nighttime

mɔ̀lī *N* early.morning

təmɔ̀ *N* sun (in isolation)

mɔ̀ *Nc* C:plant trunk; Clf for smaller plants (larger plants take bō); also ʔamɔ̀ *N* trunk

mɔ̀rəká *N* car car (English, prbly via Burmese); also mɔká

mɔ́ *N* sky

mú *P* at:I at: invisible; precedes item known by inference or hearsay, not in sight

múmè *V* ugly

mwī *V* same.name to have the same name as

təmwī *V* crazy

mūū *V* hit to hit, hammer; Classifier for strokes, hours o'clock

ʔimūū *N* stick

mɯ *V* drunk

mɤ̃ *N* town also Classifier for id.

nālī *N* watch

na *Nc* year

nachi *N* gasoline

kənē~tənē *Pv* about.to about to V, incipient; khwe-class Preverbal Particle

ʔíne *V* fart

kəne *Pv* almost

ne *Np* 2s you (singular)

ne *V* think; also təne *V* think Modal V

nenāchá *N* cheek

nè *N* self self, body, main part; often modified e.g. vē nè myself, ʔa nè him?herself

pənè *N* buffalo

nē *Pv* high.time high time to V, must V because hasn't V'd in so long

kəne *N* youngest youngest of siblings; often kəneə

nɛbɛce *N* owner owner, master

nɛkū *Pv* when when . . .then; rʌ́-class Postverbal Particle

nínè *V* real; also nɛ~nɛne~nɛnejʌ́ V or Pv really

nɛ́ *P* OBL backgrounded participant, oblique relation, quasi-coordination

nɛ́kū *Pv* when when . . . , must be followed by 'then' clause; rʌ́-class Postverbal Particle

tənɛ́ *V* steep

kəneə *N* youngest youngest of siblings

tənī *N* bee

nì *V* get also *BRE* able

nìdā *V* listen

nìhō *V* hear

ní *PsC* EMPH strong assertion or imperative, be sure and pay attention to what I say

nʌ̄ *Nc* day

nʌ̄ *Q* two

nʌ *D* that

nʌ *Ps* NØ marks neutral assertion, restatement of previously-mentioned propositions, nominalizer

nʌhō *Pnf* consequently if . . . then, whenever

nʌíma *Pnf* consequently consequently, if . . . then

nō *V* enter

pənō *BRE* inwards Orientational Bound Directional

nō *V* command variant of Directive Verb nō

no *Pv* afterward Movable Descriptive Postverbal Particle

no *V* smell

nomὲ *V* stink

nomú *V* fragrant

noso *V* rotten rotten, as cooked food

novi *V* sniff

nó *N* swamp

nɔ̄ *V* use use; also nɔ̄~nɔ̄cɔ̀ *V* command command, tell sbdy to V; Directive Verb

nɔ *N* horn also Classifier for horns

nɔ́ *Pnf* if

nɔ́ *Pv* at.all emphatic or unexpected negative, must co-occur with to; rʌ́-class Postverbal Particle

ʔinú *N* breast also V 'to suck at breast'

ŋjā *V* laugh

ŋara *N* sin

ŋē *N* part

ŋē *Nl* front

ŋē *N* banana k. of banana

ŋē *Q* five

ŋjā *V* long.time

ŋjá *V* encounter have stg bad happen

ŋò *V* language

ŋò *V* weep

ŋūlē *Nl* downhill downhill from

ŋūthé *Nl* uphill uphill from

ŋu *N* price

ʔa *Np* 3 third person pronoun, unmarked

ʔa *Pfx* ITS prefix combining with Bound nouns to form compound nouns

ʔà *V* bite

pəʔá *N* mud

ʔe *V* eat

ʔe *V* exploit use; often second verb meaning to V for a purpose

ʔeho *V* steal

ʔehí *V* steal.CP cp. of ʔeho

ʔé *V* many

ʔé *V* call

ʔɛ *Pv* (not)much not much, not very; must co-occur with to 'NEG'; General Descriptive Postverbal Particle

ʔɛ *V* lucky

ʔíʔɛ *V* dirty

351

ʔécuɨ́ *V* pretend Modal V

ʔī *V* sticky

ʔi *N* excrement also V to defecate

ʔʌ̄ *D* this

ʔō *V* drink

ʔo *V* exist exist, be located, dwell, have (X Y ʔo X has Y)

ʔojwā *V* wait

ʔolē *V* for.fun V for fun

ʔomʌ̄ *V* lie.down lie down, usually implies sleep

ʔone *Pv* against General Descriptive Postverbal Particle

ʔonē *V* sit

ʔó *BRE* hidden be hidden, in hiding, out of sight

ʔó *V* blow blow with the mouth

kəʔɔ̄ *V* deafening deafening, noisy

ʔɔ *N* pond pond; usually thʌ̄ ʔɔ

ʔɔ́ *V* mildew

ʔɔ́lò *N* cloud

ʔū *Np* 3i third person pronoun, indefinite, backgrounded; ʔū . . . pē who?

ʔɨʔu *V* row

ʔúɨ́ *V* smolder smolder, burn without flames

pā *PsA* IRR irrealis, future hypothetical, upcoming

pā *V* cut cut with knife; hack, cut as bones

pāhénɨɨ *Adv* yesterday

pāro *Adv* tomorrow

pa *Pv* DUR durative, still, to V more; rʌ́-class Postverbal Particle

təpa vā *PsC* excl see vā

pē *PsC* who in ʔū . . . pē

təpē *V* kick.stg

pe *Np* 1p first person plural pronoun

pè *Pv* able able physically, strong enough to V; Movable Descriptive Postverbal Partice; cf.next

pè *V* win win; cf. preceding

pè *Pv* TRN transfer of possession; General Bound Result Expression

pè *Pv* BEN benefactive/malefactive, V to sbdy's benefit or detriment; rʌ́-class Postverbal Particle

pé *Pv* turn.out new negative situation, not after all, will turn out that not; rʌ́-class Postverbal Particle

pé *V* dumb

pé *V* be.as V pé Clf 'to V by the Clf', can incorporate Classifier into VC

pē *Nc* bottle

pī *V* go.out go out (as fire), be extinguished

pīchaə *Ins* complete intensifier with lɔ̄ 'exhaust, use up'; cf. plī 'clean, slippery'; variant of plīchaə 'id'

pīló *N* flute panpipes

Pímò *N* (name)

pípè *N* butterfly

ʔipiə *V* narrow

pjā *N* bag

pja *N* beehive beehive, hive of bees or wasps; also Classifier for id.

pjà **Pv** BEN benefactive, rʌ-class
   Postverbal Particle; cf. pè

pjá **V** ruin be ruined, spoiled,
   no good

pō **PsC** urge urging, let's, want
   to . . . ? why don't you? also pō

po **N** coop pen, corral; finial of
   the Ilū

pothé **N** pigpen

pò **N** YSib younger sibling

pò **Pv** additionally additionally,
   more, again; rʌ-class Postverbal
   Particle

pó **PsC** urge urging, let's, want
   to . . . ? why don't you? also pō

pɔ̄ **Ptc** PTC unknown function,
   in (47.3)

pɔ̄cí **N** pagoda

pɔ̄khī **N** tiger

pɔ **N** pot pot (metal)

pɔ **V** thresh

ʔípɔ **N** hammer

pɔ **V** enough

pɔ̀ **V** crack crack or split with
   a bang, go off (of gun)

pɔ̀ **V** collide

pɔɔ **N** childs.spouse child's spouse,
   son/daughter-in-law (address term)

pū **N** straw in bópū long
   (unbroken) rice straw

pù **N** ox

pwā **Q** every

pwe **V** celebrate have a festival

təpwī **N** longan

pɯ **Nc** C:cloth

təpɯ **V?** heedless heedlessly,
   V just anywhere, not keeping to
   the right place

pù **V** catch

pɤ̀ **V** finish

phā **BRE** out.of.the.way təlwá-class
   Bound Directional Expression

Phāʌ **N** (name)

pha **V** drop let fall, put down,
   add as ingredient to food

phá **N** skin skin, hide

phákɔ́ **N** sleeping.pad

phjá **N** large.headed.fish

phē **N** father; also ʔíphē N Father
   one's own father

Phēlúídu **N** (name)

Phētɯəʔaphē **N** (name)

phe **Pv** supplanting appropriating;
   General Descriptive Postverbal
   Particle

phé **V** crack crack, be cracked
   as wood, hatching egg

phē **N** branch usually ʔaphē, sɔphē

phé **Pv** simply only, just; rʌ-class
   Postverbal Particle

phé **V** hug

təphé **N** cotton

phjá **V** take

phʌ̄ **N** grandmother

phō **N** grandfather also ʔíphō N
   Grandfather one's own grandfather

phō **Nc** (thing) in blindmen, prh
   error for phō C:blooms or pho
   C:places

phō *Nc* C:blooms clf for flowers; also N 'a flower', V 'to bloom, to flower'

phō *V* pound

phō *V* cook cook in water, boil

phōchase *N* soap.pod k. of plant whose pods are boiled to make soap used for laundry and shampoo

phōʌ *Pnf* and.then

pho *Nc* C:place

təpho *V* swollen swollen, e.g. blister, goiter

phó *Nc* C:time Classifier for events

phɔ̄ *N* winged.insect

phɔ̄chí *N* mosquito

phɔ̄dī *N* housefly

təphɔ̄ *V* stub stub toe on stg, hit stg horizontally with the foot

phú *P* like

phú *N* child child (Bound) must have preceding modifier

phúcè *N* child child (Free)

phú *Sfx* small

phú *Sfx* DIS diminutive/- instantiating suffix

phwī *V* lightweight

phɯ *V* near

phrā *N* intestine

phra *V* to.sound make sound, be noisy

phre *N* human; also Classifier for id; cf sí

phrekhū *N* man

phremɔ̀ *N* woman

təphreʔukhrɛ́ *N* (name) a protago- nist in the Kayah Li origin story

phrè *N* Shan

phrèjwi *N* Thai.Yuan Northern Thai, khon myaŋ

phré *N* swidden

phrē *V* fast

təphrɛ *V* (die)badly in sā̄ təphrɛ 'die badly'

phrè *N* shelf shelf for storage, above head height

phré *V* vomit

phri *V* buy also ʔíphri

phrɔ *V* cave.in collapse

plā *N* arm

plānɔ̀ *N* shoulder

plá *V* wrong.CP Bound couplet- partner of súí

ple *N* crack crack; cf. next

ple~plekū *Nl* between in (the narrow space) between

təple *N* cabbage

təple *V* instead reversed, turned around

plè *N* arrow cf. 'cubit'

plè *Nc* cubit cubit: distance from elbow to fingertip; cf 'arrow'

plē *N* grain.ear ear of grain

plē *V* late.morning

plè *V* slap slap, clap, beat drum with hand

plī *V* clean clean, slippery

plīchá *Ins* completely intensifier with lɔ̄ 'exhaust, use up'

pli *N* tongue

plí *V* whip

plʌ *N* string string, line

təplotəpjā *V* hurry

plò *N* storage.box storage box of woven bamboo with short legs

plò *V* smear smear, paint, rub on

təpló *V* put.on put on or wear stg that encircles or encases (ring, glove, pullover, leather shoe, finial of Ilu)

plɔ *Nc* C:small.round Clf for e.g. stars, buttons, eggs, grains of sand, seeds, letters of the alphabet

plu *V* piled be piled up; also Classifier for piles

təplu *V* search look for; also mé təplu

plú *V* punch hit with fist

plwā *V* release

plúí *BRE* to.the.end General Bound Result Expression

rāmá *V* write.down

təra *Pv* anyway Post-verbal Particle or Sentence Particle

rē *V* go.across

pərē *BRE* across Orientational Bound Directional Expression

tərē *Pv* almost almost V'd; khwe-class Preverbal Particle

re *Pv* unrestrained unrestrainedly, often connoting an undesirable extent; General Descriptive Postverbal Particle

tərecū *Pv* regularly regularly, all the time; General Descriptive Postverbal Particle

rè *N* trellis trellis, frame for vines

təré *N* wax

kərēpē *N* umbrella

ʔíre *V* work

ré *V* good also *V* should you'd have thought that, should (counterfactual); Modal Verb

ri *V* good good result of divination, heal (of wounds); cf. ré

təri *V* dress dress sbdy, get dressed

rí *Q* thousand

tərā̄ *N* luck luck, fortune

rʌ *Pnf* rØ indicates pause, unmarked

tərʌ *N* tobacco

rʌ̀ *Pv* beforehand Movable Descriptive Postverbal Particle

rʌ́ *Pv* RØ participant obliquely involved; rʌ́-class Postverbal Particle

ʔírō *V* sing sing, esp. traditional song/chant

rō *Nc* C:morning

rōʔe *V* hew hew, make even

ro *Np* other in ʔū ro other people, dɣ́ ʔaro tə-X another X

ro *V* early

təro *V* timid

rò *V* cold

rò *V* many many, plural action (of animates)

rɔ̄klē̄ *Nl* beside

rù *N* snake

Rùsɔ̄lē̄ *N* [place]

tərú *Pv* go.ahead go ahead and V, feel free to V; Quasi-modal Preverbal Particle

rwá **BRE** along təlwá-class Bound Directional Expression

rwì *N* root

rūɯ *N* silver silver, money

sálá *V* used.up

sárá *N* teacher

sē *Nc* split.with.wedge

sē *Nc* night

sē *V* new

sērē *V* prepare prepare, straighten up, tidy up

ʔíse *N* salt

ʔísechūɯ *N* sugar (salt + sweet)

se *N* fruit also V to bear fruit

sedē *V* come.forth form, as new fruit

seʔo *V* useful be useful, have meaning ('fruit exists')

seklē *V* daytime in time-of-day expression mɔ̀ seklē 'during the day, daytime'

sé *N* machine

séʔiché *N* sewing.machine

sé *V* breathe sé síplɔ breathe; kè lɛsé wind blows

kəsé *V* itch

sethūɯphē *N* (name)

setè *V* suppose suppose wrongly, mistakenly think that

sé *Pv* in.reaction again, completing one half of a cycle; rʌ́-class Postverbal Particle

sé *V* put.in put in; wear or put on stg with buttons

sɛə *V* same be the same as, resemble closely

sī *N* and.them with preceding modifier X: X and that lot, X and that sort of thing; X=NP or clause

sī *Np* 2p you (plural); also 3p they, them (third person plural); Upper dialect

sī *V* wash wash (hands)

sí *Nc* C:hum Clf for humans, suppletive with phre and zero

sí *Pv* want want to V; Modal Preverbal Particle

sídō *V* gently gently, carefully, softly (heart + thick)

síjɔ *V* care care for, love

síjɯ *V* want.to.get want stg

sílù *N* caterpillar

sínè *V* awake Vi: be awake, (person) wakes up

sínɛ *N* gun

sínɛthi *N* trigger

sínō *N* west

sínìso *V* miss miss sbdy

síŋē *V* know know, understand, recognize

síʔiché *V* fear (heart + hurt)

síphrá *V* tired

síplɔ *N* heart

síplɔdu *V* angry (heart + big)

síplɔnō *V* understand (heart + enter)

síplɔtō *V* like (heart + strike.correctly)

sísɔ̄ *V* raw

sítərē *V* ashamed

təsí *N* horse

sɅ̄ *V* die

sō *N* (name)

sō *Q* three

sō *V* green green/blue

sōswá *Q* six literally 'three doubled'

ʔaso *N* liver

so *N* louse head louse

sokhrè *N* b.louse body louse

sɔ̄ *V* rot rot, ferment (of food)

sɔ *N* tree tree, wood

sɔba *N* board

sɔkhō *N* snag snag, fallen log

sɔklⱺ *N* boat

sɔphōba *N* glv.metal galvanized metal for roofing

sɔse *N* fruit plant + fruit

sɔtō *N* weed weed, grass, vegetable

sɔ́ *Q* ten.thousand

sɔ́ *V* slide.in slide stg in by pushing

təsɔ́ *V* disordered disordered, every which-way

sūre *V* difficult difficult, poor (not rich)

ʔasú *N* oil

súba *N* hemp

súplⱺ *N* rope

súplī *V* wash wash (utensils, objects other than clothes)

súsē *N* bamboo.splint

ʔiswá *V* teach teach; ʔiswá NPx NPy teach sbdy(x) stg(y), ʔiswá V NP teach NP to V; cf. ʔiswá study, learn

ʔiswá *V* learn study, learn; ʔiswá NP learn stg; ʔiswá V (NP) learn to V (stg); cf. ʔiswá teach

swá *N* leech.w water leech, smaller

swá *N* friend cf. V 'be a pair'

swi *N* blood

ʔiswí *N* curry cooked dish to be eaten with rice

sú *V* wrong

sɣ́ *V* insert insert, put in

sɣ́ŋjɣ́~sɣ́rɣ́ *Ins* very Intensifier with lɔ 'black'

tā *V* fall downwards, fall through space

ʔítā *V* get.down descend, get down from a vehicle

tālē *BRE* downwards Orientational Bound Directional

tà *Nc* C:meals

tē *N* what what, in question words ʔitē what, me tē why? (do what), etc.

tē *V* measure

tēkhu *N* medicine

tēú *N* fish tē in compounds

te *N* thing (Bound); possessive (with modifying pronoun)

témoə *N* whatsit whatsit, whatchamacallit

tétabō *N* pencil

tɛ *Pv* on.time Movable Descriptive Postverbal Particle

pətɛə *V* small cf. pətí

tɛɛ̄ *PsC* let's also tɛ; urges hearer to join speaker

357

tɛ̀ *Pv* about.to about to V, incipient; khwe-class Preverb Particle

tɛ̀ *Pv* wrongly wrongly, V the wrong one; General Descriptive Postverbal Particle. Cf. tātɛ̀ 'unskillfully', sɔtɛ̀ 'suppose wrongly'.

tɛ̀ *Pv* don't don't, shouldn't, strengthens negative imperative; rʌ́-class Postverbal Particle

tīkwa *N* flute k. of flute

ti *V* stuff

tì *V* different

pɔtí *V* small cf. pɔtɛə

tí *P* X.big as big as, the size of

títí *Pv* constantly

tʌ *N* tuber

tō (a) *V* correct be correct, strike accurately; (b) *V* should should, time is right to V; Modal Verb; (c) *BRE* correct correctly, V with precise, wished-for effect

tōútē̄ *Adv* where

to *PsA* NEG negative marker

too *PsA* only

toíma *Pnf* otherwise if not for X, then Y

tò *V* arrive

tɔthé *N* iron

tɔ̀ *N* ant

twa *N* split.flattened.bamboo bamboo, split and flattened, used for floors and walls

twà *V* beautiful

tūī *V* sever severed, broken off, e.g. tree, log; Vi

tɯ *V* together V or Postverbal Particle

túɯ *Pv* just.now khwe-class Preverbal Particle

tɯə *Pv* alone alone; Descriptive Postverbal Particle or Verb

tɤ́ *P* x.long as long as, _ long

tə- *Q* one

ʔithā *N* felled.brush cut-down brush in swidden, before burning

kɔtha *N* magic

tha *N* sesame

tha *Nc* 20.liters measure for husked rice

thá *V* plow

thē *N* bear

thē *N* gold

the *V* go.out go out, emerge

pɔthe *BRE* outwards Orientational Directional BRE

ʔithé *N* Crataeva plant with sour edible leaves (Thai phàk kùm)

thé *N* cloth cloth being woven, usually as Object of bɔ́ 'weave'

thé *N* needle

thé *V* to.chisel

thépɔnā *N* chisel

tɔthé *N* iron

tɔthé *N* centipede

thē̄ *V* wound to wound, be wounded

thē̄ *V* sharp sharp (edge)

thɛ *V* ascend

kɔthɛ *V* go.up (Agent moves)

pɔthe *BRE* upwards Orientational Bound Directional Expression

thέ *N* pig

pith∧̄ *N* saliva

thi *N* penis

ʔithá *N* plow

th∧̄ *N* water

th∧̄klō *N* ditch

th∧̄mē *N* water container

th∧̄ʔidékū *N* water.hole

th∧̄ʔɔ *N* pond

th∧̄ʔíphrὲ *N* whiskey distilled
rice liquor

th∧ *V* see

thō *Pv* finish

thō *V* go.over go to someplace
near, move a short space,
move over

tho *V* heavy

thorəsap *N* telephone telephone
(Thai)

thó *N* eel.like.fish in tē thó

ʔithoə *N* knife

thɔ̄ *N* drum drum, long with
flared base

thɔ̄likheú *N* (name) name of
a magic drum

thɔ̄ *N* container container,
enclosure, pocket

kəthɔ *V* stand

thɔ́~ʔithɔ́ *V* cover to cover, as
person with blanket

thɔ́bí *V* covered.up

thū *V* long long, tall (humans),
high (sound)

thuú *N* bird bird (general)

thupwi *N* bird.nest

thú *Pv* probably probably is the
case [analysis uncertain]; Modal
Preverbal Particle

thwā *V* be be (something),
become, grow (of plants), be alive

thwā *V* lucky.CP Bound couplet-
partner of ʔɛ 'lucky'

thwākhwí *N* king

thwá *N* cat

thwi *N* dog

thwí *N* lime lime (mineral)

thūu *Nl* edge beside, on the edge
of

ʔíthuu *N* post

thuú *V* rub rub, wipe, scrub

thɤ́ *P* X.long as long as; also tɤ́

vā *PsC* sure! sure it's true that X,
medium-strong assertion; also
təpa vā

vā *V* cross cross, e.g. bridge

vā *V* cooked

təva *V* encircle go around stg in a
circle, either as literal motion or as
extent, as bracelet around wrist

và *V* again

vē *N* husband

vē *Nc* C:seasons

vē *V* dig

ve *N* bamboo

vē *Np* 1s first person singular
pronoun

vɛ *V* copulate copulate, have
sexual intercourse

vὲ *N* OSib older sibling (Bound)

vī *V* wind wind up, twist; drive
(car); grind

vī *V* throw throw stg large with one hand

ʔívī *V* whistle

ʔívī *V* scratch.for.food

vi *V* delicious

víju~víjuə *N* radio radio

vɔ ***BRE*** circumventing go around an obstacle; contrast təva 'encircle'

English-Kayah Li Index

b.hair chɯ
b.louse sokhrɛ̀
back khjā
backwards kəkhjā
bad hā
bag pjā
bamboo ve
bamboo.splint súsē
banana bō
banana dīklwí
banana ŋē
base lē
basis jò
bathe ʔílò
be thwā
be.as pé
be.companion béswá
be.so ma
bean kúbī
bear thē
beat dɔ
beautiful twà
bee tənī
beehive pja
beforehand rʌ
beg kwī
behind békhjā
believe jùʔe
BEN pè
BEN pjà
bend jɔ́
beside rɔ̄klē
between klēmē
between klēmēkū
between plekū
bicycle lòtɔthé
big du

binturong təci
bird thuú
bird.nest thupwi
bite ʔà
bitter khe
black lɔ
bland təcù
blanket ʔikē
blink bɔ̄klé
blood swi
blow ʔó
bmb.shoot ʔíbɛ
board sɔba
boat sɔklʌ̄
bone khrwí
book liʔú
bored bəche
bottle pē
bottom kē
bow klʌphé
bowl bēlɔ̀
brain kuklɔ́nɔ̄
branch phē
bread khɔ́mū
breast ʔinú
breathe sé
broken.off kè
broom ʔidū
buffalo pənè
bug khrɛ̀
Burmese mɛ
burn kē̄
but mané
butterfly kúpɛ̀
butterfly pípɛ̀
buy phri

362

C:animal dō
C:beehive pja
C:bit ki
C:blooms phō
C:cloth pɯ
C:ditch klō
C:flat be
C:gen ko
C:group he
C:group klɔ́
C:handful cɯ
C:hum phre
C:hum sí
C:kind cɤ
C:language klō
C:large mē
C:long bō
C:meals tà
C:morning rō
C:packages cɔ
C:pile plu
C:place pho
C:plant mɔ̀
C:pole+thatch bē
C:ravine lē
C:seasons vē
C:sheet ba
C:small.round plɔ
C:sort mjō
C:time phó
C:town mɤ̃
cabbage təple
calabash khrā
call ʔé
call ʔíla
car mɔká

car mɔ̀rəká
care síjɔ
carry.on.shoulder jɛ́
cat thwá
catch pɯ̀
caterpillar sílù
cave.in phrɔ
celebrate pwe
centipede təthé
chase lɯ
cheek nenāchá
chicken chā
child phú
child phúcè
childs.spouse pɔə
chilled chwí
Chinese hē
chisel thépənā
chop kwā
chop.contact klē
chop.hole kò
chop.up do
chop.up təkō
chopping.block jòklē
circumventing vɔ
clean plī
clear chʌ́
clear là
close.eyes bɔ́khri
closed bí
cloth bēʔū
cloth thé
clothes hʌca
cloud ʔɔ́lò
cock chāphē
cold rò

363

collide pɔ̀

COM kā̄

combine ʔílū

come.forth sedē

command nō

command nɔ̄

companion khō

complete pīchaə

completely plīchá

confronting chɯ

consequently loíma

consequently nʌhō

consequently nʌíma

consequently ɤ́ma

constantly títí

constantly təmō

constantly? titē

container thɔ̄

container təkɔ̄

cook phō

cooked vā

cooked.rice dī

cool pəlwī

cool təcʌ́

coop po

copulate vɛ

core lò

correct tō

correct tō

cotton təphé

cough təkhuí

country kè

cover klớ

cover ʔithɔ́

cover thɔ́

covered.up thɔ́bí

crack phé

crack ple

crack pɔ̀

Crataeva ʔithé

crazy təmwī

cross vā

crossbeam təcɔ

crossbow klʌ

crotch dā

crown.of.head kúdū̄

CtrA lé

cubit plè

curry ʔiswí

curse ʔíchɔ̄

curved təka

cut duí

cut klè

cut pā

dam khɔ

dangle lúlɤ́

dare bɯ

dark khí

day nʌ̄

daytime seklē

deaf kēleko kəʔɔ̄

deafening kəʔɔ̄

decide dɛsíplɔ

deep jē̄

delicious vi

descend kəlɛ

descend lɛ

die sʌ̄

(die)badly təphrɛ

different tì

difficult jè

difficult sūrɛ

dig kúvē

dig vē

dip.up dé

direction təkjā

dirty ʔíʔɛ

DIS phú

disordered təsɔ́

district lú

ditch klō

ditch thʌ̄klō

divine bá

do me

doctor mɔ

dog thwi

don't me

don't tὲ

door kədā

downhill ŋūlē

downwards tālē

dream mὲ

dress təri

drink ʔō

drop pha

drum thɔ̄

drunk mɯ

dry khrā

dumb pé

DUR pa

dust heso

dwarfed təké

dye ce

each.other lʌ~lʌ̄

each.other lū

each.other.CP ke

ear kēleko

early ro

early.morning mɔ̀lī

earring kusē

earring kūcɛ

earth he

earth ʔíkhu

easy jū

eat ʔe

edge thū̄

eel.like.fish thó

egg dʌ

eggplant kɛ́

eight lwīswá

elbow cúmākē

elephant təchē

EMPH jʌ́

EMPH ní

encircle təva

encounter ŋjá

endure càphrʌ̄

enough pɔ

enter nō

entire chī

equally khrɯ

European kulā

evening hɛ́

evening mɔ̀hɛ́

every pwā

excessively təlwá

exchange bulɛ

EXCL mē

excl təpa vā

excrement ʔi

exist ʔo

exploit ʔe

extremely chílūū

eye béseplɔ

face bése

fall lɛkhuí

fall tā

fall.as.hail cà

famous midu

far ja

fart ʔínē

fast phrē

fat bá

fat bɯ

Father ʔíphē

father phē

fear ʔichē

fear síʔichē

feed kē

felled.brush ʔithā

female mò

field lè

fingernail kúmʌ

finish pɣ̀

finish thō

fire mi

firewood khru

fish tē

fish tēú

five ŋē̄

fixed ma

flesh ja

flesh ʔíja

flute pīló

flute tīkwa

fly jo

fold kèkjá

follow khrwā

food che

foot khɛle

for.fun ʔolē

forge dā

forget chōtəpa

four lwī

fragrant nomuí

friend swá

frog di

front ŋē̄

fruit se

fruit sɔse

full bā

full kó

gasoline nachi

gently sídō

get nì

get.down ʔítā

ghost lō̄

ghost lōné

give dʌ́

glv.metal sɔphɔ̄ba

gnaw təkli

go cwá

go.across rē

go.ahead tərú

go.and já

go.on dūú

go.on ú

go.out pī

go.out the

go.over thō̄

go.until tədɯ

go.up kəthɛ

if dā
if ke
if nɔ́
Ilu ʔilū
IMP mʌ
in.front bésēŋē
in.half kékwa
in.law khī
in.reaction sé
insert sɤ́
inside kū
insistently cɔ́
inspect kò
instead láte
instead láteá
instead təple
inter lɔ́
intestine phrā
intrusively lā
inwards pənō
iron tɔthé
IRR pā
itch kəsé
ITS ʔa

Japanese jepu
Jesus jechuə
jiggle ʔíjē
joint mā
jump ʔícha
just.now tuí

Kayah kəjēliú
keep.on dītùɪ
kick.stg təpē
kilogram kīlō
kindle chuí

king khonokhá
king thwākhwí
knee khɛmā
knife ʔithoə
knife ʔídɯ
know síŋē

lack chōdō
language klō
language ŋò
large.headed.fish phjá
late.afternoon cha
late.morning plē
laugh kléŋē
laugh ŋjā
lazy təklē
leaf le
learn ʔiswá
leech.l tədō
leech.w jɛ
leech.w swá
leg khɛ
leg khē
leggings khɛbɔ́
leisure kō
lest he
let's tɛē
lick jà
lid kɔdɔ́
lid kədɔ́
lie.down mʌ̄
lie.down ʔomʌ̄
lift cɔ̄
light lī
lightbulb miplɔ
lightweight phwī
like hú

371

skin   phá

skinny   khrē̄

sky   mɔ́

slanted   kəlwa

slap   plɛ̀

sleeping.pad   phákɔ́

slide.in   sɔ́

slow   jō̄

slow   pəjɛ̀

slow.loris   təchɔə

small   phú

small   pətɛə

small   pətí

smart   limē̄

smear   plò

smell   no

smoke   kho

smolder   ʔú

snag   sɔkhō̄

snake   rù

sniff   novi

soap.pod   phōchase

soft   cè

some   ə̄

soon   chápā

sour   cha

sparse   là

speak   ʔíbe

speechless   détəklwà

speechless   təkhwa

spicy   hé

spill   klō̄

spin.thread   ʔihí

split   ʔíchi

split.flattened.bmb   twa

split.with.wedge   sē̄

spoon   dīcò

spread   dé

sprout   déplu

squeeze   ci

squirrel   jòlɛmō̄

stab   chū̄

stand   kəthɔ

star   che

steal   ʔeho

steal.CP   ʔehí

steep   təné

step   khē̄

stick   ʔimū̄

stick   ʔíkwa

sticky   ʔī̄

still   təkoʌ

stink   nomɛ̀

stomach   hɔ́

storage.box   plò

straw   pū̄

strike   be

string   plʌ

striped   kʌ

strong   chwa

stub   təphō̄

stuff   ti

stunted   təklùʔ

stupid   təkhrō̄

sugar   ʔísechū̄

sugg.   mʌ̄

suggest   kɔ

sun   mɔ̀

sun   təmɔ̀

supplanting   phe

suppose   sɛtɛ̀

suppose.wrongly   chɛtɛ̀

sure ʔíkɔ̄

sure! vā

surrender khjɔ́

swamp nó

sweat kusā

sweep dū

sweet chɯ̄

swidden kúklē

swidden phré

swollen təpho

tail kúmì

take phjá

teach ʔiswá

teacher sárá

teak lehʌ

tears bése thā̄

telephone thorəsap

tell décho

tell ʔiché

tell.legends donē

temporarily kó

temporarily kóʌ

ten chʌ́

ten chā̄

ten.thousand sɔ́

Thai.Yuan phrɛ̀jwi

that nʌ

thatch.tree təhā̄

then bōrʌ

thick dō

thigh khēkʌ

thing te

(thing) phō

think ne

think təne

this ʔā̄

thorn ʔaché

those.who cé

thousand rí

thread lo

three sō

thresh pɔ

throw vī

tick təkhʌ

tie cō̄

tiger pɔ̄khī

tight təcā

tilt.hammer kɯ̄chɯʔiphō

timid təro

tired síphrá

to.chisel thé

to.sound phra

to.the.end plɯí

tobacco tərʌ

together tɯ

tomorrow pāro

tongue pli

tooth kukhā̄

town mɤ̄

trample jì

transport dɛ

trap ché

trap təcē̄

tree sɔ

trellis rè

trigger sínɛthi

TRN pè

trough klɔ́

trunk ʔamɔ̀

try me

tuber tʌ

turn.out pé

turtle təklí

two nāˉ

ugly múmè

umbrella kərēpē

understand síplɔnō

unrestrained re

untie chijá

unwilling ko

uphill ŋūthé

upper.garment ca

upwards pəthɛ

urge pó

urge pō

urge tɛ

urinate ʔíchʌ

use nōˉ

use.up lōˉ

used.up sálá

useful seʔo

vagina lì

vehicle lò

vertical.surface lo

very lāˉ

very liə

very lōˉ

very sɤ́ŋjɤ̀

very sɤ́rɤ̀

village dōˉ

vinegar cha

vomit phrέ

wait ʔojwā

wall dɔ́

want sí

want.to.get síjɯ

warm le

wart jòthúɪ

wash ʔícho

wash súplī

wash sī

watch nālī

water thāˉ

water container thāˉmē

water.hole thāˉʔidékū

wax təré

wear kūˉ

weave bɔ́

weed sɔtōˉ

weep ŋò

west sínō

wet co

what ʔitē

what tē

what.all khrɛ́

whatsit témo-ə̂

when bɔ́kētē

when nɛkū

when nékū

when:FUT chá

where tōūtē

whip plí

whirlwind təlʌbɔ́vī

whiskey thāˉʔíphrè

whistle ʔívī

white būˉ

who ʔūpē

who pē

why metē

wick cʌ

wife mē

win pè

wind vī

wind.blows lɛsé

wind.on.spool ʔíkhu

wing dá

winged.insect phɔ̄

winnow ʔikhré

woman phremɔ̀

work ʔírɛ

wound thē

wrap cɔ

wrist cúkē

write.down rāmá

writing li

wrong súí

wrong.CP plá

wrongly tè

X.big tí

X.long thɤ́

x.long tɤ́

X.much bá

yawn təkhā

year na

yellow bē

yes.but mó

yesterday pāhénɯ

yet lāí

youngest kəne

youngest kəneə

YSib pò

1p pe

1s vē

2p sī

2s ne

3 je

3 ʔa

3i ʔū

3OBV lū

3p jesī

3p sī

8.khwe dɛ

20.liters tha

References

Benedict, Paul K. 1972. *Sino-Tibetan: A Conspectus* (Princeton-Cambridge studies in Chinese linguistics 2), contributing editor James A. Matisoff. New York, Cambridge University Press.

Bennett. J. F. 1991. Two more Kayah Li dialects. Presented at the 24th International Conference on Sino-Tibetan Languages & Linguistics, Bangkok and Chiangmai.

———. 1993. Kayah Li script: a brief description. Manuscript, University of Illinois at Urbana-Champaign.

Brown, J. Marvin. 1965 And 1985. *From Ancient Thai to modern dialects.* Reprinted by White Lotus, Bangkok.

Chafe, Wallace L. 1970. *Meaning and the Structure of Language.* Chicago, University of Chicago Press.

———. 1976. Givenness, contrastiveness, definiteness, subjects, topics, and point of view. In Charles N. Li (ed.) *Subject and Topic.* New York, Academic Press.

Chao, Yuen Ren. 1968. *A Grammar of Spoken Chinese.* Berkeley, University of California Press.

Dowty, David. 1991. Thematic proto-roles and argument selection. *Language* 67.3, 547–619.

Duffin, C. H. 1913. *A Manual of the Pwo-Karen Dialect.* Rangoon, American Baptist Mission Press.

Egerod, Søren. 1957. Essentials of Shan phonology and script. *Bulletin of the Institute of History and Philology,* Academia Sinica 29, 121–29.

Foley, William A., and Michael L. Olson 1985. Clausehood and verb serialization. In Johanna Nichols and Anthony Woodbury (eds.) *Grammar Inside and Outside the Clause.* Cambridge, Cambridge University Press.

Foley, William A., and R. Van Valin. 1984. *Functional Syntax and Universal Grammar.* Cambridge, Cambridge University Press.

Haas, Mary R. 1964. *Thai-English Student's Dictionary.* Stanford, Stanford University Press.

377

References

Haudricourt, André-Georges. 1946. Restitution du karen commun. *Bulletin de la Société de Linguistique de Paris* 42.1, 103–11.

———. 1953. À propos de la restitution du karen commun. *Bulletin de la Société de Linguistique de Paris* 49.1, 129–32.

———. 1975. Le système des tons du karen commun. Bulletin de la Société de Linguistique de Paris 70, 339–43.

Henderson, Eugénie J.A. 1961. Tone and intonation in Western Bwe Karen. Burma Research Society Fiftieth Anniversary Publication I, 59–69.

———. 1979. Bwe Karen as a two-tone language? an inquiry into the interrelation of pitch, tone and initial consonant. Nguyen Dang Liem, ed. *Southeast Asian Linguistic Studies,* 301–26. Canberra, ANU.

Jones, R. B. 1961. *Karen Linguistic Studies* (University of California Publications in Linguistics v. 25). Berkeley, University of California Press.

Lehman, F. K. 1967a. Ethnic Categories in Burma and the theory of social systems. P. Kunstadter (ed.) *Southeast Asian Tribes, Minorities, and Nations,* v.1. Princeton, Princeton University Press.

———. 1967b. Kayah society as a function of the Shan-Burma-Karen context. J.H. Steward (ed.) *Contemporary Change in Traditional Societies* vol 1, 1–104. Urbana, University of Illinois Press.

———. 1979. Who are the Karen, and if so, why? Karen ethnohistory and a formal theory of ethnicity. Charles F. Keyes (ed.) *Ethnic Adaptation and Identity: the Karen on the Thai frontier with Burma.* Philadelphia, Institute for the Study of Human Issues.

Li, Charles N., and Sandra A. Thompson. 1981, 1989. *Mandarin Chinese: A Functional Reference Grammar.* Berkeley, University of California Press.

Luce, G. 1959. Introduction to the comparative study of Karen languages. *Journal of the Burma Research Society* 42.1, 1–18.

Matisoff, James A. 1973. *The Grammar of Lahu.* (University of California Publications in Linguistics v. 75). Berkeley, University of California Press (second printing: 1982).

———. 1978. *Variational Semantics in Tibeto-Burman.* (Occasional Publications of the Wolfenden Society on Tibeto-Burman Linguistics 6). Philadelphia, Institute for the Study of Human Issues.

———. 1986. The languages and dialects of Tibeto-Burman: an alphabetic/genetic listing, with some prefatory remarks on ethnonymic and glossonymic complications. In John McCoy and Timothy Light, eds., *Contributions to Sino-Tibetan Studies* (Cornell Linguistic Contribution v. 5). Leiden, E. J. Brill.

Mazaudon, Martine. 1985. Proto-Tibeto-Burman as a two-tone language? Some evidence from proto-Tamang and proto-Karen. In Graham Thurgood, James A. Matisoff, and David Bradley (eds). *Linguistics of the Sino-Tibetan Area: the state of the art* (papers presented to Paul K. Benedict for his 71st birthday, 201–29. Pacific Linguistics Series C, No. 87 (Special number). Canberra, Australian National University.

Okell, John. 1969. *A Reference Grammar of Colloquial Burmese* (Part I and II). London, Oxford University Press.

———. 1971. *A Guide to the Romanisation of Burmese* (James G. Forlong Fund publications 27). London, Luzac.

Purser, W.C.B., and Tun Aung. 1922. *A Comparative Dictionary of the Pwo-Karen Dialect, Part I, Pwo-Karen-English.* Rangoon, American Baptist Mission Press.

Searle, John R. 1975. A taxonomy of illocutionary acts. Keith Gunderson, ed., *Language, Mind and Knowledge,* Minnesota Studies in the Philosophy of Science. University of Minnesota Press.

Smalley, William A. 1962. Outline of Khmu' Structure (American Oriental Society essay 2). New Haven, American Oriental Society.

Solnit, David B. 1989. Contrastive phonation in Central Karen. Presented at 22nd International Conference on Sino-Tibetan Languages and Linguistics, Honolulu.

———. 1994. When is an affix not a morpheme? Minor syllables in Kayah Li. In Karen L. Adams and Thomas John Hudak, eds., *Papers from the Second Annual Meeting of the Southeast Asian Linguistic Society* (1992), 343–55. Tempe, Arizona State University Program for Southeast Asian Studies.

———. 1995. Parallelism in Kayah Li discourse: elaborate expressions and beyond. *Proceedings of the 21st Annual Meeting, Berkeley Linguistics Society: Special Session on Discourse in Southeast Asian languages,* 127–40. Berkeley, Berkeley Linguistics Society.

Suriya Ratanakul. 1986. /phacannanukrom phaasăa thaj-kàrìaŋ sakɔɔ/ [Thai-Sgaw Karen Dictionary]. Nakhon Pathom, Mahidol University Research Institute of Culture & Language for Rural Development.

Thompson, Laurence C. 1965. *A Vietnamese Grammar.* Seattle, University of Washington Press.

Wade, J. 1896. *A Dictionary of the Sgau Karen Language.* Rangoon, American Baptist Mission Press.

Index of Topics

383